ECO-THEOLOGY

ECO-THEOLOGY

Celia Deane-Drummond

Saint Mary's Press®

For my daughters
Sara Elisabeth and Mair Clare

First published in 2008 by
Darton, Longman and Todd Ltd
1 Spencer Court
140–142 Wandsworth High Street
London SW18 4JJ

Published in the USA 2008 by Saint Mary's Press.

Printed in the United States of America

7019

ISBN 978-1-59982-013-2

Index compiled by Indexing Specialists (UK) Ltd, Indexing House,
306A Portland Road, Hove, East Sussex BN3 6LP. Tel: 01273 416777
email: indexers@indexing.co.uk Website: www.indexing.co.uk

Designed and produced by Sandie Boccacci

Cover design: Leigh Hurlock

Contents

Acknowledgements

The preparation of this book has taken a number of years. My first contact with religious environmentalism came in the early 1990s through working with Martin Palmer at the International Consultancy on Religion, Education and Culture (ICOREC), then based in Manchester. The book I wrote then as part of my work with ICOREC, and sponsored by WWF, was intended to support Christian groups and enable them to link environmental issues with theology. It was published eventually in 1996 under the title of *A Handbook in Theology and Ecology*. Since then I took up a teaching post at the University of Chester and Martin launched the Alliance in Religion and Conservation (ARC), engaged with practical environmental projects worldwide. I realised from the continued popularity of the *Handbook* that there are still relatively few good accessible resources to help laity and others understand and appreciate eco-theology. The idea for the present work was first conceived through a conversation I had in early 2003 with Sarah Lloyd from Ashgate publishers, who subsequently moved to hardback-only publications. Bearing in mind the financial needs of the student community, I looked elsewhere. I am grateful, therefore, to Virginia Hearn of Darton, Longman and Todd for taking on this book, intended to appeal to a lay audience, students as well as established scholars of theology, religious studies, or indeed, the environmental sciences. The book was delayed by the arrival of my second daughter, Mair Clare, in December 2005, along with further delays due to the strictures of the British system of research assessment, which somewhat woodenly resists giving value to pedagogical texts, and so has an impact on the kind of work that it is possible to complete during periods of sabbatical leave. However, although this book has taken a number of years to compile, in view of the increasing intensity of popular and public interest in environmental concern, it seems timely to be publishing this book now.

I am especially grateful to other scholars who have either read and commented on sections of this book, or made their work available before publication. In this respect I would like to mention in particular Sigurd Bergmann, Ernst Conradie, Denis Edwards, Michael Northcott, Peter Scott and Christopher Southgate. I would particularly like to thank Ernst Conradie for helpful conversations during his stay at Chester in February 2008, just as final corrections to this book were being addressed. I am also indebted, as is so often the case, to the resources and welcome of St Deiniol's Library, where I have had the opportunity for reading and reflection away from the demands of University and family. I am grateful for the feedback from my students at the University of Chester, who helped me refine some of my ideas for this book while taking the module *Ecotheology and Environmental Ethics*.

Some of the material that is presented here has also been delivered to various other audiences. Sections on eco-justice and environmental justice, for example, were delivered to the Catholic Women's League in Birmingham in March 2007. My article 'Environmental Justice and the Economy: A Christian Theologian's View', published in *Ecotheology* in 2005, was prepared for the 'Religion and Environment in Europe' workshop that met at the Theological Philosophical College of the Bendiktbeuern Monastery in southern Germany in June 2005. I have drawn on this article and aspects of my other published works in preparing this volume. I also spoke to a public audience at St Paul's Cathedral in Westminster in November 2006 as part of the *Costing the Earth? The Quest for Sustainability* programme, drawing on some of the material that forms the final chapter of this book.

In order to suit the pedagogical intent of this book, it is substantially different to any of my previous publications that I have drawn upon, and in as much as this book includes a critical review of other published work, it is completely new. I have also sought to develop my own ideas in a more focused way towards an eco-theological agenda, so in this sense, it seeks to provide the starting point for an original contribution to the field.

I would like to thank my family and my husband Henry, who has had to endure my confinement to my study over many evenings, periods of annual leave and weekends – no sabbatical could be granted to pen such a text, for reasons given above. Finally, this book is dedicated to my daughters, Sara (7) and Mair (2), who are innocently expectant of so much. Let us hope that the earth will be kept not just for them, and the generations that follow them, but for the myriad other creatures that co-exist with us on planet earth.

The turn to ecology

CONTEMPORARY CONCERN FOR THE ENVIRONMENT, broadly understood as a turn to ecology, takes its bearings from secular concerns about the environment that have developed and intensified over the last few decades. The rise of religious environmentalism in particular adds its own voice to the debate, for it seeks to trace the malaise of environmental decay as rooted in spiritual issues, along with its potential solution to environmental understanding, by a retrieval of religious symbols and traditions. In a recent survey entitled *A Greener Faith*, Roger Gottlieb traces the rise of religious environmentalism in different religious traditions, including Christianity.[1] His purpose is to survey the different possible religious responses to environmentalism, rather than analyse their validity from within a particular tradition. The intention of this book is rather different. Its aim, as the title suggests, is to offer a resource book that highlights and seeks to evaluate the merits or otherwise of different contemporary eco-theologies, drawing from different Christian theological traditions and contexts. It represents an attempt to map out a burgeoning field in a way that is accessible to university students or other readers with a serious interest in the topic.[2] It aims to introduce the reader to critical debates in eco-theology, and encourage further reflection and analysis. In bringing together something of the diversity of the field, my hope is that the student will be encouraged to listen to different emerging voices and form his or her own view on the merits or otherwise of particular positions. I have, accordingly, often left open-ended matters that arise as a result of the considerable diversity in opinion among those who engage in eco-theology, in order to encourage students to situate themselves within this debate. I have tried to invite students to ask questions of the literature in offering some of my own critique, but I also offer more general discussion questions for each chapter in order to allow students to begin such critical reflection.

I am fully conscious of the fact that there are areas of eco-theological discussion that I have been forced to omit, or have treated somewhat superficially. The field has also grown so large that every chapter could, in itself, be expanded into a monograph, or even a series of monographs. A work that was fully comprehensive would be more like an encyclopaedia in its proportions and take several volumes. This would suit a more corporate international effort, and plans are underway to implement such an ambitious project.[3] I have also, necessarily, focused on the work of *contemporary* writers rather than historical figures, except where those writings become important in the work of contemporary authors.[4] I have also concentrated on *theology*, rather than what loosely might be termed eco-spirituality and Christian eco-ethics, even though, of course, any lines of demarcation are somewhat blurred.[5] Finally, I have confined my discussion to Christian theology, rather than attempt a broader, multi-religious perspective. I recognise the importance of other religious traditions in their engagement with ecological concerns. This is true of the other Abrahamic faiths as well as religions within Buddhist or Confucian traditions. However, there are existing resources that do attempt such a breadth,[6] and I am conscious of the primary need for Christian theologians to take on board the scale and extent of the development of eco-theology right across the globe from within their own traditions. This has often been recognised insufficiently, if at all. Perhaps only then a more articulate dialogue with other theological positions can begin. I find it astonishing that courses on eco-theology do not exist in many university departments of theology and religious studies in the United Kingdom. This book will, I hope, encourage tutors to take this issue far more seriously than to date, and place eco-theology firmly in the curriculum of contemporary theology. In addition, my intention is that this book will be suited to the wider context of educated laity for discussion and reflection, though I have presupposed a certain amount of theology.

The first premise that this book presumes is that it is possible to combine concern with the environment and an understanding of God. Eco-theology, as defined here, is that reflection on different facets of theology in as much as they take their bearings from cultural concerns about the environment and humanity's relationship with the natural world. It is, in other words, broadly speaking a particular expression of contextual theology that emerges in the particular contemporary context of environmental awareness that has characterised the late twentieth and early twenty-first centuries.[7] Given the widespread secular engagement with environmental issues at global, national and local levels, such expressions of theology are highly significant. This development is not simply the concern of a minority interest group, but reaches out to include all those who are aware of global and local environmental problems. Given that this affects human survival as well as the survival of all creatures on our living planet, such issues touch deeply our sense of meaning and purpose. In other words, it is hard to talk meaningfully about ecology in such a context, without also speaking about religion and theology as well. This is also true the other way round, so that for theology to be meaningful, it also, I suggest, needs to encompass an awareness that is beyond the human, inclusive of the natural world in which humanity is embedded. Ecology here means the broader context of ecological concerns, as well as that described by ecological science as such.

The fashion in much contemporary academic theology has been to shift towards radical postmodern deconstruction, taking its cue from authors such as Derrida and Foucault. While such studies have their merits in raising un-substantiated assumptions brought to bear in philosophical and theological reasoning, the spectre of relativism and nihilism looms, and unless carefully handled, leads to inactivity and disillusionment. Moreover, we should be fully conscious of the relativism of the turn to postmodernity in a way that is often insufficiently recognised. In other words, we need to view the swing to post-modern deconstruction as *itself* culture bound, often tied into particular Western traditions that form the basis of its criticism. What will be the next fashion *after* postmodernity? In such a climate, the tendency for theology might be either to resort to confessional positions that ignore such criticism, or bend to it through lack of confidence in any constructive proposal. In a loose sense, all eco-theology is postmodern in that it takes *context* as its start-ing point, and challenges the presuppositions of much theology emerging in the so-called modern period.[8] *EcoSpirit: Religions and Philosophies for the Earth* is published as this book goes to press.[9] *EcoSpirit* engages specifically with philosophy, and in particular, postmodern thought, but it assumes that grounding theological reflection in environmental and other practices is nec-essarily postmodern in its orientation – in other words, rejecting any notion of 'foundation', while affirming a sense of being 'grounded'. *EcoSpirit* is also wider in its brief compared with the present volume, gathering together a range of different religious and cultural traditions. It recognises that facts alone about environmental issues are not enough; what is needed is something more elemental, that probes the background assumptions pervading modern thought in a way that leads to denial – what the editors term 'apocalyptic insomnia'.[10] Such sensitivity to context echoes something of the concerns in other contextual theologies.[11] In the main, eco-theology turns against the tide of radical postmodern relativism or confessional counter-reaction in that it accepts that environmental problems have a substantial and reasonable basis in reality. At their best, postmodern critiques show up the limitations of scientific analysis and theological dogmas. Eco-theology can survive such criticism by also challenging the secular idea that the sciences are sufficient to solve en-vironmental problems. Moreover, I suggest that even at a secular level the various forms of eco-theology need to be viewed as important contributions to myth making and symbol making, where 'myth' is not intended to imply the lack of truth, but rather shows its capacity to reach beyond the rational to include other dimensions of knowing. It is disentangling the roots of such myths and their impact, negative and positive, that forms the basis of much eco-theological reflection. In other words, religious thinking and practices are as much part of the root of the problem as they are part of the potential way forward.

Overall, eco-theology seeks to uncover the theological basis for a proper relationship between God, humanity and the cosmos. Humans are understood in Christian tradition to be created, but alienated from the natural world through their own tendencies towards domination. Many approaches to eco-theology are those that seek to recover our sense of place on the earth, a reminder that the earth is our common home, that the story of the earth and that of humans are one. This may also be broadened out to include the economy, the *oikos* or household of God. Such reflection naturally enough leads to a great deal of literature on ethics as that which needs to be practised to re-order the household. Yet, as Ernst Conradie has pointed out, moving too readily to a sense of humanity at home on earth misses out the concrete experiences of natural suffering, finitude and the pervasiveness of human sin.[12] Like Conradie, I believe that we need an ecologically informed anthropology, yet one that is more consciously aware of the limitations of simply trying to recover a sense of being at home on the earth. At the same time, other aspects of Christian theology need to be teased out through an ecological hermeneutic as well. Like Conradie, I believe that the agenda for eco-theology must be bold enough to encompass the main tenets of faith, without being reduced to environmental ethics.[13] He also acknowledges that while many publications have emerged from North American, British and German contexts, 'perhaps more important is the sometimes unarticulated ecological wisdom that has been gathered from impoverished local communities in Africa, Australia, Central America, India, Latin America, New Zealand, the Pacific Islands, the Philippines, South East Asia and also in North America itself.'[14] This 'rich mosaic' of different cultures, traditions and contexts informs ecological theology, and is one reason why I have sought to highlight the global nature of ecological reflection, while being acutely aware that the scope of such reflection is limited in a work of this length. I hope, at least, to give something of the flavour of such diversity in eco-theology. At the same time, eco-theology has as its horizon environmental praxis; it is theology worked out at the coal-face, as it were, of environmental concerns and problems.

The purpose of this book is threefold. The first task is pedagogical. The first two chapters in this book raise secular environmental and economic dimensions of the debate in order to set the scene for more rigorous theological discussion. Issues such as climate change, biodiversity, and secular ecological values are raised, alongside particular practices that affect the economy, such as globalisation, sustainability and genetically modified crops. Such coverage cannot be exhaustive, but it is intended to be sufficient to give a flavour of the issues and problems for those readers encountering eco-theology for the first time. It also raises some of the ethical issues that have been the subject of intense debate. Ethical controversy sets the scene for theological discourse and arguably far more has been written on religious environmental ethics compared with eco-theology, though the lines between the two are also very blurred in many cases. The next four chapters (3 to 6) review something of the diversity of eco-theological thought, emerging from different global contexts. The designations 'North', 'South', 'East' and 'West' in the chapter headings are loosely intended to highlight the global variety of the discourse, rather than imply that this book can ever hope to encompass the full extent of theological reflection on the issue from different starting points. Moreover, all these chapters are illustrative, rather than exhaustive reviews, and aim to encourage further reading, rather than being fully comprehensive. For example, Chapter 3 deals with deep ecology, the mystical creation theology of Teilhard de Chardin and Matthew Fox, while Chapter 4 discusses ecology and liberation theology in comparison with indigenous theologies. Chapter 5 outlines the particular approach to the doctrine of creation from the perspective of Eastern Orthodox theology, alongside its commitment to grounding theology in liturgical practice. Chapter 6 is more concerned with sociological interpretations and the extent to which social and political insights might be incorporated into eco-theology. All these chapters to some extent are reviews of existing work as a basic primer in eco-theology.

The second task of this book, as exemplified in Chapters 7–12, seeks to go beyond merely critical literature review, and attempt more active theological construction. Chapter 7 begins the discussion by raising alternative interpretations of the Bible that draw on eco-justice principles. While such alternative readings could form the topic of a textbook in its own right, its purpose is primarily one that serves subsequent theological construction. The word 'construction' is not intended to mean an overarching or foundational position in the sense that it cannot be revised, but at the same time it seeks to go further than more timid renditions of theology that are becoming more popular in some quarters, where it is described as simple fragments to a discussion. It is, in other words, one way of reading systematic theology that arguably is helpful in the context of environmental concerns. All these chapters argue for the importance of the tradition of wisdom in theology and its potential for eco-theology. Different chapters focus on different systematic concerns in the light of ecology, ranging from Christology to Theodicy, Spirit, Eco-Feminist Theology and Eschatology. The doctrines of creation, Christian anthropology and the doctrine of the Trinity are also woven into the discussion of the book as a whole, rather than forming separate chapters. This is partly because I have written on these issues elsewhere,[15] and also because the other systematic themes are perhaps less obvious to students in terms of their potential ecological readings.

I am painfully and acutely aware that a book of this size could not cover all aspects worthy of consideration and some may be offended by my omissions or compressions of areas of work. There are also no specific chapters devoted to ecclesial perspectives, for example, but I have tried to give due consideration to these issues in other chapters, representing authors from Eastern and Western traditions. My hope is that this book will be a resource for reflection in different churches, which is why I have deliberately not flagged up a particular denominational stance, such as a particular emphasis on the Roman Catholic tradition in which I now stand, or my roots in the Anglican tradition. The context in which I teach is one where students are welcomed from all faiths or none, and while I do not claim to be neutral with respect to my own faith position, I also believe that those who do not share a religious faith will find this book gives insights into the interweaving of faith, theology, and practices that form the basis for the development of eco-theology. In other words, a student does not have a requirement to be a believer in order to gain something from this book.

I am also aware that the layout of this work could have been very different, given the sheer size and scope of material relevant to eco-theology. For example, full chapters could have been devoted to gleaning the relevance of different aspects of the tradition from a historical perspective, such as Franciscan, Benedictine or Celtic traditions, for example. Such traditions do, I suggest, influence the authors that are represented in this book, so that those who are more influenced by Franciscan traditions will be inclined to a more sacramental approach, those by Celtic traditions towards a deeper affinity with the land, and those by Benedictine traditions will allow for some active change by human involvement, fostering notions such as stewardship, for example. Yet it also seems to me that sources relating to such traditions are relatively easy to access, so that the student or interested reader should not have difficulty finding such material. In fact, my hope is that those who read this book might feel inclined to delve more deeply into these traditions than has been possible in this very compressed survey. I could also, perhaps, have organised the material around what might be called loosely models of eco-theology, according to, for example, the sacramental and stewardship traditions already mentioned, but also according to eco-feminist and ecumenical approaches. By devoting a full chapter to eco-feminist thought, and by deliberately representing different theological traditions, my hope is that these issues will be clear to the reader. There is also a disadvantage in such modelling in as much as many authors draw from many different approaches and models, so fitting the work of one author to a given way of thinking is somewhat artificial, even if it lends some clarity. I hope that the reader will be alert to such different styles as they read this text.

As a pedagogic text this aims to highlight how it is possible to interpret more traditional doctrines in ecologically friendly ways. I have, of course, been limited by the scope of what is achievable in one relatively short volume, but I hope that I have been able to demonstrate the starting point for more reflection and more questions. I have woven in soteriological themes throughout, as well as considering such issues under the broader heading of Christology. My intention is to open up the field so that others will be encouraged to enter it, rather than even attempt a fully comprehensive survey. Given the diversity and contextual variety of much eco-theological literature to date, even providing such a starting point proved extremely challenging. I hope that any readers who are disappointed with the selection that I have made will bear patiently with the intention of this book, namely one that seeks to encourage more interest and research in the topic. Moreover, I will argue that such an analysis implies not simply that ecology is an option for theology, but also that it is *necessary* if theology is to be correctly understood.

The third task of this book is to encourage readers to engage in active reflection and positive action. I suggest that the re-reading of theology sketched out in this book has important implications for eco-praxis. The closing postscript points towards such an interpretation, though I am fully aware that a full text on theological eco-praxis would be desirable from such an analysis. I am using praxis to mean the liturgical life of the church as well as the particular ethical boundaries for individual actions. I have also included discussion questions emerging from each chapter that can be used in order to stimulate either individuals or groups to think further about the issues raised. This book has also benefited from being used as a source on a taught module entitled *Eco-theology and environmental ethics* for students at the University of Chester. The feedback from these students was interesting and slightly surprising to me. Almost all said how, as a result of taking this module, they found it necessary not only to re-think their theological beliefs, but also to change their lifestyle and practice. I am delivering this book to the publisher on 11 July 2007, appropriately the Feast of St Benedict. For him, as many others, Christian belief could never be divorced from practices that were in tune with the land. If this book contributes in any small way to this task, then it will have succeeded in its intention.

Chapter 1

Trends in ecology and environment

THIS CHAPTER SEEKS TO HIGHLIGHT SOME OF THE MORE important environmental concerns raised by the rapidly expanding knowledge of environmental problems and ecology. It also forms the background in which eco-theological discussion is situated, and it is therefore appropriate to name these issues at the outset. It would be impossible to do full justice to the complete range of issues that need to be addressed; instead I will highlight areas that seem to me to be crucial in demonstrating the extent and complexity of the problems involved. I am also deliberately avoiding using the language of 'crisis' to discuss these changes, not because I see a lessening of the problems at the dawn of the twenty-first century, but because this language has been around since the early discussions of environmental issues in the 1970s, and it has often been used as a rhetorical, polemical device for particular political purposes. I am also not implying by this move that political issues are irrelevant for discussion, but I will return to more particular political questions in later chapters. This chapter sets the scene for subsequent political and economic debate. I will briefly review population, resource use/pollution, climate change and biodiversity. This list will give some indication of the state of the planet and likely trends in the future. The final section explores values emerging from ecology that also feed into later theological discussion.

Population

Population growth is often one of the first issues that come to mind when reflecting on why the earth is suffering environmental strain. We are, in R. J. Berry's words, simply 'running out of world'.[1] The exponential rate of population growth alarmed many writers in the 1960s, Paul Ehrlich, for example, likening the population explosion to a 'bomb' that would soon wreak havoc on human survival on planet earth. Others are less pessimistic today, believing that indefinite population growth is not inevitable. Demographic studies calculate population growth from live births and immigrants minus the number of deaths and emigrants.[2] The global population in 2000 was twice that in 1960, reflecting a staggering rate of exponential growth in the last half of the twentieth century. In 2005 global population grew by 74 million, so that the world's population topped 6.4 billion, more than twice the number in 1950. Although the population growth rate has dropped from 2 per cent in the 1970s to about 1 per cent in 2006, the overall trend is an increase in population.[3] Over time medical improvements in health care in some populations have increased the rates of population growth by reducing the death rate, even when birth rates are falling. On the other hand, complex social issues, including sex education, the availability of contraception and abortion, attitudes to women, homosexuality, and economic incentives, all affect birth rates. Often improvements in economic and social gains are correlated with declining birth rate, but the question here is which comes first, the improvement in economics, or the reduction in birth rate? If the former comes first, then improving social conditions and economics should lead to a decline in birth rate, but if the latter, then a targeted approach to birth control is favoured. The total fertility rate (TFR), or average number of children born to a woman in her lifetime, has fallen in many populations, including not just the USA and Europe, but also Japan and China. However, this shift does not mean that overall population size is declining, for reasons mentioned above. In addition, other poorer nations of the world that show a much higher TFR have a corresponding lower average population age; but medical disadvantages and other social conditions such as poor hygiene also lead to high infant mortality rate. The overall effects are global increases in population size, so that even if the exponential rate of growth is slowing slightly, overall global population size is still increasing.

Resource use and pollution

But is population growth itself the only variable worth considering? It is recognised that global resources such as energy, soil and water are insufficient to meet the needs of a growing population. Yet many environmentalists believe that over and above population growth, the distribution and extent of resource use by some privileged groups leads to gross differences in energy and pollution burden per head in different populations.

In spite of vast increases in the global productivity of grain, world hunger still prevails. The production of food through monocultures has reached its limits. The world grain harvest dropped slightly from 1869 million tons in 1999 to 1840 million tons in 2000, but by 2005 it had reached a steady level of 2015 million tons.[4] Yet the high grain production levels do not eliminate world hunger for economic reasons and because of difficulties of distribution. The modern system of producing food is dysfunctional. Not only are there mass migrations to cities in poorer communities, leading to a collapse in the rural economy, but there is also a failure to meet the basic need for food for many of those in poorer nations. This contrasts with excessive over-consumption in other nations. Four billion people live on less than $2 per day, while 20 per cent of the world's population is responsible for 90 per cent of consumption of resources and energy. The richer, Western nations are primarily responsible for over-consumption, leading to considerable global environmental strain.[5] The largest cause of death in 2000 was due to cardio-vascular diseases, which killed 16.7 million people. Infectious diseases and parasitic diseases, including AIDS, tuberculosis and respiratory diseases, malaria and diarrhoeal diseases, killed 14.4 million people, mostly in impoverished communities. Cancers also led to 6.9 million deaths. Cardiovascular diseases and cancers affected primarily those affluent populations who have sedentary lifestyles and consume unhealthy foods.[6]

In addition, 40 per cent of the world's population is short of fresh water, and this is projected to rise to over 50 per cent by 2032. In 2000 the World Heath Organisation estimated that 1.1 billion people could not meet their basic need for clean water, contributing to the deaths mentioned above. In Asia 693 million people lack access to clean water. An estimated 3.4 million people die each year as a result of water-related disease and many more suffer disabilities as a result of water-related pathogens. It is estimated that 64.4 million Disability Adjusted Life Years (DALTs) come from water-related pathogens, often linked to inadequate sanitation. The most recent report suggests that 2.6 billion people still lack adequate sanitation facilities.[7] Other data suggest that up to 1.1 billion people lack access to a clean water supply.[8] This effect is compounded by the growing use of artificial fertilisers in agriculture, leading to an increase in groundwater and leaching of minerals, reducing long-term productivity of the soil. Eutrophication is a process by which particular pollutants are washed into water supplies – be it a lake, river, wetland or shallow sea – and overload it with organic and mineral nutrients. Common sources are nitrate fertilisers washed from the soil and phosphates from fertilisers and detergents in municipal sewage. There has also been a massive increase in global livestock populations, increasing 60 per cent since 1961. Pig and goat populations have doubled, chickens quadrupled. Industrial forms of production are on the increase, 43 per cent through feedlots where animals are kept in a confined space in factory-like conditions. For 200 million people living in arid areas, livestock is the only option. Overall there has been a fivefold increase in the global consumption of meat since the 1950s. In developing countries meat consumption between the early 1970s to the mid 1990s increased threefold over that in industrial countries.[9] Farm animals consume 37 per cent of the world's grain harvest, cattle being the least efficient in this respect. Overgrazing has degraded 20 per cent of global rangeland; and half of rainforest destruction is the result of cattle ranging. Moderate, severe or extreme degradation affects 7–14 per cent of farmland, so that each year some

5–8 million hectares go out of production as a result of degradation.[10] The waste from livestock also contributes significantly to environmental damage, including consequences such as toxic algae blooms and global warming through methane production.

Global fossil fuel consumption has expanded by three and a half times since 1950. World oil use reached 3.8 billion tons (83.3 million barrels a day) in 2005, with the USA the largest consumer at 20.8 million barrels a day. Europe came a close second at 15.6 million barrels a day, China 6.6 million barrels and Japan 5.4 million barrels. Overall per capita, the USA uses two thirds more compared with Japan and 13 times more than China.[11] Natural gas use is rising, and replacing use of coal. There is debate about the projected trends in energy use. For example, World Energy Outlook 2000 was more pessimistic than some about projected energy use. In North America and Western Europe there are no firm plans to increase nuclear power, though, ironically perhaps, under the pressure from anxiety about climate change, political talks have resumed in the United Kingdom, and this may spread to other jurisdictions. China, Japan and South Korea continue to fund new projects. There has been a mixed response in other countries, some such as Cuba and Taiwan responding to public pressure not to continue, others such as India and Brazil still completing projects. Global wind power increased by 24 per cent in 2005, and in 2004, the latest year for available data, global hydroelectric power increased by 5 per cent. The latter is hampered by lack of appropriate sites for development. In 2005 the global production of photoelectric cells increased by 45 per cent from the previous year, representing a sixfold increase since 2000, making it the world's fastest-growing energy source.[12] These changes in energy use are, unfortunately, not yet sufficient to halt the overall trends in carbon emissions.

Climate change

The projected rate of climate change this century is far greater than anything experienced by the earth in the last 10,000 years, mostly caused by human activity through the burning of fossil fuels.[13] There have always been sceptics who challenge the detailed predictions anticipated through climate change models. The *extent* of change anticipated is debated, rather than whether there is any change taking place at all. The most recent analysis suggests that we are close to the tipping point on climate change. Action needs to be taken in the next 15 to 35 years in order to stabilise the climate. Accumulated scientific evidence points to increasing unpredictability. The intergovernmental panel on climate change (IPCC) accumulated detailed empirical evidence from a network of hundreds of distinguished scientists.[14] The overall consensus is that, in spite of the uncertainties, most of the observed global warming over the last 50 years is due to changes in greenhouse gas concentrations. Hence, it would not make any sense to ignore such warnings, for even if the sceptics are right, change will inevitably take place, but it will just take slightly longer compared with more pessimistic estimates.

The ten warmest years have occurred since 1980. 2005 was among the warmest years on record since records began in 1880, and six of the warmest years on record have occurred since 1998.[15] NASA Goddard Institute for Space Studies (GISS) in New York City has reported that 2007 tied with 1998 for Earth's second warmest year in a century.[16] The average temperature of the earth's surface gives an even more sensitive measure of this trend. The increased concentrations of carbon dioxide and other greenhouse gases are likely to be responsible. Carbon dioxide levels have risen by 30 per cent from pre-industrial times, due to burning fossil fuels, land use changes, especially deforestation, and agriculture. If nothing is done, it could reach double the level in 2100. So far the concentration of carbon dioxide as predicted by emissions has not normally taken into account the effect of climate change itself on the carbon cycle,[17] so that at higher temperatures there is an increase in respiration from living organisms in soil, as well as dieback of forests. Hence the problem is likely to be even worse than that predicted on the basis of emissions originating purely from human activities. If this is taken into account, then a tipping point may be reached whereby the earth becomes a net emitter of carbon dioxide.[18] Oceans could turn from being carbon sinks, to carbon emitters; tropical rainforests would be depleted further by enhanced temperature rises, and more carbon released from decomposing peat and release of frozen methane. By mid 1995 the IPCC agreed that the anthropogenic effects (that is, effects as a result of human activity) could be positively detected, and stronger support for this view has emerged since then.[19] The simulation climate models, such as that from the Hadley Centre, take into account anthropogenic and natural factors, such as solar variation and volcanic activity. Increased temperature leads to increases in water vapour and decrease in ice cover, especially in the Polar Regions, leading to further positive feedback, that is, further temperature increases. A doubling of pre-industrial carbon dioxide would lead to an overall global 1.5–4.5 degree change in temperature. This might seem a small change, but the difference between having an ice age or not amounts to a mere 5 or 6 degrees. Hence 2.5 degrees over a century is massive in terms of climate change. It will also vary enormously over the earth's surface. Predictions of regional variation in temperature are very difficult because of uncertainty in profiles of greenhouse gases; extent and feedback from cloud formation; changes in ocean circulation and changes in composition of the biosphere.[20]

The impacts of climate change on the ecology of both human and non-human communities are through factors such as rising sea level and the increase in number and frequency of climate extremes, floods and droughts becoming more common due to a more intense hydrological cycle.[21] The changes that have a 90–99 per cent probability, if trends continue, include higher maximum temperatures and more hot days as well as higher minimum temperatures, fewer cold days and frost days over nearly all land areas; reduced diurnal temperature range and increase in heat index over most land areas; and more intense precipitation events over many areas. Weather-related disasters affect millions of people; the overall cost in 2005 hit a record of $204 billion, way in excess of the previous record of $112 billion in 1998.[22] Three of the ten strongest hurricanes ever recorded occurred in 2005; high-profile cases include Hurricane Katrina that hit the United States coast at the end of August. In addition, at the very end of the previous calendar year, on Boxing Day 2004, the mega-tsunami that hit the Indonesian region left thousands of people dead, and thousands orphaned. Although this tsunami was related to geological changes, rather than climate change, it represented the extent to which poorer nations are unprepared for such catastrophes. Those nations that are the most subject to change are the poorer subtropical parts of the world. The projected impact of climate change for the end of the twenty-first century includes:

- *Increase in sea level rise* from 0.1 to 0.9 metres for delta regions like those in Bangladesh, Egypt and China. Low-lying islands in the Pacific and Indian Oceans will be particularly vulnerable. Geological data suggests that the eustatic sea level (that is, estimated global sea level) has changed at an average rate of 0.1–0.2 millimetres per year over the last 3000 years, one tenth of that occurring in the twentieth century alone. Significant sea-level rises could lead to swamping of entire communities. Millions of people are likely to be displaced. Such devastating loss will lead to a huge number of environmental refugees, estimated to be 150 million by 2050 if present rates of change continue.
- *Impact on water availability.* The hydrological cycle will be affected by climate change, leading to greater evaporation, more rainfall in some places and drought in others, with a tendency for greater extremes – that is, dry places become drier and wet places become wetter.
- *Change in the distribution of food production.* This is most likely to be felt in the subtropics, leading to further environmental refugees.
- *Negative effects on human health.* This comes from heat stress, increased disease, such as malaria, and damage to some ecosystems.
- *Economic loss.* Direct effects of climate change, such as flooding, are estimated to be about 1.0–1.5 per cent of GDP in the Western world, and 2–9 per cent in poorer countries. These estimates do not take into account indirect factors such as the immigration of environmental refugees.

The social problems resulting from these impacts inevitably raise the issue of environmental justice, namely the proportionally greater impact of climate change on the poorer communities of the world, which are, in relative terms, contributing significantly less to the anthropogenic effects on climate change. Climate scientists have proposed a contraction and convergence approach in order to share out the impacts of climate change in a more equitable manner on a global scale. This approach adopts the following principles:

- *The precautionary principle*, in this context meaning that the existence of scientific uncertainty should not preclude action.
- *The polluter pays principle*, using measures such as carbon taxation.
- *The principle of equity*, both international and intergenerational, so that the burden is shared out evenly.

A drastic shift in global emissions of carbon dioxide from the burning of fossil fuels would be required to bring about stabilisation of CO_2 levels to 450 parts per million. This is called the contraction principle. But how are these reductions to be shared out? Using the above principles, the fairest way is to set the limit by allowing an equal share of CO_2 per capita, reaching this (convergence) by 2030. Having given allocations to each nation, based on population size, trading would be allowed, so that technical and economic resources would be given in exchange for greater pollution 'debt'.

While this might seem idealistic at first sight, it is well within the economic sights of richer nations to reach such a target. The estimated reduction in carbon dioxide emissions required to stabilise the climate exceeds that of the Kyoto Protocol.[23] In the UK a reduction in carbon dioxide emission by 60 per cent from current levels might seem overly optimistic. However, the actual cost of making such a change would amount to 0.02 per cent, or six months' economic growth over a half century to 2050.[24] The economic case for action has been robustly defended by the Stern report, published in 2007. Nicholas Stern has also responded strongly to critics who argue against the economic case for action.[25] The United States has still not yet signed the Kyoto agreement. The G8 summit in July 2005 did not come to satisfactory conclusions in this respect either. The latest figures from Defra show that the basket of greenhouse gas emissions in the United Kingdom have fallen significantly to within the Kyoto target.[26] However, the overall emission of carbon dioxide was only 0.1 per cent lower in 2005 compared with 2004. The greatest proportion of carbon dioxide emission (37 per cent) comes from energy industries, 22 per cent from road transport, 18 per cent from other industries and 15 per cent from residential use of fossil fuels. While there has been an overall 12 per cent reduction in emissions from the energy industry since 1990, this has risen again since 2004, suggesting that the overall trend downwards has stabilised. Overall the UK contributes about 2 per cent to total emissions from human sources. Taxing and fining those companies that are polluting provides a legal mechanism to manage the over-production of carbon dioxide, but it is certainly insufficient as a moral response, and some might argue, ultimately destructive.[27] As Michael Northcott aptly points out, 'the climate is not a social construct; instead it represents a real biophysical limit on the freedoms of corporations and consumers to maximise their preferences and profits.'[28] Even more surprising, perhaps, is that those ecological systems that are necessary for human life, including climate regulation, food and fresh water production, are now becoming known collectively as 'ecosystem services'. Bulked together, 62.5 per cent of these 'services' are being degraded or used unsustainably, but the attitude of mind that considers ecological systems as 'services' for human life shows the extent to which a focus on human needs dominates even the secular environmental agenda.[29]

Environmental impacts and biodiversity loss

There are a staggering number of species in the world today, between 5 and 80 million, probably around 30 million. Only 100,000 species have been described in any detail out of the total 1.5 million identified so far. Yet 1–11 per cent of the world's species are becoming extinct every decade. The International Union for the Conservation of Nature has drawn up a comprehensive list of those species that are extinct, extinct in the wild, critically endangered, endangered or vulnerable. As well as an increase in extinction rate, there has been a huge increase in the number of species that are critically endangered. The colonisation of land by human populations has always led to some loss of biodiversity, even among prehistoric peoples. Since 1600 researchers have identified over a thousand recorded cases of extinctions of plant and animal species.[30] Ecological knowledge helps define biological diversity, though the species that have so far been identified represent only a small fraction of the actual diversity, especially in areas such as the tropical rainforest. Conservation is, at best, a safety measure for known species. There are others that are disappearing well before they can be identified.

Overall plant diversity is also threatened, so that from an estimate taken in 2004, 70 per cent of all species assessed and 3 per cent of all plant species are threatened with extinction, and 45 per cent are endangered or critically endangered.[31] In 2005, of the 9900 bird species, 12 per cent were threatened with extinction.[32] In addition, about a quarter of all mammals are threatened, with 73 mammal species already extinct, and 4 extinct in the wild. Within the next 50 years chimpanzees and other primates may be extinct in the wild. Black rhinos suffered a catastrophic loss in population numbers between 1970 and 1992 due to hunting.[33]

In general, species may be lost through (1) direct exploitation by humans, and in areas such as the tropical rainforest it is difficult to estimate original wildlife diversity because there are virtually no regions entirely free from human exploitation. Exploitative practices include bush meat, as well as fuel wood, which overall exceeds replacement planting. Direct exploitation also includes hunting, especially in parts of Indonesia, for luxury items or for the pet trade. About 50 per cent of traded birds end up in the USA.

As well as direct exploitation, (2) loss of habitat is a common reason for species extinction, correlated with population density and clearance of land as well as climate change mentioned above. Although habitat loss has been a feature of human history since the dawn of civilisation, its extent has increased rapidly with the march of technology. The main habitats under threat are the tropical rainforests, wetlands and coral reefs. The former is better known than the latter two examples.

Forest clearance, especially the tropical rainforest, has led to loss of a myriad of species, many not yet identified. Global forested area contracted by 36.6 million hectares, or just less than 1 per cent between 2000 and 2005, according to the 2005 Global Forest Assessment from the US Food and Agriculture Organisation (FAO). This is a net figure, so that actual losses were 65 million, with offset by expansion of plantations and natural re-growth.[34] While the destruction of tropical rainforest is well known, less appreciated is the destruction of mangrove forests on the coastlines, leaving coastline ecologies vulnerable to destruction.[35]

The planet has lost over half its wetlands in the last hundred years. These are highly fragile ecosystems. Most loss is through drainage for agricultural use. There are secondary effects as well: water tables can fall, leading to salinization; and the change in water flow in rivers can harm coastal ecosystems and ultimately lead to water shortages in some places and flood-related disasters in others. Many environmental problems are concentrated in coastal areas, including the mismanagement of fisheries and damage to coastal land by poorly planned land use through badly managed urbanisation, industrialisation, tourism and flood control. Wetland degradation also accounts for some of the decline. Wetlands cover up to 6 per cent of the earth's surface. The Mesopotamian marshlands of Iraq and Western Iran make up the largest remaining wetland system in the Middle East and Western Eurasia. This ecosystem had shrunk to 10 per cent of its original size, mostly due to draining projects in the 1990s by the Iraqi government.[36]

The rapid loss in coral reefs is one of the most dramatic changes seen since 1992. The latest World Watch Institute report is horrifying:

> As of late 2005, an estimated 20 percent of the world's coral reefs had been 'effectively destroyed', showing live coral losses of at least 90 percent and no immediate prospects for recovery, according to the Global Coral Reef Monitoring Network. Another 24 percent face imminent risk of collapse as a result of human pressures and 26 per cent face longer-term loss – bringing the share of world reefs now threatened or destroyed to 70 percent, up from 59 percent in 2000. The greatest destruction has occurred in the Caribbean Sea, Indian Ocean, Gulf regions, and Southeast Asia.[37]

Coral reefs are among the world's most complex and productive ecosystems.[38]

Loss in coral reefs is through human pressures, including fishing, coral mining, coastal development, waste dumping, inland deforestation and farming; nearly 60 per cent of all reefs are threatened in this way. Yet the greatest threat is global warming: just a one-degree rise in temperature makes the corals expel their living parts and turn white, a process known as bleaching.

Another major factor in species loss is through (3) introduced species. About 400,000 species have been introduced over time. While some may be intentional, others have come through transport routes between human populations. In about 10 per cent of cases, introduced species have effects on existing ecology, leading to negative impacts, including species extinction. Endemic species in lakes and islands are particularly vulnerable to predation and parasitism by introduced species. For example, the accidental introduction of the brown tree snake, *Bioga irregularis*, to the island of Guam in 1950 resulted in the loss either directly or indirectly of 12 species of an original fauna of 22 native birds, reduction in the remaining forest species to a mere remnant, and the loss of over a third of native reptiles.

The Convention on Biological Diversity represents international political recognition that sustaining biodiversity is within the scope of international interests. It attempts to arrive at an international consensus towards protecting biological diversity in different national regions. The convention has three aims: first, to conserve biological diversity; second, to use biological resources in a sustainable way; and third, to share any benefits arising from genetic resources fairly.

The relationship between biodiversity and ecosystem function is a major research area within ecology.[39] In some cases a species may be lost without any effect, known as 'redundancy'. In other cases there are crucial species whose loss disrupts the ecosystem, an effect known as 'rivet popping'. In a third 'idiosyncratic' scenario it is not possible to predict accurately the impact of the loss of a particular species, because each species has complex and varied roles. An ecosystem with a large number of species is more likely to show species 'redundancy'. Yet the value of conserving biodiversity is not simply related to ecosystem function. The benefits of biodiversity relate to (a) direct uses – that is, instrumental uses for human benefit; and (b) indirect use, achieved through biogeochemical cycling (cycling of basic nutrients including carbon, nitrogen and sulphur, released as appropriate gases into the atmosphere). Such cycling is necessary both for the maintenance of global ecology and climate stability. So-called 'redundant' species may also be indirectly useful as food sources for other species that are of instrumental use. Other indirect uses could include tourism and recreation. There are also (c) four values that do not relate to present usefulness. Future generations may have (i) instrumental or other uses for biodiversity, known as (ii) bequest value. There is also (iii) existence value, which is the value of species as such for human beings. Finally, the value of species in and of themselves apart from human valuation leads to the notion of (iv) intrinsic value.

There are other disturbances to ecology related to human activities in addition to degeneration in biodiversity. Algal-carrying biological toxins are on the increase, along with the appearance of novel toxic species.[40] The increase is related to wash-off nutrients, especially nitrogen, from the land. Three hundred out of the 4,1000 species of phytoplankton produce red tides; about 70 per cent of these are toxic tides that then poison marine species and sometimes people as well. The overall phytoplankton population has declined by up to 30 per cent in Northern oceans since 1980 as a direct result of climate change, or more indirectly through changes in carbon dioxide levels. Changes in ocean temperatures also increase algal blooms. Paralytic shellfish poisoning, linked directly to harmful algal blooms through the food chain, is also on the increase. Rehabilitation of coastal habitat areas, which act like natural filters, is the best preventative strategy.

A thousand major agricultural pests, including 550 insects/mites, 230 plant diseases and 220 weeds, are resistant to pesticides. These changes threaten to lead to a loss in food security. Repeated pesticide over-use encourages the evolution of resistant species. Multiple resistances to pesticides are also soaring, so even a cocktail will not eliminate all pests. Herbicides, antibiotics and fungicides used to control plant disease are also diminishing in their effectiveness. The overall crop loss due to pests has not changed in spite of a tenfold increase in pesticides. Genetically modified crops engineered to produce pesticides throughout the growing season are likely to exacerbate the problem. Data on extent of genetically modified crops showed a 23-fold increase between 1996 and 2000. The bulk of transgenic crops are grown in the USA, Canada and Argentina.[41] Integrated pest management, which uses less pesticides and non-chemical methods such as crop rotations, intercropping and release of beneficial insects, may help to slow down the trend.

Values in ecological science

How might humanity respond to this somewhat gloomy account of escalating environmental problems? One of the core values in ecological science is the challenge to anthropocentrism – that is, the view that humanity is the centre of the universe. Authors such as Anne Primavesi and Mary Midgley have argued that James Lovelock's Gaia hypothesis presents an even deeper challenge to the place of humanity on the earth.[42] Lovelock's hypothesis addresses the interaction between the sum of living organisms on the planet, known as the biota, and global geochemistry. In its strongest version, Lovelock's hypothesis argues for the homeostatic regulation of the earth's atmosphere by the biota in order to keep environmental conditions constant.[43] The values implicit in this hypothesis are more commonly interpreted in terms of cooperation and symbiosis. Yet, it is equally possible to interpret Gaia's theory along more Darwinian lines, which includes the idea that those species that are the most influential in setting the environmental state become the most dominant. In this respect Lovelock's Gaia hypothesis is rather more ambiguous as a guide for ethics than some of its proponents allow. In so far as it raises the importance of cooperation and symbiosis, it can serve the function of reminding humanity of the varied ways in which species relate to each other – competition, in other words, is not the only or last word that might be said from an ecological perspective.

Alongside a paradigm of interrelatedness and cooperation, there is an equally strong notion of 'balance' that has served ecology for many years. Of course, it is a disputed point as to what extent the idea of the 'balance of nature' arose from ecological science; more likely it was already embedded in cultural assumptions about the natural world, and ecology just reinforced this notion.[44] This idea of balance continues to dominate the discourse among many contemporary Christian theologians, who find it congenial in relation to the concept of connectivity and community expressed in idealised terms, and serving as a pointer towards ethical conduct.[45] Yet ecologists themselves in their current practice are less attuned to this notion now compared with the past. Instead, the notion of flux, unstable equilibrium, openness to external influences, disturbance from internal and external forces, including humanity, is much more to the foreground of the way ecologists perceive their tasks.[46] This shift illustrates the difficulties of using ecological science as a basis for values, for as further research is conducted, other values appear that undermine the original notions. Ideas related to balance include integrity, which fits in well with the notion of balance, and serves to inform some ethical positions.

The concept of balance cannot be dispensed with altogether, since just as Newtonian mechanics proved accurate at the broadest level, but was eventually supplemented by Einstein's ideas, so too the concept of ecological balance can persist at the crudest level, even if flux is a more accurate description of what actually happens. Balance is also crucial in consideration of broad global processes such as climate change, but here too, research shows that such balances are subject to disturbance, often anthropogenic in origin. The concept of ecosystems being in fragile balance, subject to disturbance, is important to *inform* the way humanity thinks about ethical conduct in relation to the environment – that is, we need to be aware that this is the case, but it should not become paradigmatic as a *value term* for ethical behaviour. Why not? I am reluctant to adopt a strong philosophy of naturalism – that is, deriving how we *ought* to behave from the way things are. This is not the same as saying we can ignore ecological science; rather, such aspects of the way ecology *is* serve to help us interpret how to treat the environment even if, to some extent, this knowledge is always provisional. If flux became a value, this would lead to chaos, and shows how inappropriate it is to derive or read off values from the natural world. There need, in other words, to be other reasons why humanity has decided that balance serves the common good, and reflects the goodness of creation understood as God's gift, rather than being derived as such from ecological science.

A case might be made for ecological wisdom, arising out of a perceived sense of the interrelationships and integrity of biological nature. In one sense natural wisdom exists, arising from the way creatures are so marvellously attuned to their environment and converge into particular patterns during the course of evolution.[47] The meaning of wisdom is itself elusive. Wisdom as a particularly human capacity is, according to Jeffrey Schloss, that ability to critique culture in the light of human evolutionary history. He suggests that 'Wisdom is living in a way that corresponds to how things are.'[48] The way things are could helpfully include ecological insights and knowledge. Wisdom, then, would be living in accordance with our knowledge of such sciences, but in such a way that gave meaning to existence.

Wonder, like wisdom, is also a virtue, or a particular habit of mind, that is common to many of the sciences, including ecology. Wonder among ecologists largely springs from the marvellous fecundity and diversity of life on this planet, in spite of multiple extinctions that threaten this diversity. Edward O. Wilson contends that humans possess an innate tendency to focus on life and life-like processes – a tendency he calls *biophilia*.[49] He argues that modern biology is a genuinely new way of looking at the world that happens to be in tune with this tendency. It is through such a search that he believes we can discover the core of wonder, due to the rich abundance of life.[50] Wilson wonders at biological facts, such as the fact that a handful of soil is home to hundreds of insects, nematode worms and other larger creatures, alongside a million fungi and ten billion bacteria. Other amazing facts include the genetic information required for one particular insect – if printed as standard-size letters, would stretch over a thousand miles. He is aware, as are many other biologists, that 90 per cent of species are not even named, and species are disappearing faster than they can be identified. Amidst a tropical rainforest, the sheer diversity of life is such that there are literally thousands of undiscovered species, with the number of discoveries per investigator greater than anywhere else in the world.

Wilson tries to argue for uniting the natural sciences and the humanities.[51] He intends the humanities to be absorbed by the sciences and reconfigured through the latter's knowledge. He does the cause of biology a disservice in using rhetorical devices such as the language of conquest and imperialism, which imply an underlying arrogance on his part in favour of biological knowledge. This imperialising tendency is opposed to the very wonder that he is trying to foster among fledgling ecologists. One of the reasons why he may have thought that this strategy would work is that it appeals to both group instincts and inter-group hostility, as according to him territorial expansion is 'an epigenetic rule'.[52] The fact that his strategy failed shows that there are values in human nature that do not conform to his model of human values. Instead, the project of uniting natural sciences and the humanities becomes more relevant when each is allowed to contribute to the overall discussion. Environmental problems are too complex to be the prerogative of one field of study, even if the scientific study of ecology is highly relevant to such discussions.

Rachel Carson, a biologist writing in the era before E. O. Wilson developed his sociobiology, argued passionately for the wondrous appreciation of the natural world.[53] However, this appreciation did not lead her to announce the tyranny of biology over other forms of knowledge in the manner of Wilson's rhetoric; rather, it came from a more fundamental anxiety about what might happen to the world if humans continued to despoil the environment. Although Wilson used the language of wonder to express his forays in natural history, he appealed to baser aspects of human nature as a basis for environmental protection. The natural world was valuable for its instrumental use to humans, so that it could be viewed as an untapped source of new pharmaceuticals, crops, fibres, and so on. Carson believed that the despoliation of nature was not in humanity's best interest.[54] She believed that wonder is a prelude for care for the earth, and in this her views are directly contradictory to those of Wilson. For example, she claimed that 'The more clearly we focus our attention on the wonders and realities of the world about us, the less taste we shall have for destruction', and 'A child's world is fresh and new and beautiful, full of wonder and excitement. It is to our misfortune that for most of us that clear eyed vision, that true instinct for what is beautiful and awe inspiring is dimmed and even lost when we reach adulthood.'[55] It is unlikely that she was advocating a return to childhood in a way that is detached from science, for where such romanticism means a total rejection of science it fails to convince. Carson was hinting at something profound about wondering, for it allows us to pay attention to what is, and in this sense comes closer to the religious instinct in wonder that Wilson only partially expressed. Wonder includes a sense of the aesthetic, an acknowledgement of what might loosely be termed 'beauty', but it also allows for recognition of what, to us, would be an awareness of horror, the dark side of creaturely being.[56] The capacity for wonder does, I suggest, go a step further than a simple awareness of creatureliness – humans understood as contingently embedded in a network of relationships, that Michael Northcott has correctly identified as being essential in order to counter more destructive attitudes to the environment.[57] For Christian believers both a sense of creatureliness and wonder are related to an understanding of God as Creator, but this is to anticipate theological discussion that will follow in later chapters.

Conclusions

The story of environmental damage outlined in this chapter shows the complexity of the issues involved, even using a few illustrative examples. While population issues do need to be addressed, it is more important to address the lifestyles of the existing populations in order to begin to contain some of the more negative effects of human activity on the environment.

Inequality in distribution of resources, alongside over-consumption by richer nations of the world, contribute to depletion of energy reserves, water shortages, pollutant damage, health impacts and biodiversity loss. International cooperation is called for in order to address what might be called the tragedy of the commons, shared resources that are then abused, as no nation feels directly responsible. Human activities contribute to climate change that then adds to problems created by direct effects of pollution and energy shortages. In particular, those countries of the world that contribute relatively little to greenhouse gases suffer the worst impact, with the prospect of environmental refugees looming in low-lying areas and islands likely to be subject to flooding due to rising sea levels, or other areas exposed to climate extremes and soil erosion. While climate scientists have called for a greater degree of equity in calculating allowable pollution rates per person, there is little sign of a real desire by nations to make the necessary changes. Ecological science has contributed significantly to our knowledge of biodiversity and its loss due to anthropogenic activities, both due to direct exploitation and indirect loss of habitat and introduced species. Ecological science offers a reminder that ecological systems are fragile and subject to disturbance, including disturbance by humans. Humanity, in other words, is an integral aspect of the ecology of an area, though the global impact of humans is far greater than other species.

Are there values implicit in ecology that might be helpful in addressing some of the environmental problems that have become more pressing with each generation? Viewing the earth as a whole system through the Gaia hypothesis has been inspirational for some authors. Others point to the feeling of wonder possible through the study of the natural world in all its diversity and complexity. Such wondrous appreciation can be a prelude to more responsible behaviour. In addition, the cooperative integrity of living things points to a kind of ecological wisdom, though of course in making this suggestion we need to bear in mind other features of evolutionary history, 'red in tooth and claw', that appear less attractive. Human wisdom, in particular, can mean living in tune with the way things are in the sense of not undermining the very basis for biodiversity, understood in ecological and well as evolutionary terms. Such a discussion lends itself to theological analysis, for it points to the issue that environmental problems are not simply about scientific discoveries of what those problems might be, but also the underlying crisis of values in the human community.

Yet before we trace some of the different religious responses to such crisis, it is important to spell out more clearly than we have so far some of the global trends in economics which seem to have paralysed human political will to change in line with the suggestions presented above. In addition, one of the main reasons for the growth in biotechnology has been economic gain, and it illustrates how such direct human intervention in genetics can further the ecological impacts that are already in place through the widespread use of industrialised agriculture. The arguments in favour of such technology are often couched in terms of the requirement for food, but more often than not, the economics might suggest alternative motivations. The following chapter deals with economic issues and environmental justice in order to set the scene for the alternative theological positions that follow.

Further reading

Berry, R. J., *God's Book of Works* (London, T. & T. Clark/Continuum, 2003)

Carson, R., *Silent Spring* (Boston, Houghton Mifflin, 1961)

Deane-Drummond, C., *Wonder and Wisdom: Conversations in Science, Spirituality and Theology* (London, Darton, Longman and Todd, 2006)

Gaston, K. J. and Spicer, J. I., *Biodiversity* (2nd edn, Oxford, Blackwell, 2004)

Gottlieb, Roger, *A Greener Faith: Religious Environmentalism and Our Planet's Future* (Oxford, Oxford University Press, 2006)

Houghton, J., *Global Warming: The Complete Briefing* (3rd edn, Cambridge, Cambridge University Press, 2004)

Lovelock, J., *Gaia: A New Look at Life on Earth* (2nd edn, Oxford, Oxford University Press, 1987)

McDonagh, S., *Climate Change: The Challenge to All of Us* (Blackrock, The Columba Press, 2006)

Northcott, M., *A Moral Climate: The Ethics of Global Warming* (London, DLT, 2007)

UNEP, *Global Environmental Outlook 3 Report* (London, Earthscan, 2002)

Wilson, E. O., *Consilience* (London, Abacus, 1999)

World Watch Institute, *Vital Signs 2006–7* (New York, W. N. Norton, 2006)

Chapter 2

Economics and environmental justice

THE STUDY OF ENVIRONMENTAL PROBLEMS AND ECOLOGY illustrates the depth of the extent of global damage related to human activity. Such problems are intensified by the socio-political structures in which human societies are embedded, especially in the Western world. In particular, the market economy that currently dominates world trade fosters, rather than curbs, the tendency for spiralling habits of over-consumption. Overall, globalisation brings some benefits, but skews power away from nation states. Hence, even if there is a multinational desire for more sustainable living, other forces counter such trends. Biotechnology is illustrative of the way multinational activity has dominated the global market in a way that is highly ambiguous for global ecology. Broader issues of environmental justice illustrate the disproportionate suffering in human communities through environmental dislocations. In addition, future generations stand to suffer as a result of human activities in the present. This chapter intends to highlight these issues and offer a critical commentary prior to more specific theological responses in later chapters.

Market economics

According to the neo-liberal view of the market economy, free trade leads to inevitable growth. Justice is then related to the fixing of prices according to the market equilibrium in relation to individual preferences. This theory postulates that the reason that there is a persistent tendency to damage the environment is that there is no price tag or economic burden associated with such activities. The solution, therefore, in this case is to ensure that such a price does reflect environmental goods; either by giving tradable property rights to those goods, or by constructing prices on the basis of what individuals would pay if there were a market for such goods. From this follows a cost-benefit analysis whereby proposed projects take into account such goods in accordance with the market value either directly or indirectly constructed. Where value is constructed, monetary values can be estimated by asking how much people are willing to pay (WTP) or how much they would be willing to accept in compensation if it were hypothetically in a market.

The idea that an environmental good can be given a monetary value directly equivalent to property rights is one resisted by many philosophers.[1] This trend towards 'commodification' of environmental goods through extension of property rights runs up against the same sort of objections that one might have in the sale of, for example, body parts and so on. As well as direct valuation, many object to the spread of dominating market norms into ecological valuation at all; other areas of life that are deemed inappropriate as sites for such norms would be religion or education. Ecological concern reflects human values as citizens, whereas the economy presupposes preferences as consumers, hence giving monetary value to environmental goods is a category mistake. In surveys designed to see how far people are willing to pay (WTP) for environmental containment, people habitually refuse to give specific monetary values for environmental protection.[2] In other words, many object to the assumption that environmental problems arise because of a failure to apply market norms; rather, the fault is in the spread of those very norms. In addition, extending market systems to environmental problems exacerbates these problems indirectly by adding to the existing global market system that has fostered over-consumption and a depletion of resources along with associated effects of climate change.

The question for Christian theologians is also how far the market economy as a system reflects Christian ideals. Harvey Cox has suggested that the global market economy functions as an implicit religious system, showing key characteristics of a religion, such as (i) a story about the purpose of human life; (ii) a particular interpretation of human identity expressed as freedom; (iii) a doctrine of what is wrong and how to repair this – in religious terms, sin and redemption; (iv) sacramental rituals – for example, shopping; (v) exemplary heroes; and (vi) an assumption that all will work together for the good. Everything is turned into a commodity. The market tries to expose the secret desires of its adherents through market researchers, the new priests of the religion. Advertising re-presents wants as consumer needs; even spirituality becomes a market commodity. Cox's commentary on land is particularly instructive in an ecological context:

> For millennia of human history, land has held multiple meanings for human beings – as soil, resting place of the ancestors, holy mountain or enchanted forest, tribal homeland, aesthetic inspiration, sacred turf. The Market transforms all these complex meanings into one: land becomes real estate; there is no land that is not theoretically for sale, at the right price.[3]

His critique provides a sharp rebuttal of those who assimilate and endorse fully a market economy as expressive of Christian faith – the so-called prosperity gospel. Those who oppose the market system from a Christian perspective seem to do so only when human parts are up for sale, such as human genes. The critique does not go to the deeper trends in the market towards acquisition and consumerism. Cox is correct to expose the market economy as an idol of our time that needs to be challenged and kept in check. You cannot serve God and Mammon.

Globalisation and sustainability

Globalisation
The trend towards globalisation of markets means not so much the end of politics, but its escape beyond the boundaries of the nation state, and arguably beyond the age-old distinction between the political right and left. Transnational corporations (TNCs) are able to export jobs to those parts of the world where labour is cheapest and workplace obligations are lowest. Information technology furthers such a spreading of the net into different parts of the world. Trading between nations allows the cheapest possible investment conditions and the most favourable infrastructure to be selected. In addition, investment, production, taxation and residence are all bargained for on the basis of what is best for company profits, with the components possibly separated spatially from one another. Ulrich Beck points out that such shifts have come about without any political or democratic discussion. The process itself has escaped into a sub-political sphere where power dominates over and above the normal political processes. He states:

> The transition to a politics of globalisation has crept in on velvet paws, under the guise of normality, rewriting the social rules of the game – with the legitimacy of a modernization that will happen come what may.[4]

In Europe corporate tax has not kept up with company profits, which have soared, along with downsizing in labour. There are also important distinctions to be made:[5]

- *Globalism* refers to the view that the world market eliminates political action; it reduces the multi-dimensional aspects of globalisation through economic processes. The central task of politics, which in the past has helped to define the legal, social and ecological conditions for economic strategies, disappears from view. Various forms of protectionism are a reaction to globalism, viewed as inevitable.
- *Globality*, on the other hand, refers to society as a world community, so that there is a sense in which different countries and groups intersect with each

other in a way that has to be taken into account. It is the premise of this book that such globality exists, reminding the reader of differences across different cultural, social and political boundaries. It also allows for differences to be expressed and aired in a way that recognises human distinctiveness.

- *Globalisation* is the sum of processes through which transnational players undermine nation states. Note that such transnational players also include not just TNCs, but also organisations such as the United Nations and non-governmental organisations, including those campaigning for environmental action (NGOs). The critique of globalisation needs to be qualified with this in mind, though for the most part globalisation has deleterious environmental impact by, on the whole, operating in a way that either takes little account of environmental harms, or isolates these from wider considerations of human development.

Beck also believes that awareness of such processes is the first step in breaking down the ideology of globalism and associated globalisation. Those pushing for globalisation in markets recognise that sensitivity to local context is important – in other words, the market products should be appropriately clothed in the cultural symbols of the local society. This makes the spread of global markets all the more successful. There is also the possibility of transformation of TNCs so that they become more accountable in their use of power, perhaps being willing to subscribe to benefit sharing and being willing to pay adequate taxes instead of deliberately separating taxation from production.[6] In other words, TNCs need to be supported in projects that work for the common good, including environmental goods, rather than simple self-interest. Pressure could be brought to bear through consumer boycotts in order to force TNCs to be more democratic and more ecologically aware. Such a shift would alleviate some of the difficulties associated with the shift in power to TNCs, but it would not provide lasting solutions to the underlying political issues raised by globalisation.

Sustainability in a risk society

In the context of environmental concern, there is also the issue of the risk of ecological destruction caused by affluence itself, leading to the unpredictable impacts of processes such as biotechnology. Ecological devastation is also, however, associated with poverty, so that those communities that are concerned with their own survival needs do not have the wherewithal to take appropriate ecological responsibility. There is, in addition, the ecological threat of weaponry, and military conflict arising through movement of environmental refugees. Alongside the awareness of risk we find growing demands for sustainability – that is, a style of living within the limits of the earth's resources. Some authors, on the other hand, define sustainability in terms of the needs of future generations.[7] Ironically, perhaps, sustainability has taken on its own rhetoric within world markets, to such an extent that it becomes accommodated within globalisation. So-called 'sustainable' products are sold on the basis of a global market among all of those in different nation states who are environmentally aware. More radical is the idea of *sustainable economics*, one that seeks to challenge the market system as such, by making production decisions not on the basis of market or consumer demand, but on the basis of the rate at which resources could be replenished.[8] In addition, the level of production of waste would be set on the basis of the earth's capacity for assimilation, rather than willingness to pay.

Does the carbon trading through contraction and convergence and through the Kyoto agreements suggested in the last chapter provide an adequate economic response to climate change and promote a sustainable future? Michael Northcott is deeply sceptical of its potential, for similar reasons to those discussed on page 18 regarding the commodification of ecological goods. He suggests, correctly in my view, that such an approach creates the illusion that human activity can be regulated through supply and demand, and provides significant opportunities for corruption and evasion. He suggests that the solution to the problem is not simply acquisition to the existing market economy, but moral and political deliberation in parliaments, courts and local forms of governance.[9] The difficulty, of course, as in all criticism of the market economy, is that the market is so deeply embedded in Western societies that it is hard to shift to alternative strategies.[10] What is clear is that carbon trading is not enough, though I fear that if it were removed altogether, the result could be worse. Clearly, there are deceptive practices that are encouraged through such schemes, such as allowing multinationals to engage in projects to grow eucalyptus tree plantations in tropical areas as a trade-off for more polluting industries in Europe. In this case the eucalyptus plantation has negative environmental impacts, even though, ironically, it is approved as a 'carbon sink'.

Are there strategies for achieving alternative sustainable economies compared with the current market economy? John Cobb has argued for the establishment of small regions that are self-sufficient in terms of basic survival needs through the decentralisation of the economy.[11] Such regions would impose tariffs on goods that are produced elsewhere where the wages are low, or where there is pollution or poor working conditions generally. He believes that regions may be national in some cases, but in others may be villages that culturally can operate in a self-sufficient way. Of course, the idea of small economic units has been around for some time, ever since Schumacher proposed that small is beautiful.[12] The difference, perhaps, today, is that the need for such alternatives comes from a realisation that justice and sustainability are impossible with policies orientated simply towards growth. Further, there is a growing underclass that would support change, and a growing interest in communitarian thinking.

Biotechnology

The impact of genetic biotechnology has local, national and international ramifications that impinge on global ecology as well as being interwoven with global economic considerations through patenting of plant and animal varieties. It is a visible expression of the globalisation process discussed above. The development of new genetically modified (GM) crops is primarily motivated by market considerations. Strong public objections to GM food have more recently shifted this advantage against the commercial use of GM crops, especially in Europe.[13] Environmental risk factors associated with genetic engineering are related to the power of the technology to bring about irreversible changes in the hereditary material of plants, animals and bacteria. Genetically engineered rapeseed and maize, for example, which contain resistance to specific herbicides, have escalated in production since their first release, with the majority of the crop grown in the USA, though a significant portion is grown in Canada, Argentina and parts of Europe.

There are strong advocates of and opponents to genetic engineering.[14] Those who are supportive of genetic engineering argue that it is simply an extension of normal plant breeding and cultivation that has been going on for years. They also suggest that world food problems cannot be solved without genetic intervention. Those opposed to genetic engineering have pointed to the possible environmental risks associated with biotechnology. They argue that the belief that GM crops will feed the world is a self-deception. Such a technological fix to the problem is neither desired by those in poorer nations, nor realistic. They argue that problems of starvation and lack of access to healthy diets cannot be whitewashed by simple technological 'solutions' that cover up the underlying social and political causes of poverty. Moreover, opponents suggest that far from improving environmental conditions, GM crops lead to risks to the environment and potential damage to ecosystems and the food chain, as well as loss of biodiversity. Such effects are very difficult to test or predict in advance. Who is really to gain from the new genetic engineering products? In most cases it seems as though it would lead to an even further redistribution of wealth, to the detriment of poorer nations. Furthermore, at a cultural level it is worth considering not just the possible benefits to the cultural wealth of richer nations, but also the potentially damaging effects on traditional subsistence agriculture which relies on less chemical inputs.

GM crops reinforce the culture of modern industrialised farming, orientated as it is towards increase in yield regardless of the social consequences. The increased dependence of the farmers on herbicides for weed control encourages an equal dependence on the hybrid seed sold by the same company. Hybrid seeds do not breed true, so the traditional method of saving seed for the next year's crop is only possible with loss of yield. The impacts of these stipulations are of particular significance for farmers in the poorer communities in the world, where recycling seed is seen as an integral part of their lifestyle. The World Council of Churches (WCC) undertook a Global Consultation on Genetics in Johannesburg in December 2007. The accounts of the impact of GMOs (genetically modified organisms), especially on the poorest communities of the world, were particularly poignant. The introduction of GM maize in Mexico, for example, has not only impacted the ecology of the native varieties, but also undermines the close association between people and the cultivation of specific varieties of maize built up over centuries of farming. Indigenous peoples speak of humanity being made by maize, and maize as a gift of God to the people, a reflection of the religious as well as social affiliation between maize and people that suffers radical disruption with the introduction of genetically modified crops.

Such stories are also repeated in other parts of the world, leading to profound injustices for those on the receiving end of the technology. Following the global consultation, the WCC reported that the case of maize in Mexico represented an exploitative pattern that was also characteristic of other parts of the globe:

> These themes were echoed again and again, from the canola fields of Canada to the sugar cane field in the Caribbean, Africa and the Pacific, to those who struggle with the agro-export model of genetically modified soy in Latin America, and to 120,000 cotton farmers who committed suicide in India because of crop failure. Violation of the human rights of the farmers often went hand in hand with violence against women and children and other groups, which was reported from many countries. Driven by the global market economy and unjust political systems, biotechnology promised increased production, but in the context of injustice and violence it results in dependency and threat to biodiversity. The new emphasis on agrofuels threatens to further monocultures, expulsion by peasants, land speculation, pollution, and disease, while raising food prices.[15]

Another indirect risk of GM crops, which is also characteristic of conventional plant breeding, is the overall loss in genetic diversity. Wild strains have a much greater variability that protects them naturally from pests and disease. When a crop is genetically engineered (or bred) the resultant uniformity brings the desired increase in yield, but also carries a greater vulnerability to disease. In order to find new sources of variation, researchers have sought wild strains that have retained their genetic variability. These wild strains are on the whole confined to the poorer Southern continents, but the patent payments are more often than not accrued by the company developing the technology. There are also indirect effects on genetic biodiversity by environmental impacts of genetically modified crops over and above that resulting from conventional agriculture.

Genetic engineering also allows genes to be modified so that the plant produces novel products.[16] Oilseed rape plants, for example, can be GM and grown in the northern hemisphere so that their oil is very similar to that normally produced in the Southern continents by palm and coconut trees. The UK currently imports 400,000 tonnes of palm oil and coconut oil; hence locally produced GM oilseed is likely to be a commercial advantage depending on particular economic conditions. Genetic engineering can also be used to render plants more tolerant to frost. Such developments can cater for the demand for strawberries in the Western world well ahead of the normal growing season. More money has been spent on developing GM strawberries than all research on basic subsistence crops such as cassava grown in poorer communities.

Other experiments are underway to enhance the tolerance of crops to a range of unfavourable conditions, including high acidity, high aluminium, drought and high salt conditions. Drought and salt tolerance in crops is complicated by the fact that these attributes are coded for by many different genes, and there is no guarantee that such plants would not become 'invasive' species, taking over ecological niches that were once occupied by native varieties. This is one reason why ecologists are conscious of the real environmental risk of GM crops, in spite of their seeming attractiveness as a resource.

There are, however, some good examples of successful GM control of plant disease.[17] The use of genetic technology to control nematode pests in bananas and potatoes is an important, but relatively rare example of the careful use of GMOs in order to support farmers in developing countries who would otherwise have very poor crop yields. It is also important to note that such introductions were not imposed, often against the will of the local populations, as in the examples cited earlier, but took place through careful consultation with the farmers themselves. There are no organic methods of control of nematodes, and nematicides are environmentally very damaging. About 50 per cent of the crop in Bolivia is lost to nematodes. The proteinase inhibitor, cystatin, is a rice gene that can be introduced into potato or banana crops in order to control nematodes effectively. It is harmless to eat and reduces the exposure of animals or humans to toxic nematicides. Of course, in these instances it is also worth asking a broader question – namely, are the farmers getting a fair price on the banana and potato crops and who are the recipients?

These illustrations show that GMOs have more often than not been used for the purpose of commercial gain for particular specialist markets, without adequate consideration of the overall impact on either local ecology or global trade, and in many cases leading to gross injustices towards those who are most vulnerable to exploitation. However, there are some exceptions, in that GM may be usefully used to control plant disease or to assist in plant breeding and cultivation. Yet it is worth bearing in mind that the collapse in market support means that even the commercial justification of GMOs in the richer nations of the world has now also been challenged in the light of the poor return experienced by US farmers. This may, of course, be one reason why there are strong attempts at proliferation in other nations that have less tight regulatory controls and are more vulnerable to exploitation by those transnational companies that are finding a dwindling market in the more industrialised Northern nations. Yet even in these nations, in many cases there were no public consultations prior to the release, which may be one reason why there has been a severe backlash in Europe, and increasing resistance in the USA. In the UK the consultation that took place in 2003 seems to have been ignored by government policy-makers. While the companies concerned deny any risk to the environment, it is not proven. If anything, the *science* suggests the opposite, since rapeseed can cross-fertilise with wild mustard plants.

Some field research conducted in the UK and published in 2003 has indicated that biodiversity is reduced when GM oilseed rape and GM sugarbeet are grown in place of conventional intensive agriculture, but not when GM maize is grown. These results reflect changes in agricultural practices, rather than direct impacts of genetic engineering as such. Subsequent reports that GM genes can spread into surrounding weeds indicate more direct effects that were unknown and so unaccounted for earlier. However, the earlier field research gave the British government ammunition to argue for the introduction of GM maize, in spite of widespread public resistance to such a development in a survey conducted in the same year that was known as the GM Nation report. The government action in spite of strong objections by the public implies that the democratic processes are themselves susceptible to pressure from the biotechnology lobby, tied up with lucrative patents, rather than fulfilling their democratic role as the representatives of popular opinion. Of course, those companies involved are more likely to refrain from development of such technologies where there is no support from the market, leading to an overall result that reflects current public opinion. The premise is still that the market boundaries will be sufficient.

Patenting

The development of genetically modified crops is also intricately bound up with the economics of patenting and patent rights.[18] Henry VI first granted a UK patent to John of Utyam in 1449 for his method of making stained glass. John had to teach others his trade, in return making his method public; a more common reaction by manufacturers then was to keep the methods secret. Patents gradually became part of the commercial life of the nation. At the turn of the last century ornamental plant lobbyists campaigned to include plants within patent law, so that in 1930 a US Plant Patent Act established the right to patent new cultivated varieties, but held back from permitting patenting of 'wild' varieties in the field. At this stage the Act limited protection to those plants that could reproduce asexually. Human intervention was, of course, required in order to gain a patent licence. There was a general consensus that anything 'natural' could not be patented. By 1970 the US Plant Variety Protection Act had extended to allow intellectual property rights (IPR) for sexually reproducing plants (in other words, seed-bearing varieties), though such rights were not, strictly speaking, patents as they were less extensive and, significantly, allowed farmers to save protected seed for their own use or for sale on other farms.

Patenting is the reward given to groups or individuals for a specific invention, rather than a 'discovery'. This invention has a requirement to be *novel* (that is, it is not obvious to others), and also *useful* (that is, it has some application that is of economic value). The reward of issue of a patent takes the form of a 'negative right' in that those who make use of this inventiveness are required to pay a fee covered by patent law. The fee is justified on the basis that the time and money spent on research and development requires a payback, over and above the marketing of the final product. If a patent is not granted, this does not prevent the research going ahead; it merely means that others can use the methods published without penalty. Scientific discoveries are not subject to patenting because scientific advance grows from pre-existing knowledge, which should be accessible to all for further research, without penalty. Such knowledge is very broad in its applicability. Hence, if it were subject to a patent, it would, in effect, grant a reward to a single group and curtail further research. In theory patent law was designed to facilitate socio-economic functioning at a national and global level by providing incentives to develop innovative and useful research that will benefit the whole community. The 'secrets' become 'shared' through patent protection. This is balanced by the need to reward individuals for their creative contribution to the process – though increasingly, and ironically perhaps, the reward is not given to individuals so much as to multinational companies. Companies have their own means of rewarding employees who are responsible for achieving patentable commodities.

In a famous case, Ananda Chakrabarty filed a US patent for a bacteria (*Pseudomonas*) that was genetically modified in order to degrade components of crude oil. His application in 1976 was initially rejected on the basis that nothing 'natural' could be the subject of a patent. He worked for General Electric, a company that was more used to dealing with processes as 'inventions', compared with, say, other biologically based companies, that would have more readily assumed that patenting on biological organisms would be refused, as they could not easily be put under the traditional patenting bracket of 'inventions'. The US Supreme Court in 1980 made a landmark decision by a narrow five–four majority in ruling that in *Diamond v. Chakrabarty* the GM bacteria could be protected by a patent. The court held that 'his discovery is not nature's handiwork, but his own', and is 'the result of human ingenuity and research'.[19] This was a watershed decision, as it allowed an increased number of filings for patents of living things, including newly developed plant varieties that had previously had more restricted protection. The patents were, in some cases, far too broad. For example, they covered all genetically engineered seeds and plants of a particular species. By 1987 provision was made to extend patentability to non-human living multicellular organisms, which included animals. By 1988 a mouse genetically engineered so that it developed cancer, known as the Harvard oncomouse, had been patented.

Environmental justice

The situation of environmental injustice understood as unfair distribution of environmental harms and goods needs to be addressed urgently, prior to any desirable revolution in the economy. Extreme poverty, social exclusion and environmental injustice appear in tandem in communities all over the world. This is one reason for the environmental justice movement.

Considerations of environmental justice also bring political issues to the fore. For many scholars environmental injustice is inevitably wedded to liberalism and the market economy. It is worth considering whether we can formulate some *intermediate mediating strategies* between the market-led system that has dominated the political economy to date and more radical idealistic alternatives mentioned above on page 21.[20] Such mediating strategies need to be viewed as interim emergency measures prior to more widespread change, rather than a reformist strategy as such that is content merely to stay with reform measures.

Environmental justice includes both the opportunity for all to take part in environmental decision-making, which is a form of procedural justice, and also more substantive environmental rights. It is also worth naming a contrast here. While economic justice is normally couched in terms of monetary goods to be distributed, environmental justice has been about the extent of distribution of harms, mostly to health. A long history of research shows that low-income groups are also subject to a higher proportion of pollutants. Of course, such environmental injustices could also now include, ironically perhaps, introduction of so-called carbon sink crops in poorer nations, where these are displacing other native crops or being imposed without proper consultation. The environmental injustices of much GMO proliferation, especially in the poorer nations of the world, also provides good examples of harms. More recently there has been a shift in interest to include not just harms, but also environmental goods. This is beyond basic goods such as clean air and water, towards a right to a minimum standard of environmental quality at home and reasonable access to those higher quality environments in the countryside. In the UK an Economic and Social Research Council Briefing Paper on environmental justice highlighted the lack of adequate provision for fuel for heating homes that are energy inefficient, and lack of access to affordable healthy food due to the growth of out-of-town superstores.[21]

John Rawls' difference principle states that where economic and social inequalities exist, then they must be conditional on being of greatest benefit to the least advantaged in society.[22] Rawls uses income and wealth as a measure of advantage. Rawls' theory cannot be applied to ecological justice, understood in terms of giving rights to non-humans, but it can be used to support environmental justice, and justice to future generations.[23] It is important to consider how public money might have been spent in alternative ways, such as education, or medical care, while recognising that a minimum standard of environmental quality to sustain basic health needs to be met. The goal in this case is not so much zero pollution, as reducing the levels of pollution in order to allow individuals to be fully cooperative members of society. The difference principle requires that pollution be reduced to this minimum standard in terms of impact on otherwise socially disadvantaged groups. Access to a clean environment at home and in the countryside would improve health, and so be a justifiable expense. However, it falls short of recommending quality environments as a good in themselves.

A Rawlsian vision takes us in the right direction towards environmental justice, but it is far too thin a standard to satisfy most advocates. In the first place, who is to say that providing the bare minimum level merely to assure health is sufficient? Why, in other words, should access to quality environments be restricted simply to those instances where it is proven to have a positive impact on the health budget? Tim Gorringe argues strongly that the injustices in the built environment call for empowerment for those marginalised through poverty and exclusion.[24] Rawls' account, which asks us to imagine what it might be like to be in the situation envisaged, is insufficient in this respect; we need to go further than this in the interests of human equality.

Rawls' account also fails to tackle international global issues of injustice, for it assumes a democratic society where the possibility of wealth creation impacts on members of that society alone. It does not take into account wider issues of environmental impact outside its particular jurisdiction. This position excludes considerations of world international trade and the powerful dominance of some countries and TNCs over others through trading agreements that are more often than not distorted in favour of the most powerful groups. The World Trade Organisation (WTO) is guided by values embedded in the economy of the richer Western European nations and the USA towards increased trade liberalisation. Its rhetoric of sustainable development rings hollow to those concerned with more radical shifts in economic policy that aim to include those who have become marginalised in such discussions. Mary Grey and Sallie McFague have offered a sharp critique of these trading relations from a religious perspective that puts more value on the earth as bearer of the sacred.[25]

I have suggested so far that the use of Rawls' account provides an intermediate step in terms of the implementation of environmental justice understood in a narrow sense. Its inadequacies are highlighted once we consider international trade relations and the global economy. Another of the reasons for its inadequacy is a failure to appreciate the basic environmental condition in which human beings are situated. This is an issue recognised by environmentalists, namely that sustaining environmental goods such as biodiversity and climate stability is necessary for the ultimate sustaining of human society as such.

More promising, perhaps, is Amartya Sen's capability approach.[26] He is influenced by Rawls, but considers that the choice of variable is critical in measurement of equality, so that people may be equal in one respect, but lacking in others. He draws on Rawls' notion of the original position, but suggests that rather than using income as such as a measure, we should use capability that is related to the well-being of an individual. Well-being is measured by being happy, having self-respect, taking part in the life of the community and so on. Sen's capability approach underscores freedom of the individual to choose one type of life over another. He believes that Rawls is incorrect to assume that primary goods, such as income, rights, liberties and opportunities are what every person wants. Rather, the focus should be on the person's freedom to live the life that they have reason to value. For him, poverty is about *capability failure*, rather than simple deprivation of income.

In the light of deeper awareness of environmental issues, Sen's capability approach would include environmental goods as an important aspect of well-being. Yet because he suggests capacity for full functioning is the most important indicator of human well-being, it becomes possible to stretch this to the non-human community in terms of its capacity for functioning – in other words, ecological justice. It is the mutual capability of all members of the human and non-human community that needs to be sought. In the broadest sense it also includes the capability of the earth to maintain itself in order for biodiversity to flourish – in other words, climate stability. This seems to me to be more reasonable than campaigns for animal 'rights', for justice is now considered in terms of capabilities, rather than narrowed to single-issue primary goods that are difficult to extend to non-human species.[27] The ethical difficulties pertain to how to adjudicate between different demands of living systems, though, as indicated below, given that environmental goods such as climate change impact on all life forms, including humans, such goods need to take a high priority.

Future generations

Consideration of the place of future generations also forces us to consider the basic ecological pre-condition for sustaining human life in a way that is sometimes lacking if the focus is purely on present communities.[28] Reflection on future generations pushes us to the limit of our conception of human rights, and by association, justice. Consideration of future generations is one area where rights language comes up against its own limits, since reciprocity is impossible.[29] Such a conception relies on theories of justice that are more contractual in tone. Future generations can be included where it is recognised that they are valid *recipients* of justice, though of course, some would argue that even this status would be inappropriate to beings that do not yet exist. Some philosophers hold to the narrow view that future generations have no rights, as they do not yet exist.[30] Other philosophers, however, argue for the rights of future generations. For example, non-existence at the time when obligations are discharged is no excuse for negligence, as in the example of a young child that falls down a mineshaft that was left uncovered years before his/her existence.

Finally, it is worth mentioning the idea of eco-justice towards future generations of non-human communities. As we noted in the previous chapter, it is not just human beings who suffer from environmental decay; habitats are wiped out with reduced health of the existing populations where pollution is present. Even greater changes to habitats are wrought by climate change. Some life forms are particularly sensitive to pollution, such as lichens, and can even be used as 'pollution indicators'. If environmental justice is to become extended to the non-human community and become *ecological* justice, then while there needs to be some discrimination between different species in terms of priority, the political will in the richer economies needs to be redirected towards environmental protection and sustainability.

One way to achieve such a goal may be through curtailing the discretionary powers of governments by raising the issue of obligations to future generations.[31] This is a sensible strategy in many respects, as the notion of 'rights' of non-human species is unlikely to gain widespread political support. When the loss of biodiversity fails to impinge on the economy of present generations, it is often not taken sufficiently seriously, even though we are entering the 'sixth major mass extinction of all time'. Yet this is a 'tyranny of the majority', namely the present human generation against future ones. We have obligations to future generations that include, for example, preservation of biodiversity, and this could be achieved by constitutional constraint. The limited measures in liberal democracies in existence so far are insufficient to meet the needs of future generations. A legal restriction on destruction of biodiversity is a more convincing strategy compared with economic incentives, as long as it can be enforced. Some sort of retributive penalty for past errors in damaging environmental goods may also contribute to changing the way society perceives the seriousness of the problems.

Conclusions

I have suggested so far that the relationship between the market economy and environmental issues is a complex one. On the one hand there are those who argue that the market system is the root cause of environmental problems, because it fosters the kind of over-consumption that is ecologically irresponsible in terms of energy use, pollution, waste of resources and so on. On the other hand, there are those who believe that market systems are here to stay, so that the only way of providing some kind of protection for the environment is to give environmental goods market value such that they will be taken seriously in the market-place. There is also the added complication of globalisation, which threatens to undermine the democratic structures of nation states, and allow a free exchange of goods and commodities in a way that escapes national and international scrutiny. Questions arise now as to whether it is possible to reform the practice of TNCs, or whether alternative means of trading in a more sustainable way need to be found, or perhaps both in tandem. Biotechnology offered a case study in the growth of global products, but this time these products have potential direct effects on the environment, as well as indirect effects through global market mechanisms. In this case, wider social impacts are also relevant in as much as the spread in global biotechnology often disrupts indigenous lifestyles and cultures, and may even in some cases be associated with violence against the most vulnerable.

The protection of intellectual property rights through patenting of life systems raised other issues for consideration, namely how far it is appropriate for living systems to be the subject of patents. In addition, the widespread growth of such technologies poses significant challenges not just for the present generation, but also in the context of future generations, who will receive the legacy of those decisions made for or against the planet. But what is the most appropriate response to such shifts? So-called 'Deep Ecology' attempts to construct its own platform based on perceived threats to the environment. The next chapter will consider its claims and ask how far such claims are relevant both culturally and from a theological point of view in the light of the issues discussed in the previous two chapters.

Further reading

Beck, Ulrich, *What is Globalisation?*, trans. Patrick Camiller (Cambridge, Polity Press, 2000)

Bruce, Donald and Bruce, Ann, *Engineering Genesis* (London, Earthscan, 1999)

Cobb, John B., 'Towards a Just and Sustainable Economic Order', in Andrew Light and Holmes Rolson III (eds.), *Environmental Ethics: An Anthology* (Oxford, Blackwell, 2003), pp. 359–70

Cox, H., 'Mammon and the Culture of the Market: A Socio-Theological Critique', in Roger S. Gottlieb (ed.), *Liberating Faith: Religious Voices for Justice, Peace and Ecological Wisdom* (Lanham, Rowman and Littlefield, 2003), pp. 274–83

Deane-Drummond, C., 'Environmental Justice and the Economy: A Christian Theologian's View', *Ecotheology* 11.3 (2006), pp. 294–310

Dobson, A., *Justice and the Environment: Conceptions of Environmental Sustainability and Dimensions of Social Justice* (Oxford, Oxford University Press, 1998)

Schumacher, E. F., *Small is Beautiful: Economics as if People Mattered* (London, Blond and Briggs, 1973)

Chapter 3

Eco-theology from the North

HOW CAN SOME OF THE ENVIRONMENTAL PROBLEMS identified in earlier chapters be addressed? Writers in the Northern hemisphere, notably from the United States, became conscious in the early part of the twentieth century that their treatment of the earth was not in tune with natural ecosystems and ecological cycles, leading to environmental destruction on an unprecedented scale. Others believed that the social and political situation prevailing in democratic societies needed to be confronted by direct action, and sought to find philosophical roots to the problems, alongside a campaign for political activity. Still others sought to create an alternative approach to theology that stresses the value of the whole of life and creation, rather than sin and redemption. This chapter focuses on firstly the influence of the land ethic of the conservation ecologist Aldo Leopold, and secondly on the development of Deep Ecology. More theological developments of holism are found in the work of Matthew Fox, Teilhard de Chardin and Thomas Berry, and we will consider the significance of each for creation spirituality. We will also consider the adequacy of these claims both theologically and in the light of the ecological and economic analysis raised in the first two chapters.

Ecology and the land ethic

Aldo Leopold (1887–1948) worked in game management in the United States. He originally held a view that was fairly typical of conservationists at the time, namely that game should be managed like 'crop', and treated as a resource for human benefit. He also believed that natural predators were vermin, competing with humans for the valuable crop, and so should be destroyed. Gradually he began to question this view, seeing that the simple destruction of predators had other, unforeseen long-term impacts on the overall ecology of a region. He tells the story of how he watched a wolf that he had shot die slowly in front of him, the light in its green eyes glazed over slowly in death. This experience seemed to have a powerful impact on him, for after this he started to question the policy of eliminating wolves, believing, in a famous phrase, that we should learn to 'think like a Mountain' and get in touch with the needs of the overall ecology. He developed his land ethic arising out of his experiences on a sand farm in Wisconsin in a series of essays published posthumously, known as the *Sand County Almanac*.[1]

His land ethic postulates that we should extend our ethical concern to waters, plants, animals *and* the land. This refutes the idea of land just as property to be managed for human benefit alone. He began to challenge the focus on individuals' needs; rather, his overarching claim was that 'a thing is right when it tends to preserve the integrity, stability and beauty of the biotic community. It is wrong when it tends otherwise.'[2] The ecological understanding that he used was the one current at the time, namely that each species were layered in a series of trophic levels, each level decreasing in size and predatory on the layer below, setting up lines of dependency known as food chains. His model of ecology was one that stressed stability, harmony and interdependent relationships. He believed that only very slow changes in ecosystems took place over evolutionary history and abrupt changes, such as that introduced by human activity, could be disastrous. His focus on the ecological whole showed an underlying philosophical holism, so that hunting and other activities were still permitted as long as the ecology was not disturbed. His work also inclines towards the view that the land itself is living, rather than dead matter, a concept that James Lovelock takes much further in his Gaia hypothesis developed half a century later.[3]

Leopold's land ethic is significant in developing an ecological consciousness, one that is more in tune with the longer-term impact of human activity. Yet a number of criticisms may be levelled at his work.[4] The first is a philosophical one known as the 'naturalistic fallacy', namely the legitimacy of moving from perceived facts about the natural world, namely ecological integrity and so on, to an ought, or what should be done. Secondly, why does Leopold attribute significance to the particular stability of the ecosystem as he finds it? Contemporary ecologists are now much more inclined to speak of flux, dynamism and instability, which implies his notion of eco-stability is somewhat artificial and outdated.

Baird Callicott has tried to rescue Leopold's thesis in the context of a more contemporary understanding of ecology by suggesting that we can rephrase his dictum as: 'A thing is right when it tends to disturb the biotic community only at normal spatial and temporal scales. It is wrong when it tends otherwise.'[5] But who is to decide what constitutes normality? Different ecologists work at different scales of measurement, so what is normal to one will not be normal to another. Further, while at the largest possible scale there will be little apparent disturbance, there might be at lower scales. Who is to say which is the most significant? Callicott also compares the kind of dynamic community envisaged in ecology today with that of human communities bound together by loose cultural ties that are subject to change. Yet while the analogy may be closer than the previous more mechanical model of ecology according to energy states, it is still not possible from a study of ecology alone to name why one particular ecological community is to be valued. There are also important distinctions between ecological and human communities that Callicott does not consider adequately.[6] If humans serve their own good, then this will not lead to action on behalf of that biotic community. The ideal of human communities falls short in human history; examples of failure to protect basic human rights are legion. Finally, cultural norms contribute to human communities in ways that are not reflected in the idea of an overall biotic community.

The idea that a particular ecosystem or collection of ecosystems might have an overarching 'purpose' fails to convince evolutionary biologists influenced by Darwin's theory of evolution.[7] At the most we might say that there are constraints on the evolutionary process so that only some species flourish, and perhaps only some ecosystems as well.[8] Instead there may be other, more philosophical or theological reasons why we might wish to find purpose in the natural world, but to try and glean this from ecology is somewhat mistaken.

The holism implicit in Leopold's approach has also come under fire because it has been accused of being fascist, ignoring individuals, and perhaps even being prepared to kill humans where this is warranted for the sake of eco-system stability. Yet it seems unlikely that Leopold would have wanted to incite such negative consequences on human populations, as he still admitted to the possibility of using other species as a resource for human use, implying a somewhat contradictory thread in his holistic approach. But there is a lack of clarity in both Leopold and Callicott in terms of knowing how to act when interests of humans and other members of the biotic community conflict with each other.

Rather more promising, perhaps, is Leopold's admission of the need for love, respect and admiration for the land. Ecology may lead to a more intense appreciation of the land, which can then shift human attitudes. This bypasses the criticism of the naturalistic fallacy, and also could arise from a more sensitive appreciation of the dynamic flux inherent in ecological systems. If a person acts out of love and respect, then a decision is more likely to be a responsible one. Yet even this view could be challenged, as normally love and respect are given to a community that has a particular good or interests of its own, and this falls short of a broader ecological vision. In addition, sentiments alone may not be sufficient ground for ethics, for others may have sentiments that point in another direction entirely.

Some theologians have warmed to the idea of a greater valuation of the land in Leopold as an overarching model, but believe his work needs to be cor-rected in a number of ways.[9] These corrections include a greater sensitivity to the earth as dominated by water systems, not just sea; provision to protect the rights of individual humans; provision to respect other members of the biotic community; a hierarchy of values in order to discriminate between conflicts of interests; a theological transformation so that the earth is not the centre of all things; and finally the development of particular traits of character known as 'the virtues'. Yet one might ask if so many changes are made, what is left of Leopold's original proposal, other than affirmation of the land, which of course could come independently through reflection on respect for the land in the Hebrew Bible?

What is Deep Ecology?

Deep Ecology represents a collection of writers who emphasise different aspects of its broad holistic approach to the natural world. Arne Naess introduced the words 'shallow' and 'deep' in an essay published in 1973.[10] Bill Devall and George Sessions have also developed his views. Naess named shallow ecology as those attempts to protect the environment based on awareness of the depletion of resources and the extent of pollution. The incentive for both actions came from human interests alone. Deep Ecology, on the other hand, pointed to a more radical shift in philosophy and cultural norms away from the human towards the biotic community. Like Leopold, Naess recognised the essential unity of all creatures on the earth, but he sought to develop a firmer philosophical platform for his ideas. Deep ecologists also sought to challenge the predominant economic ideology, calling for its transformation in favour of other creatures. The so-called Deep Ecology Platform[11] consists of the following main elements:

- The flourishing of human and non-human life has value in and of itself – that is, intrinsic value, independent of usefulness for human purposes, or instrumental value.
- The richness and diversity of life are values in themselves and contribute to human and non-human flourishing.
- Humans have no right to reduce diversity except for vital needs.
- Current human interference with non-humans is excessive, and getting worse.
- The flourishing of human life is compatible with a significant decrease in the human population; in fact non-human life requires this adjustment.
- There are policy changes required in economic, technological and ideological structures.
- There needs to be a deeper appreciation of the quality of life, rather than just measurement in economic terms.
- There is an obligation to work either directly or indirectly to implement change.

Some deep ecologists have used the platform in order to justify political activism.[12] This might take the form of civil disobedience, where there is a commitment to non-violence and the use of open, peaceful protests, normally accepting the penal consequences where they follow. Alternatively, some actively support eco-sabotage and eco-terrorism, where violent means are used in order to highlight particular problems, perhaps at the expense of human life. In this case the activists try to avoid detection and often work under the cover of darkness in order to disguise their identity. Not all deep ecologists work in political activism, but all are committed to working out the practical consequences of their views in some form or another.

Clearly, for such committed activity, the levels of motivation need to be high. In order to encourage a shift in worldview, various strategies draw on the use of poetry, ritual, narrative and spirituality. Deep ecologists also 'sit more lightly' to the science of ecology compared with Leopold. Naess believes, for example, that ecology as a science needs to be treated as only one form of knowledge. Giving ecology too great a weight in ethical decision-making would, for him, bypass the need for more philosophical analysis. It might also, he fears, lead to an attitude that simply leaves decisions to the experts, in this case ecologists. Yet ecology is still inspirational for alternative metaphysical philosophies that stress the importance of the whole.

Holism in Deep Ecology seeks to shift consciousness away from individualism and scientific reductionism.[13] Humans are not so much separate individuals, but an aspect of the whole biotic process. Deep Ecology challenges the distinction between subject and object, where subjective elements are labelled as arbitrary and objective 'facts' are labelled as testable and true. Once humans are viewed as a unity with the world, the distinction between subjects and objects becomes broken down, and from this it follows that judgements based on the value and beauty of wilderness, for example, are as rational as judgments of science. In other words, such judgements are not simple 'sentiment'.

The ultimate norm for Deep Ecology is one of self-realisation and biocentric equality. Self-realisation comes through a discovery of interconnectedness with the larger Self or whole. This contrasts with the Western idea of self-realisation through the development of an individual, separate and personal nature. Such self-realisation in the context of Self challenges self-gratification of wants, rather than basic needs. All organisms have equal weight and intrinsic value through the notion of biocentric equality. This is, of course, inconsistent with one of the principles of the Deep Ecology Platform that states that humanity's vital needs can be met at the expense of other creatures. Nonetheless, it also opens up the possibility that where species are under threat of extinction, killing humans may be justified. The model for human society is one that is non-exploitative towards other creatures, in harmony with the natural world – an eco-topia, practising eco-Sophy, or 'wisdom' on behalf of the earth. Warwick Fox links his view specifically to pantheism, where all beings are conceived of as having a cosmic Unity. This abstract philosophy encourages Fox to argue against a personal approach to the land and identification with it. In this respect Deep Ecology contrasts sharply with Leopold's land ethic that argued more specifically for the value of human identification with the land.

Deep Ecology raises a number of questions that are worth discussing. Since it is a diverse movement, it is hard to criticise it with generalisations. Yet its overarching Platform makes sweeping claims that are hard to endorse. Many are worried by the holism in Deep Ecology that hints at forms of fascism also implicit in the land ethic. The violence against humans, even if it is hinted at in only some writers, is too extreme to be helpful. More particularly, Deep Ecology has ignored the plight of those in the poorer communities of the world. A policy of biocentric equality would, if taken to its logical conclusion, wipe out whole communities in Southern nations such as India. It also seems imperialistic, Western and specifically North American to those on the receiving end of its ideas.[14] There is also the difficulty of its pick-and-mix approach to Eastern religions for its own particular philosophical and political purposes, detaching elements of Eastern philosophy from their original cultural and historical roots. Many also argue that Deep Ecology is too abstract, for it fails to engage adequately with the social and economic structures of contemporary societies. Feminists in particular point to its failure to address patriarchal structures in human societies. Furthermore, political activism fuelled by such ideology can only lead to hostility by those who are not inclined towards its approach, as there is no attempt to forge realistic alternatives.

Creation spirituality

While the field of creation spirituality encompasses far more authors than those named below, the intention of this section is to give a flavour of the thinking of those Christian writers who have tried in one way or another to represent what they perceive as authentic Christian teaching.

Teilhard de Chardin

Pierre Teilhard de Chardin, a palaeontologist and a Jesuit priest, was one of the first authors to seek to construct a synthesis between evolutionary and cosmological science and Christian faith in a cosmic, mystical vision.[15] His influence was particularly profound in the middle of the twentieth century and he influenced subsequent theological developments, such as process theology. Many eco-theologians are wary of his work, because he seemed to endorse scientific technology and its ideal of progress without taking any account of the potential social and environmental difficulties. His vision was also thoroughgoing in its focus on Christ as the Omega Point, and arguably somewhat anthropocentric in tone.

More recently, however, scholars sensitive to environmental issues have returned to his work, and found in his writing a form of creation spirituality that is still relevant for contemporary debates.[16] His mystical thinking, in particular, is cosmic in scope and serves to affirm all of the earth's processes. He also resisted the materialism common to scientific culture, arguing instead for a vision that does not reduce everything to its component parts. In this there is an implicit empathy for ecological ways of thinking that seek a more holistic perspective. For Teilhard physical matter has psychic properties that eventually flower into complexity and consciousness. Teilhard also comes very close to 'vitalism', long resisted by biologists, through his notion of the existence of the cosmic spirit in the natural world, though his clear sense of the transcendence of God effectively steers him away from any such conclusion. For Teilhard, a particular way of 'seeing' how this complexity emerges and in particular, its appearance in humans, flows out of the dialectical relationship between matter and spirit.[17] The participation of humanity in the evolutionary process becomes what Teilhard calls the centration of persons, a discovery of the human place on earth by means of active participation in the evolutionary process.

Ursula King is convinced of the possible contribution of Teilhard to the specifically ecological imperative of spirituality that arises out of our own present context.[18] In the first place Teilhard's vision makes us conscious that we are living on one planet. In the second place, his vision enables us to see connections between ecology, spirituality and the world as a whole. In the third place spirituality becomes more deeply embedded in the biological world, through the way Teilhard envisioned the mutual interaction between the biosphere, common to all creatures, and the noosphere, characteristic of humanity. King believes his vision provides us with a spiritual heritage that is global in outlook and one that can be ecologically balanced. It is also important to note that Teilhard always intended his work to be acceptable from the point of view of the Roman Catholic tradition, even though he was condemned in his lifetime. Accordingly, he gives high regard for traditional elements such as the Eucharist and the place of the Virgin Mary. His understanding of Mary is also cosmic in tone, and in this sense his Mariology points to environmental awareness.[19]

Although he focuses on the human, he always sees humanity in a cosmological context in a manner that also shares elements with Eastern Orthodox Christianity.[20] His strong appreciation of the importance of Christ serves to unite matter and spirit, and his cosmic Christ acts as a counterweight to more anthropocentric tendencies in his thinking. In addition, his vision, informed by a 'love energy', unites themes of nature and humanity as well as creation and redemption in a way that is positive for Christian theology, which has tended to put too much emphasis on redemption at the expense of creation. The love that Teilhard pointed to is a love that differentiates and personalises, rather than one that confuses or merges individuals. In this sense the love becomes connected with all of creation, and hence forms a basis for thinking in a more holistic way about the earth.[21]

There is also the sense in which Teilhard invites his readers to engage with scientific understanding, rather than withdraw from it in a form of mysticism that is world-denying. Such engagement may be creative from the point of view of affirming human activity, even if it needs to be channelled in such a way to be environmentally responsible. The difficulty that Teilhard perceived was that in spite of great scientific understanding, humanity needed to recover spiritual and psychic energy in order to act appropriately.[22] Teilhard was also aware of strands of evolutionary science such as symbiosis and complexity that have only come to the fore in more recent research, flowering in the Gaia hypothesis of James Lovelock.[23]

Even amidst strong appreciation of his thinking for eco-theology, his cosmic vision tends to be somewhat abstract in tone, resisting the particularity of the historical Jesus as well as failing to deal with concrete problems, such as social and eco-justice.[24] His notion of Mary also tends to be abstract, offering an idealised notion of women. He restricts his understanding of Sophia, wisdom, to Mary, which in turn curtails its full potential in ecological terms.[25] There are also ambivalences in his thinking from an environmental point of view in his positive attitude towards globalisation, the market economy and development.[26] He was, in other words, comparatively naïve about the possible implications of such systems, nor could it be said that his work was explicitly aimed at creating a theology that would be relevant for those environmental issues that were not yet obvious in his lifetime. Teilhard died before concerns about ecology and environmental issues were fully recognised on the cultural landscape.

Matthew Fox

Matthew Fox also writes from a starting point in the Roman Catholic tradition, but unlike Teilhard he chose to leave that Church rather than face restriction or denial by ecclesial authority. He is also more explicit in his aim to confront the global environmental issues, believing that humanity requires a new form of spirituality if it is to face the seriousness of contemporary problems.[27] Fox claims that he is retrieving an ancient form of Christian spirituality that has lain dormant, rather than inventing a new theological tradition. Like Teilhard, he sought to recover a holistic way of thinking as a challenge to modernity with its reductionist rhetoric. He believes that Christian theology is culpable in its promotion of an Augustinian spirituality of original sin, leading to the Fall and redemption, that is thoroughly dualistic in tone, separating humanity from the earth and therefore denigrating it. Instead he actively promotes the notion of creation spirituality understood as Original Blessing, which, in turn, celebrates and honours the earth and all its processes.[28] For him, redemption is caught up with the renewal of the earth and human responsibility to act in such a way so as to restore its harmony. He also interprets the incarnation and suffering of Christ in ecological terms, so that Christ identifies with all that is alive, every creature is bearer of the cosmic Christ, and Christ's crucifixion is symbolic of ecological suffering.

His explicit emphasis on blessing brings him much closer to pantheistic notions[29] compared with Teilhard, and he is quite ready to use divine names, such as Goddess, which would have been foreign for Teilhard. One of the reasons for the difference is the cultural context in which each author presents his ideas. For Teilhard the most pressing need was the synthesis between evolutionary science and theology. Science itself was left largely unscathed, even though his emphasis on holism challenged the materialistic and reductionist metaphysics implicit in contemporary science. For Fox, on the other hand, the agenda is more specifically environmental, actively seeking to recover strands in religious traditions, from whatever source, that are helpful to his thesis. Teilhard, like Fox, has been criticised for its apparent lack of attention to sin, though I suggest that in Teilhard's case it was more a matter of re-focusing thought amidst the pessimism in modern science, rather than the explicit rejection of redemptive themes that surfaces in Fox's version of creation spirituality.

Both Teilhard and Fox were appreciative of the creative potential in humanity, though the goals for that creativity differ in that while Teilhard endorsed the modern scientific project, Fox was more inclined to see creativity in a way that encompasses themes of justice and integration with his understanding of ecology. Both believed in the harmony and inherent beauty of the cosmos. Fox named the virtue of compassion for the earth as a vital way that expresses in practice a mystical sense of God as integrated into nature. Like Teilhard he also affirmed the evolutionary history of the earth, told through a new cosmic story of its emergence from dead matter to living consciousness. Like Teilhard, he also sought to promote human awareness of cosmic interconnectedness.

Fox's theology has come under attack for a number of reasons. In the first place he seems to misrepresent key figures in the theological tradition, such as Aquinas, Meister Eckhart and Hildegard of Bingen in order to suit his own particular purposes. In the second place, he uses Scripture in a way that is unacceptable to most biblical scholars, in that he reads meanings into texts in a way that distorts the original intention of the authors. He is also heavily influenced by feminism, but in a way that is arguably one-sided, so that he focuses on the maternal birthing process in a way that is still somewhat stereotypical for women. His emphasis on pantheism also departs from traditional interpretations of Christianity, and, arguably, empties God of transcendence. Fox's spirituality is also, in common with new age spirituality, somewhat individualistic rather than communitarian, stressing the individual's path to God even though holistic, cosmic, interconnectivity themes are an inspiration for such renewed spirituality. He has also an idealistic view of ecology as balance and harmony that does not take sufficient account of more recent ecological theories discussed in earlier chapters.

Thomas Berry

Thomas Berry's version of creation spirituality takes up elements of Teilhard de Chardin's thought in a distinctive way. In his first book, *The Dream of the Earth*, he acknowledges this influence.[30] He is particularly drawn to the cosmological 'story' of creation named by modern science. Like Teilhard, he believes that this story has a sacramental quality – that it displays something of the revelation of God to the world. Like Teilhard, he puts emphasis on the importance of humanity in the overall story, and sees the emergence of humanity in terms of the emergence of consciousness, but now it is the universe that becomes conscious of itself through humanity. He also affirms Deep Ecology's notion of human Self-realisation through identity with the cosmos, but at the same time he suggests that the universe attains Self-realisation through such identification with humanity. Humanity's role as the Self-consciousness of the cosmos also has parallels with more metaphysical versions of Lovelock's Gaia hypothesis.[31] Unlike Teilhard, Berry is highly critical of the biblical, prophetic tradition in Christian faith, believing, in common with Lynn White, that it was largely responsible for creating a dream of progress, including limitless economic growth, which then has environmentally destructive consequences. The solution, for him, is a shift to a religious basis that embraces the story of the universe as unfolded by scientific cosmology and evolution. The natural world is the true home of spirituality, rather than a remote prophetic longing for heaven – an elusive state of perfection, detached from the earth.

Thomas Berry's integration of the human story with that of the earth is complete in as much as he holds that even human care for the earth stems from a cosmic caring that is embedded in evolutionary processes. Furthermore, the cosmic story is the overarching one in that it also embraces other religious stories of humankind. Religious narratives are like natural extensions of those processes that are integral to evolutionary history. Yet because the universe has become conscious of itself through humanity, it has the power to determine the earth's processes. He is highly critical of an ethic of resource management for the earth that views it simply as a means for human betterment. This theme has continued in the joint work with physicist Brian Swimme, where 'industrial assault upon the planet', including the Gross Domestic Product ignoring the Gross Earth Product, undermines the emergent processes in the universe.[32] In order to counter this trend we need to enter what they term a 'fourth biological era', an 'Ecozoic era', which stresses the idea of the universe as a communion of subjects, analogous to a living organism. This organic unity means that the well-being of the planet is needed for the well-being of other members of the planetary community. Hence:

> to preserve the economic viability of the planet must be the first law of economics. To preserve the health of the planet must be the first commitment of the medical profession. To preserve the natural world as the primary revelation of the divine must be the basic concern of religion.[33]

Human well-being is, therefore, derivative on the well-being of the planet. Above all they want to emphasise reciprocity in relationship between the processes of the earth and humanity. Where the earth becomes an object for exploitation, it leads to devastating consequences. The relationship with the earth is intimate, almost animistic in the idea that humans communicate with 'life principles in the soil', alongside a 'feeling for subjective communion' and 'mutual reverence'. They reject what they name as an alternative to the Ecozoic era – namely, a 'Technozoic era' that is gripped by an ethic of commercial and industrial growth.[34] They advocate not so much inactivity, but a tuning into the activity of the planet at every level of society, from a reformulated technology and engineering, through to economics, education and political governance. Religious traditions, too, have to learn the message that humans are sacred through participation in the larger, planetary community, where ethics takes up the cause of biocide, the destructive killing of other species. They also nod to eco-feminist concerns by suggesting that the limit to population increase opens up new roles for women, releasing new healing energy for the earth. In addition, they suggest we need to recover the languages characteristic of an Ecozoic era, one that is multivalent not just in the sense of human narratives, but one that draws extensively on non-human languages and communication in a way that is poetic and symbolic.

Thomas Berry is widely appreciated, like Teilhard, for his cosmic mysticism and vision that seeks to move away from materialistic exploitation of the earth for human benefit. His thesis has its drawbacks. In the first place, many would see that his vision is overly idealistic, ignoring some of the more unsavoury, destructive aspects of evolutionary and cosmic history. His ethic is naturalistic in as much as it takes its cues from his perception of balance in nature, in a manner akin to Matthew Fox. Not all organisms are equally valuable in the earth system, but this aspect is not really addressed. John Haught criticises Berry's dismissal of the biblical and prophetic tradition in Christianity, believing that his focus on the earth detracts from a need for eschatology.[35] I suggest that Berry does have a form of eschatology in as much as he views the earlier cyclical view of natural processes as requiring replacement with a greater sense of the irreversibility of change. However, it is not one that is derived from his religious faith, rather it stems from his understanding of the earth story. He is also drawn to other pantheistic religious traditions in a similar vein to Matthew Fox, and the criticisms levelled against Fox could be applied to Thomas Berry.

Conclusions

Aldo Leopold pioneered the idea that there is more to the earth than simply a resource for human management, though he still favoured traditional practices such as hunting as long as the overall ecosystem was not disturbed. He also adhered to a holistic philosophy that gave priority to whole systems, rather than individuals. Deep Ecology similarly criticises materialism at the expense of the earth, but attempts to make more explicit the philosophical foundation of a commitment to holism, along with elements that support radical political activism in working for change. Teilhard's, Fox's and Berry's creation spirituality have some resonance with Deep Ecology's stress on the unity of the cosmos. Teilhard wrote at a time before environmental issues were at the fore of contemporary debates, but he did recognise the dangers of scientific materialism and sought to replace this with a mystical view of nature that united matter and spirit. Matthew Fox viewed environmental problems as evidence for a deeper spiritual crisis that represented not just a failure in religious belief, but a failure of Christianity to recover those traditions supportive of earth care. His work has, however, been criticised for his use of tradition. Thomas Berry, on the other hand, has sought to embed religious traditions into an overarching story of the cosmos, for while scientific materialism may be faulted, its story has powerful implications in helping us think more carefully about the place of humans on the earth. In a manner somewhat analogous to the language used by Teilhard, he calls for a new Ecozoic era, one that resists wrongful attachment to technology in the name of progress, but instead encourages lifestyles in tune with the way the natural world is. All writers discussed so far can be faulted for their somewhat idealistic view of ecology and natural processes. While Berry mentions the possibility of new economic structures, his notions seem too far-fetched to carry weight in a secular, global market economy. All these writers fail to consider adequately the issue of global poverty and oppression, alongside the suffering of planet earth. It is appropriate, therefore, for the next chapter to address these questions, by reflecting on how far an ecological agenda has become incorporated into those forms of liberation theology that are sensitive to such issues.

Further reading

Deane-Drummond, C., *Teilhard de Chardin on People and Planet* (London, Equinox, 2006)

Devall, Bill and Sessions, George, *Deep Ecology* (Salt Lake City, Peregrine Smith Books, 1985)

Flader, Susan and Callicott, J. Baird (eds.), *The River of the Mother of God and Other Essays* (Madison, University of Wisconsin Press, 1991)

Fox, Matthew, *Original Blessing* (Santa Fe, Bear and Co., 1983)

Leopold, Aldo, *A Sand County Almanac – and Sketches Here and There* (1949; New York, Ballantine, 1970)

Swimme, Brian and Berry, Thomas, *The Universe Story* (San Francisco, HarperCollins, 1992)

Teilhard de Chardin, P., *The Human Phenomenon*, trans. Susan Appleton-Weber (Brighton, Sussex Academic Press, 1999)

Chapter 4

Eco-theology from the South

THE SCOPE OF THIS CHAPTER REFLECTS PRIMARILY the voices of those committed to various forms of liberation theology, which was embedded first of all in the cry for justice for those who were oppressed by various totalitarian regimes and other unjust political structures. The literature of those writing on ecological issues from the perspective of the Southern nations is vast, so this chapter necessarily highlights and reviews only a small selection of that literature.[1] Those concerned with 'development' of impoverished parts of the world became more conscious of the indirect importation of particular cultural values that effectively suppressed native cultures. It soon became apparent that changes on behalf of human communities needed to go hand in hand with care for the environment. Initially liberation theology focused more specifically on human survival and flourishing in the particular contexts of oppressive regimes, but as in development studies, the linking between the oppression of peoples and their land became obvious, so that the cry of the poor also joined with a cry of the earth. Yet because liberation theology also broadly concerns domination of one people over others, in this sense it also needs to be inclusive of those indigenous populations that are oppressed by the dominant majority, either directly by discrimination in access to particular goods, or indirectly through unjust economic structures.

Ecology and development[2]

In the 1940s the most powerful voices were in favour of a particular model of development known as 'modernisation'. So-called 'underdeveloped' nations were required to find ways of becoming productive in economic terms, boosted by input from so-called 'developed', richer nations. The assumption was that such a development strategy would pave the way for stable democratic societies to emerge. Andre Frank challenged the modernisation thesis through an alternative known as 'dependency theory'.[3] He directly attacked capitalism as a means for development in Latin America, arguing instead that foreign monopolies or domestic elites siphoned off profits, hence leading to overall stagnation. Although his ideas have been criticised for over-simplification, dependency theory was subsequently developed with more nuance by Fernando Cardoso. He, in turn, influenced liberation theologians such as Gustavo Gutiérrez, who argued that 'liberation' should be used, rather than 'development', for it avoided the pejorative connotations associated with the latter, and also had the advantage of linking up with more biblical themes.[4] For him, revolutionary forms of socialism are the only way to break the bonds of an unjust society, epitomised in forms of class struggle at both a national, internal level and international level. But even though dependency theory attacked modernisation, what might be more concrete solutions to political and social issues associated with development?

Historically the divide between development and environmental concern was not simply about choosing between people or pandas, but a radical difference in approach to social issues. While those on the 'red' end of the spectrum tended to view capitalism as the source of problems, those on the 'green' end generally viewed technological culture as something to be vigorously opposed. Some of those concerned with environmental issues, such as the group known as the Environmental Fund, founded in the 1970s, even advocated a form of eco-fascism. They were pessimistic about the prospect of improvement for peoples in the poorer nations of the world, and were prepared to advocate more extreme curtailment of population growth. There are also theoretical issues to consider when attempts are made to link environmental concerns with development models. For example, how might it be possible to combine an emphasis on community presupposed in environmental models, with an emphasis on the plight of working classes presupposed by those influenced by Marxist models of economy?

Yet it became obvious from about the late 1980s onwards that the destruction of the environment in the name of 'development' could no longer be ignored, regardless of the model of development used, so economic growth had to go hand in hand with ecological sensitivity in order to preserve the long-term future of peoples. Alternatives included the idea of 'endogenous' development, which is one that is aware of local and global limits. Gradually the rhetoric of sustainability emerged. Unfortunately this does not necessarily refer to encouraging styles of living that are commensurate with the earth's carrying capacity. Sometimes it is the sustainability of human societies that is being referred to in terms of population, consumption, resource use and pollution, including the obligation to future human generations.

The link between development and the environment is illustrated well by the following case study.[5] When loggers first cleared the forests in the Philippines, early settlers moved in and formed the small hillside village of Kinapat. Initially, one hectare yielded about 60 to 80 sacks of maize. By the 1980s, some 20 years later, the yield was down to one sixth of this amount, and more than half of the working population had moved on to alternative, more fertile lands, to repeat the cycle again. The agricultural authorities believed that yields were low because of outdated farming methods; instead they recommended high-yielding varieties alongside chemical fertilisers and pesticides. The best land had always been given to large agricultural business plantations, reliant on high-yielding varieties and the input of chemical fertilisers. This left the poor with only one option – farming on marginal hillside land following clearance of the rainforest. Farming is even more precarious in these conditions, with rainfall drastically reduced, and crops vulnerable to pests, drought or flash floods. Once the soil is washed away it is carried down to the sea, silting up coral reefs, and destroying habitat for fish stocks. The recommendation to use high-yield varieties and other intensive farming methods was impossible for economic reasons.

Local farmers in Kinapat believed that yields were low not simply because they were not conforming to intensive farming methods; rather, the crucial change was the gradual loss of the fertility of the soil. Three farmers decided to undertake a participatory research survey into the reasons for the low yields. They documented evidence for much higher productivity when they first moved to the site. If the soil was originally productive, then their traditional farming methods had been adequate in the past; hence it was the loss in soil productivity that accounted for the low yields. They believed that, instead, a simple alternative farming method known as sloping agricultural land technology (SALT) would prevent soil erosion and help rehabilitate viable farms. Some farmers worried that they might be driven off the land for other reasons, as they did not hold official titles to the land. However, in spite of these reservations the farmers banded together to form the Kinapat SALT Farmer's Association, believing that simply moving on to other sites would be disruptive to their communities. They also held out the hope that they could apply and obtain titles for their land, which materialised in due course. Sarah White and Romy Tiongo make the following comment:

> Overall, what comes out of the Kinapat story is a message of hope. What seemed like the end became instead a new beginning. In working towards harmony with nature, the villagers also built community with one another. Like human beings, the natural environment is remarkably resilient. The search for alternatives is not an empty option. With some give and take on the human side, environmental systems can re-establish equilibrium to accommodate changed circumstances. Shifting from relationships of exploitation to nurture holds the promise of new life.[6]

Ecology and liberation

Leonardo Boff is, arguably, one of the foremost liberation theologians who has actively sought to integrate a theology of liberation with environmental concern.[7] He writes from his experience of the threatened Amazon of his native

Brazil. He begins his book entitled *Ecology and Liberation* with a rehearsal of the need for greater awareness of global ecological issues. He is particularly critical of forms of eco-politics that focus on organic or additive-free products while failing to take into account basic human needs and global environmental concerns. He is also prepared to speak of *ecological* ethics, including the rights of other creatures and nature as a whole having a 'cosmic right', alongside human and national rights. The task ahead is to heal the 'broken alliance' between humanity and nature, individuals and community. He also believes in the need for a psychic renewal, a 'mental ecology' that seeks to recharge human affinity with nature, including a capacity for celebration and conviviality. He moves towards a cosmic mysticism in his reflections on ecology, aligning himself with the work of Thomas Berry and James Lovelock. He takes on these paradigms somewhat uncritically, before turning his attention to liberation theology as that devoted to a more specifically socialist, anti-capitalist agenda. The core means of linking the two areas comes through his demand to 'widen the meaning of the option for the poor to include an option for the most threatened of other beings and species'.[8] This is followed through by an inclusion of environmental concern into his liberation theology agenda, rather than the total transformation of the latter. He responds to the criticism that Eastern European communism has failed in social and environmental terms by pointing to the ideals behind Marxism – namely, a more equitable society. He is strongly critical of a capitalist approach, which he believes fails to meet basic human needs. Moreover, he argues that socialism does not need to go hand in hand with limitations on human freedom as expressed in Stalinism. He is also convinced that a modified form of capitalism will not work either, for its 'iron logic' is the greatest profit in the shortest possible time.[9] He views science and technology as wedded to capitalist structures in an unhelpful way, namely to forward political dependencies. Instead, he argues for political participation, so that people are actively involved in working out a solution, rather in the manner suggested in the case study outlined in the section above. Included in this process is an awareness of ecological welfare. His agenda for a new global political economy lays out the following elements:[10]

- A minimum of humanisation. By this he means that basic human needs are met, including, for example, requirements for basic food, shelter and health care.
- Citizenship that is inclusive of all people in their diversity.
- Equity – that is, a greater realisation of political equality.
- Human and ecological welfare. The goal should be an enhanced quality of life, not simply an improvement of goods and services. Human well-being includes alliances between men, women and nature, as well as a spirituality that recognises the importance of the otherness of all created beings.
- Respect for cultural differences, including different ways of expressing solidarity.

- Cultural reciprocity and complementarity, including willingness to learn from other cultures and diverse ways of fulfilling humanity.

Boff's ideas are developed in more depth in his later book *Cry of the Earth: Cry of the Poor*.[11] He spells out more specifically his alliance with eco-theology's charge against anthropocentrism, and eco-feminism's charge against androcentrism as violations of the 'first universal law; namely that we constitute an immense cosmic and planetary community, and we must live in harmony and solidarity with one another because we are all interconnected and have the same origin and destiny.'[12] He believes that modern civilisation has as its organising axis not life, or the wonder of life, but its own power and means for more power and domination. The common ground between liberation theology and radical ecology is that they both

> start from two bleeding wounds. The wound of poverty breaks the social fabric of millions and millions of poor people around the world. The other wound, systematic assault of the earth, breaks down the balance of the planet, which is under threat from the plundering of development as practiced by contemporary global societies.[13]

He believes that the focus of liberation theology on the poor is still relevant, but it is not simply concerned with basic human needs, such as food, but also desires for beauty, which can never be satiated. Above all, liberation needs to be achieved by the poor themselves, even if aided on their journey by others. Liberation theology moves from awareness, to critical judgement, to trans-formative action and celebration. He believes that not only are both accounts starting in awareness of suffering, but also both accounts of suffering in libera-tion theology and radical ecology are rooted in a similar cause, namely a social system that encourages accumulation, exploitation of people and the plunder-ing of the natural world. He seems somewhat optimistic about human beings being able to turn from 'being the Satan of the Earth' to its 'guardian angel, able to save Earth, their cosmic homeland and earthly mother'.[14]

He claims that the *priority* for liberation theology is still meeting the demand of social justice first, in that only once the basic level of social justice is met 'will it be possible to propose a possible ecological justice', understood as right relationship of human beings and nature.[15] He understands ecological justice in terms of a new covenant between humans and other beings, a new 'gentleness' towards created things, and a new ethic based on 'kinship' with other creatures in a cosmic community. He also argues for a political structure of democracy that is biocratic – in other words, one that is centred on life. Yet his manner of appropriating the ecological paradigm is of interest, for he sees human beings in similar terms to Teilhard de Chardin, as representative of the most advanced stage of the cosmological evolutionary process, yet also, as in Deep Ecology, created for the universe.

Of course, such a vision is still somewhat ambiguous in spite of the rhetoric of holism that he includes in his account. The priority for human need, as well as his conviction that humanity has the capacity to solve those needs, is one particular philosophical interpretation of Gaian theory that is arguably more anthropocentric than most protagonists would allow. He seems to be aware of this in later statements where he argues first and foremost for a broader understanding of liberation beyond the confines of the human community, affirming and enabling 'Gaia to live and all beings in creation, including human beings, to exist in solidarity'.[16] He also contradicts his earlier statements by apparently allowing for a change in priority for liberation theology, so that 'the starting point must also be redefined' so that the option for the poor is 'first' the planet Earth as a whole.[17] The option for poor humanity is then set in such a context, understood in evolutionary terms as a small minority of one species exploiting huge masses of that same species. In this respect he has gone further towards the ecological agenda, radically transforming liberation theology under the lens of a radical ecology paradigm.

Sean McDonagh has, arguably, been one of the foremost thinkers introducing themes of liberation theology as an *ecological* agenda into dialogue with Western theological traditions.[18] He writes as someone who, although not originally from the Philippines, has absorbed the concerns and plight of the people from years of working as a Columban Roman Catholic priest and serving the people on the island of Mindanao in the Philippines. He is also concerned, more perhaps than Boff, with educating his readers about the extent and nature of ecological problems and some of the social and economic factors that are responsible. Like Boff, he also takes inspiration from Thomas Berry and Teilhard de Chardin in arguing for a radical global ecology. He views traditional accounts of creation as needing to be recovered in the light of the new cosmology presented by Berry and others, and reworked in the context of Berry's story of the universe. He is critical of much of the tradition of the West that he views as responsible for destructive attitudes to the natural environment. Moreover, he situates the struggle also in the West, in the context of his native Ireland where he finds despoliation of the earth. In particular, he has sought to bring an ecological agenda to the attention of the wider global Catholic Church. He also links oppressive Western colonial-ism with modern technology that he sees is responsible for much of the despoliation of the earth.

But there are some difficulties with this interpretation of ecology in the light of the motifs of liberation theology. In the first place, the broad agenda to heal planet Earth as a whole moves towards forms of holism that, as we noted, are problematic in Deep Ecology – namely, a tendency for eco-fascism. In this respect liberation theology could be said to align itself even more strongly to a 'Western' agenda. Concepts, such as Gaia, absorbed uncritically by both Boff and McDonagh, are also more ambiguous ethically than they appreciate from the perspective of valuation of human beings, for arguably it is the so-called 'lower' organisms that form the basis for geochemical stability.[19] It is fair to suggest that all ecological models, including Gaia, have a positive role in helping to shift the agenda away from individualism and anthropocentrism, but how far this is entirely helpful for liberation theology requires further discussion. In the East, for example, liberation is achieved through a primarily spiritual or inner experience, so that the real liberation needs to be within, away from self-interest and egocentrism. Although Boff has tried to take such criticism into account by his discussion on mysticism, his cosmic mystical approach shifts the focus away from individual responsibility. Those who are critical of liberation theology have also noted that in some writers there is a tendency to critique political structures and take insufficient account of indigenous people who are truly marginalised members of society. Such theologies emerge in the context of the indigenous cultures discussed in more detail below.

Ecology and indigenous theology

Indigenous theologies are those emerging from the so-called 'Fourth World' and put far more emphasis on local inculturation. A good example of how this surfaces in practice comes through the association of maize with cultural identity and its disruption through the introduction of genetically modified organisms discussed in Chapter 2. Of course, if we move too far in this direction the advantages of liberation theology's critique of social structures may become obscured, but arguably indigenous theology is an important voice to be heard in those contexts where the more specific agenda of local communities may be forgotten.[20] Liberation theology has also moderated under the influence of indigenous theology through its attention to the importance of base communities. However, more often than not these are seen as vehicles for expression of praxis, moderating liberation theories, rather than originating sources in and of themselves for theological reflection. In particular, indigenous cultures seek to stress primarily *identification with the land*, rather than radical economic critique of capitalism through socialist ideology. Rob Cooper, for example, is a Maori of Ngati Hine descent in New Zealand. He expresses his desire in the following way:

> Our hope is that in coming so late into a world mad with materialism, our identification of ourselves as literally 'people of the land' and our harmony with our environment will reflect the way the world could be. There remains in Maori culture, in the way we live, that sense of unity in creation … Naming and knowing our world distinguishes us from the brutes. It also joins us together in responsibility for it – and them.[21]

In other words, the ecological agenda is not added on from other cultural critiques of the plight of the planet, but emerges from indigenous culture itself as an expression of its values. In this sense it offers a form of liberation that is instructive even beyond its confines, for it expresses a way of living that is exemplary for other cultures and, arguably, other religious traditions.

Indigenous traditions are also important in as much as they put due emphasis on a theology of place. George Tinker, writing from a North American Indian context, describes this as 'the full circle of liberation'.[22] Tinker is, as one might expect, highly critical of the founding messengers of liberation theology who stressed its role as a historical project, making a revolutionary socialist choice on behalf of the poor and emerging out of the praxis of the people. He believes that the particular situation of oppression of indigenous peoples is overlooked, for such peoples resist analysis in terms of class struggle; in fact labelling of such cultures in terms of class superimposes another form of oppression against their sense of personhood. In brief:

> Small, but culturally unique communities stand to be swallowed up by the vision of a classless society, an international worker's movement or a burgeoning majority of Third World urban poor. This too, is cultural genocide and signals that indigenous peoples are yet non-persons, even in the light of the gospel of liberation.[23]

For indigenous peoples, God is self-revealing not so much in the context of history and time, but in creation, space and place. A missionary endeavour automatically puts the missionary at an advantage in such a perspective, for they are the first recipients of the Gospel in a linear time-frame. One example is the Miskito Indians during the Sandinista revolution in Nicaragua. These peoples were relocated from self-sustaining, local, coastal communities to high-altitude communal coffee plantations, with little regard for their own cultural dislocation. Tinker contrasts the emphasis on history in Western traditions with that on place in indigenous cultures, so that Marxism in its historical analysis falls short as far as its connectivity with the indigenous religious traditions. In the Plains Indian context, all creatures have a status as 'personal' and the circle is the key symbol, uniting family, clans, tribes and extending out to other creatures. For such traditions the call to repentance is one that admits human place in the world understood as part of the circle of creation, with respect for all creatures and participants in the whole of creation. This departs from the individualism of creation spirituality in the West that has grown up in reaction to the dominant historical trends, as in Matthew Fox, for example. It is also, significantly, different from the trend towards a Gaian perspective that tends to obliterate local differences. Rather it is an expression of a 'theology of community' that also admits to a concern for justice and peace.

Stan McKay, writing from an Aboriginal perspective, similarly identifies his culture with that of the land. The earth is considered as mother to all, with animals as brothers and sisters.[24] Any idea of ownership of the land seems inappropriate from this perspective. Rather, life is a gift and there is a sense of profound belonging to the earth, rather than having rights over it. Other scholars concur, suggesting that Aboriginal consciousness and self-identity is rooted in ancestral place, even taking a priority in this respect over body and paternity.[25] McKay also believes that claims for 'land rights' are devastating to cultural values that are embedded in the Aboriginal way of life. Documents have to be couched in legal jargon that contains concepts of ownership that are foreign to its way of thinking about the land. But the choice is stark – either compromise or death. Like the North American Indians, there is a stress on humanity as integral to the circle of life, moving to the rhythm of creation, with the Great Spirit moving through all of life, expressed in terms of cosmic order.

Those writing from an African perspective also make a significant contribution to this literature. Samson Gitu, for example, draws on the ecological insights of the Maasai and the Kukuya.[26] Gitu compares these teachings with Christian teachings on God, creation, providence, humanity and nature. In this his work is exceptional, for in many other cases where indigenous African spirituality is retrieved there is little attention paid to Christian theology as such. Instead, the theme of harmony between humanity and the natural world comes to the fore in legends and songs. Ernst Conradie summarises this variety in a useful way:

> There is a sense of wonder at the fecundity of life, for the land and all the creatures that live from it, for the cycles of the seasons. There is an almost overwhelming emphasis on notions of interrelatedness, mutual dependence, reciprocity, ecological balance, wholeness, integrated web of life, and, especially community. The world exists as an integral balance of parts. Human beings must recognise and strive to maintain this cosmic balance. Everything, from hunting to healing, is a recognition and affirmation of the sacredness of life. Where the ecological balance and the ancestral world are disturbed it leads to suffering for human communities and other creatures. In this vein Harvey Sindima (Malawi) speaks of the bondedness, sacredness and fecundity of the 'community of life', Emmanuel Asante (Ghana) suggests the ecological category of pan-vitalism, Eugene Wangiri (Kenya) calls for an *urumwe* spirituality which sees God's presence in creation, while Gabriel Setiloane (South Africa) celebrates an African biocentric theology and ethos.[27]

Given this strong connectivity with the land, it is hardly surprising that many eco-theologians have viewed indigenous approaches to creation in a somewhat idealistic way as harbingers of a spirituality that needs appropriation elsewhere. It is certainly true that there is much to learn from this voice. However, a note of caution is worth articulating here. The historian Simon Schama, for example, in *Landscape and Memory*, explores the extent to which historically those in Europe and North America have been sensitive to the indissoluble connections between people and place.[28] In particular he emphasises that we cannot separate the natural world from human culture; the landscape is an expression of such interaction. Such a view challenges the perception that it is possible for human existence to simply tune into what is inherent in the natural world without alteration, a view that seems implicit in indigenous traditions. It is also possible to learn from this historical work that there are resources buried in the Western tradition that are more than the caricature of exploitation, capitalism and aggression implied by all liberation theologies. An idolisation of nature in its native wildness is also dangerous in as much as it fosters the belief that human beings have little or no hope of creating solutions to environmental problems.[29] In addition, a simple appropriation of, for example, spiritual traditions from indigenous cultures in a piecemeal way may have good intentions, but it can also lead to further marginalisation by exclusion from an equal place in socio-economic spheres. This is the mirror image, to some extent, of the problems with much liberation theology, where inclusion of one group or 'class' in the socio-economic processes undermined other aspects of indigenous culture. Yet, bearing in mind these dangers, it is appropriate to engage with sensitivity in dialogue with cultures and traditions other than one's own, not least for the light it sheds on one's own tradition.

The alliance of African Independent Churches (AIC) have sought to weave together insights from indigenous African cultures and Christian faith.[30] It represents a case study where indigenous religious views have become woven into a liberation approach from grass-roots practice. One hundred and fifty of these churches, inspired by the work of the Zimbabwean Institute of Religious Research and Ecological Conservation (ZIRRCON) have formed an Association of African Earthkeeping Churches (AAEC) and also collaborated with groups who were similarly concerned about environmental degradation from a traditional African religious perspective, namely the Association of Zimbabwean Traditionalist Ecologists (AZTREC), comprising chiefs, headmen and spiritual mediums. Together they have succeeded in planting between 3 and 4 million trees in Zimbabwe, incorporating tree planting into specific religious rituals. Religious leaders in the AAEC viewed such tree planting by poor and relatively underprivileged members of society as a sacred mission, fulfilling a vocation to heal the earth, and serving as guardians of creation. This task is woven into the more traditional evangelical task of conversion to Christian faith. The portrayal of the Church as guardians of creation links with the traditional Shona cosmology, where founder ancestors of tribes and clans are referred to as guardians of the land, protectors of the holy groves and sanctuaries. In association with Christian faith, Christ becomes the universal guardian of the land, prefigured in the guardianship of ancestors, yet his Spirit is understood to hold sway over generations of Shona guardians. Those who wilfully destroy the earth are labelled as 'wizards', in parallel with those opposed to the liberation struggle prior to the independence of Zimbabwe. The first president of the AAEC, Bishop Machokoto, named the connection between the two in unambiguous terms, suggesting that 'There is absolutely no doubt about the connection between our war of the trees and the former liberation struggle, *chimurenga*.'[31] The eschatology of such churches is one that is visible in the present dispensation, incorporating social justice and peace, and a means of empowering those who have previously been marginalised through colonialisation. Although the theological basis for such action has not been worked out explicitly, the practice emerges from an alliance between the struggle for liberation and indigenous traditions in a way that is focused on the local context. In the light of attention to Christ in ecclesial and cosmic dimensions, it also broadens out to a more universal perspective, mobilising the entire Church, rather than specialised local healers. The advantage of this approach is that earth care is rooted in indigenous practice rather than more theoretical socio-political agendas, yet the struggle for liberation has become woven into the debate, born of the particular historical struggle for liberation. It is also exemplary in terms of mobilising and empowering those who have very little opportunity to make a difference, and, arguably, to be agents of their own liberation. A criticism of such an approach is that it lacks an articulate theology and includes syncretistic elements of traditional religion in a somewhat uncritical way.

Conclusions

This chapter has focused on the priority to the poor that is implicit in Christian faith, but arguably has not been given sufficient attention in the richer nations of the world. Ecology and development are linked in as much as the plight of the poorest of the poor is more often than not bound up with devastation of the land. Alternative theories about development from the perspective of those who lived in Southern continents gradually challenged the modernisation hypothesis, the thesis that capitalism was equipped to enhance the lot of those in less 'developed' nations. Such theories are incorporated into the discussion of liberation theologians, though initially the plight of the earth was ignored in such debates. The focus on human survival seemed a more pressing need compared with that of the environment. Yet, with time, liberation theologians such as Leonardo Boff have enlarged the liberation theology agenda, so that not only is it forced to take into account the earth as a global system, but it also includes elements of cosmic mysticism. The difficulty with such views is how far the message of liberation is also bound up with Western culture through its reliance on forms of socialism influenced by Marxist philosophy. The earth story of Thomas Berry, which serves as a springboard for discussion of global ecology, fares no less well in this respect. Indigenous peoples have also felt marginalised by the liberation theology discourse, and have taken steps to show how their own traditions are deeply embedded in a culture of land and place as sources of identity and resistance. Indigenous cultural reflection on the land is rooted primarily in environmental practice, rather than engaged more specifically in education on globalisation and the economy, or conscientisation programmes characteristic of liberation theology as such. Themes such as the cosmic Christ help to enlarge the vision beyond the local indigenous community. In this respect it is worth asking how far and to what extent this coheres with other religious traditions of the Eastern Orthodox Church that have had a long tradition of cosmic Christology, as well as concern for the environment and ecology. A discussion of Eastern Orthodox approaches will follow in the next chapter.

Further reading

Boff, Leonardo, *Cry of the Earth: Cry of the Poor* (Maryknoll, Orbis Books, 1997)

Boff, Leonardo, *Ecology and Liberation: A New Paradigm* (Maryknoll, Orbis Books, 1995)

Edwards, D. (ed.), *Earth Revealing, Earth Healing* (Collegeville, The Liturgical Press, 2001)

Hallman, D. (ed.), *Ecotheology: Voices from South and North* (Geneva, WCC, 1994)

Hessel, Dieter T. and Ruether, Rosemary Radford (eds.), *Christianity and Ecology: Seeking the Well Being of Earth and Humans* (Cambridge, Harvard University Press, 2000)

McDonagh, S., *To Care for the Earth: A Call to a New Theology* (London, Geoffrey Chapman, 1986)

McDonagh, S., *The Greening of the Church* (London, Geoffrey Chapman, 1990)

White, Sarah and Tiongco, Romy, *Doing Theology and Development: Meeting the Challenge of Poverty* (Edinburgh, St Andrew's Press, 1997)

Chapter 5

Eco-theology from the East

THEOLOGIANS FROM THE EASTERN ORTHODOX TRADITION offer a distinctive approach to theology that is reflected in their engagement with ecological themes. In particular, a strong sense of the transcendence of God is complemented by a keen awareness of the ongoing participation of all creatures in God as one who not only creates, but also sustains all of creation. Above all, the liturgical celebration of the Church is cosmic in scope. The priesthood of humanity is affirmed, though debates exist as to the exact role of human beings in the cosmic liturgy. Traditional Orthodoxy has allowed for an affirmation of creation by pointing to the *logoi* present in all creaturely being, corresponding to the divine Logos. Sergii Bulgakov's understanding of creaturely Sophia (wisdom) present in all creation provides an alternative way of affirming creaturely being while maintaining its distinction from divine Sophia. In addition to these more theoretical bases for acknowledging the worth of creation, a strong tradition of asceticism encourages environmentally friendly practices.

Introduction

Those in the Orthodox tradition will often resist developing a particular ethics understood as a system of rules to live by, and this is no less true of environmental ethics. Why? The reasoning is that it is not enough to know what might be right and true; rather, humanity does not behave in a rational way. In addition, the underlying motivation is often not explored through such ethical systems, for people will continue to waste energy even if they know such actions are 'immoral', or even irrational, based on current knowledge of, for example, climate change. Instead, theologians need to encourage a deeper awareness of the mythological and imaginative tasks facing humanity, countering a post-Enlightenment trust in the power of reason alone to solve pressing issues. John Zizioulas, for example, argues strongly that the alternative and somewhat reactionary 'pagan' route is not the only answer; rather, the sacred and secular, rational and mythical, and so on need to come together.[1] Judging by the almost exponential growth in interest in pagan and 'new age' spiritual traditions, his words have either not been heeded sufficiently by the wider Church, or those who have an interest in such matters have felt alienated from the Church for other reasons. He suggests, therefore, that in striving to create an alternative ethos we need to recover a stronger liturgical dimension, with humanity given a crucial place as priest of creation. Paulos mar Gregorios identifies the particular vices of human greed and aggression that need to be overcome in addressing environmental problems. He also resists the idea of reunion with nature as an answer to environmental questions, for it presupposes that Christianity somehow 'desacralised' nature. Instead, he believes that the early Church fathers understood nature as 'the constitutive and identifiable qualities of each separate type of being', rather than, as commonly supposed today, 'the reality that surrounds us and can be known through our senses'.[2] The constitutive quality of created reality is that its being is changeable and changing, moving in space and time, in contrast to God's being which is *sui generis*, without beginning or end, and neither spatial nor temporal. Such a contrast sets up a *diastema*, or standing apart, between the being of creation and the Creator. However, the *diastema* does not apply in the opposite direction – that is, there is no gap between the Creator and the creation, as the whole of creation is permanently co-present with the Creator. In order to overcome the one-way *diastema* set up between creation and the Creator, the possibility exists of *metousia*, or participation in the *energeia* of God. How might humanity and creation participate in God in this way? The answer is, characteristically, through liturgical celebration.

Liturgical theology

Those less familiar with Orthodox liturgy may wonder how liturgical celebration can help reinforce connectivity with creation, for many such liturgies in the Western tradition have tended to focus almost exclusively on human salvation history.[3] For the Orthodox, the created world is not simply a 'stage' in which salvation history is played out in the manner famously indicated by Protestant theologians such as Karl Barth, but rather, the whole of creation as a work of God is intimately bound up with salvation and expressed accordingly through liturgy. Elizabeth Theokritoff has articulated the extent to which non-human creation permeates the liturgy in Orthodox worship. First, she points to texts that celebrate the praise that the earth in all its diversity offers at the birth of Christ, or at the salvation of humanity. Such texts draw on a Hebrew theme attesting to such praise, such as found in Isaiah 49:13, which points to the joy of the earth, or in the New Testament in Romans 8:23, where all of creation is caught up in the story of salvation. In the liturgy for Nativity it is expressed explicitly as:

> Every creature made by Thee offers Thee thanks. The angels offer Thee a hymn; the heavens, a star; the Magi, gifts; the shepherds, their wonder; the earth, its cave, the wilderness, the manger: and we offer Thee a Virgin Mother.[4]

Similarly, the joining in of creation at other key moments in the liturgies for Good Friday and Easter shows that this involvement of creation permeates the liturgy.

Secondly, some remarkable texts show that in some instances the non-human creation actually takes the lead. Examples include the way texts such as the Jordan turning back (Psalm 113:7) are applied to Christ's baptism, so that in some cases the Jordan addresses the Baptist and says:

> Why do you prevent the cleansing of many? He has sanctified all creation; let Him sanctify me also and the nature of waters, since for this He has been made manifest.[5]

While such language is, of course, a literary device, it is unlikely just to have 'decorative' significance. Rather, since, according to Athanasius, only humanity erred from God's purposes, then other creatures are likely to set the example in recognising and serving God. An early third-century text known as *The Apostolic Tradition of Hippolytus* encourages Christians to pray alongside the stars, the forests and the waters. Later amendments seemed to put more emphasis on the special role of humanity in articulating that praise.

Thirdly, the incarnation of Christ builds on an existing relationship between God and creation. In a similar way, Christ's names take up material creation through natural images used to describe him; Christ's image is human, but Christ's imagery is in other creatures as well. Similarly, Christ's death on a wooden cross is significant for trees in general. Theokritoff comments:

> Humanity misused a tree and polluted the world: God cleanses his world by the tree of the Cross. The misuse culminates in the instrument of torture and execution, the quintessential tree of death: God's use of the tree reveals it as a tree of life. And this has implications for trees in general.[6]

In this way,

> The new use of the tree does not ignore the purpose for which it was originally created but builds on it … Its functions such as giving food and shelter, purifying water or enriching the soil are thus seen to have a certain spiritual counterpart. We have come full circle: the life-giving tree now revokes the curse upon the earth.[7]

Yet, crucially we might ask what salvation means for non-human creation that suffers the effects of the Fall of humanity. Liturgical texts point to a recovery of sacramental potentiality of all of creation, a restoration to its original beauty, which is the original intention for creation, a return to its 'natural' state. Crucially, perhaps, intense awareness of the importance of salvation as mediated through creation means paying it special attention, expressed in hagiographic stories of lifestyles that express that awareness of God's presence. Theokritoff suggests that we see this in practice

> In the Athonite elder who calls on a basking lizard to testify to its faith in God before a sceptical student – and it does. In the saintly Alaskan priest's wife whose winter funeral is marked by an unseasonal thaw, and attended by a flock of birds who should have flown south long since. In another Athonite elder who bends down painfully to collect every spilled lentil, so that nothing goes to waste, and delights in the company of the 'voiceless theologians', the rocks and weeds among which he lives. In the villagers who make the sign of the cross over a loaf of bread before cutting it, and cense their livestock too when they cense their homes. In every believer who venerates an icon or relic or holy place, because God's material creation is not without participation in His sanctifying grace. And in the renowned Athonite elder who can give a visiting pilgrim a leaf in place of a photograph to remember him by, and speak of a blade of grass as an icon through which we can venerate the Creator.[8]

Humanity as priests of creation

Given the worth of all of creation celebrated through liturgy and stories of the lives of saints and others, the spotlight now needs to come on the role and place of humanity. This theme is taken up by John Zizioulas, who argues passionately for a restoration of the sense of the importance of humanity as priest of creation. He believes that far too much emphasis has been placed on human rationality – only to be thwarted by Darwinian science that shows rationality is not confined to human beings. Humanity, uniquely perhaps, goes against the inherent rationality in the natural world, making *freedom* the measure of what humanity is like, rather than rationality as such. Such freedom, he suggests, is restricted by the givenness of the world, unlike the absolute freedom of God. Yet while humanity aspires towards absolute freedom, it can never attain it. The Fall is about humanity mistakenly retaining a claim to absolute freedom, and as such Zizioulas believes that even at the Fall something of the image of God remains, even if it is against his own good and that of creation. Distorted freedom, too, means that humanity uses creation as its own possession in a purely utilitarian way, in dissociation from the rest of the natural order. Yet if humanity tried to make the world its own by elevating the world to a personal level, it would become 'humanised'. What does the traditional claim that the consequence of the Fall was death mean? Zizioulas suggests that this cannot mean a literal introduction of death, for this makes no sense in evolutionary history. Rather, he believes that the Fall amounts to the inability of humanity to overcome the mortality *already* inherent in the natural world. Death came about as humanity made itself the ultimate reference point, rather than God. Taking the personhood of humanity as a guide, Zizioulas posits humanity as *the link* between God and creation. In a hypostatic sense humanity achieves this through embodiment. In an ecstatic sense humanity achieves this through offering the world to God. He believes that this hypostatic identification and offering up to God liberates creation from its limitations and lets it be itself. Priesthood, understood in such terms, engages far wider activities than simply the ceremonial, for it amounts to a 'broader existential attitude encompassing human activities that involve a conscious or even unconscious manifestation of these two aspects' of personhood'.[9] As might be anticipated, Christ fulfils this role of Priest of creation and models the proper relation between human- ity and the natural world. In the Eucharist, also, humanity offers the creation back to God, in such a way that creation is brought into relationship with God, freed from its natural limitations and transformed into a bearer of life. Creation 'acquires for us in this way a sacredness which is not inherent in its nature, but "acquired" in and through Man's free exercise of his *imago Dei*, i.e., his personhood.'[10] Of course, given the high place Zizioulas has placed on human beings in this role, humanity now has 'an awesome responsibility for the survival of God's creation'.[11] Zizioulas concludes that there are two alternatives possible: the pagan alternative which posits the world as sacred, but never worries about its fate, as it is deemed eternal; and the Christian way which views humanity as the 'crucial link between the world and God ... the only way to respect once again the sacrality of nature'.[12]

The high place that Zizioulas gives to humanity is theocentric rather than anthropocentric, but its emphasis on the crucial role of the human in contra- diction with paganism is drawn too sharply for other contemporary Orthodox writers. Given the place of creation in the liturgy already alluded to, I would agree with Theokritoff that his characterisation of humanity as *the link* between God and creation is too stark, even among contemporary Orthodox writing – for creation as a whole can express its praise regardless of the presence of humans.[13] Of course, Zizioulas' scheme is clear and attractively simple – distorted human freedom is embedded in the Fall, from which fol- lows a turning away from the potential to overcome mortality in creation. This is opposed to right use of human freedom in relation to God, and as priests of creation expressed supremely in the Eucharist, through which all creation now lives. Other theologians prefer to emphasise in cosmic priesthood thanks- giving for creation, another strong element in the eucharistic liturgy.[14] This allows for a rather less stark view of the place of humanity as cosmic priest compared with Zizioulas' view. Instead, all of creation is caught up in an inter-dependent model of praise to God. Hierarchical arrangements within the created order are, according to this view, by providential design, which indicate a distinctive relationship to the Creator, including direct relationships, rather than simply that mediated through human persons. Humanity, according to this view, does not so much displace the offering of other creatures, but furthers that offering. Accordingly, priesthood is about an offering, but also points to a belief in the need for transfiguration in Christ. Such transfiguration is required in the light of not so much a Fall from initial perfection, as a failure to reach potential. The priestly role could be said to point to the possibility of transfiguration of the cosmos, but it is one that is marked by non-human creation as 'concelebrants in the offering of glory to God'.[15]

Logos and *logoi*

Alongside this understanding of priesthood, we find other Orthodox writers developing the notion of the natural world as expressing *logoi* or patterns after the divine *Logos* or Word. This view separates clearly the *essence* of God and God's *activities*, manifested through God's energies (*energeia*) and described through God's words (*logoi*).[16] *Logoi* are the principles and ideas in the sensory world as we know it in different manifestations, but which ultimately express their source in the divine Logos. Maximus the Confessor believed that the *logoi* are pre-existent in God, but then realised in the natural order. In this respect, *logoi* are both transcendent to, yet immanent in, the natural world. Alexei Nesteruk suggests that *logoi* are not, therefore, created or part of the created order, for they are rooted in the divine Logos. In other words, in their origin they are transcendent, but in their manifestation they are immanent, in a way somewhat analogous to radii on the circumference of a circle. Yet, bearing in mind the *diastema* between the world and God mentioned earlier, this connectivity works in one direction only, that is from Logos to the world. The possibility for a relation from the world to God exists through participation in the energies of God as that which relates to the *logoi*. Such reflection allows reason a higher place in Nesteruk's theology compared with Zizioulas, for 'humans, as a divine image, were granted reason in order to be in a dialogical relationship with another reason, the reason of God'.[17]

Kallistos Ware also affirms the relation between God and the world in terms of transcendence and immanence, expressed through notions such as *pantokrator*, a term that means not just 'almighty', but 'holding everything together in unity'.[18] Ware puts particular emphasis on the omnipresence of God in all created being, so he can state with confidence that 'Our primary image should be that of indwelling. Above and beyond creation, God is also its true inwardness, its "within".'[19] The active presence of God as one who sustains everything in being is dependent on the creative word of God, without which everything would collapse into non-being. This strong sense of co-presence with creation is expressed through the *logoi*, 'which is God's intention for that thing, its inner essence, that which makes it distinctively itself and at the same time draws it towards the divine realm.'[20] This, of course, gives value to created things, for they are not simply objects, but a personal word spoken to us by the Creator of all that exists. Ware, following Maximus the Confessor, claims that *logoi* may be created or uncreated, depending on perspective. They are *created* in as much as they inhere in the natural world, but in terms of preconception they are *uncreated*. This interpretation is useful (compare Nesteruk who claims *logoi* are simply uncreated) in as much as it puts more emphasis on the indwelling presence of the *logoi* in a way that is not separable from material being.

Ware also suggests that the relationship between God's being (*ousia*) and God's energies (*energeiai*) is a complementary approach to Logos/*logoi* in understanding more fully the relationship between God's transcendence and immanence. God's essence is utterly transcendent and removed from human knowing, while God's energies serve to maintain all that exists in its being. Such energies are uncreated and eternal, while allowing all things to become a sacrament of God's presence. In speaking of God's being, Ware is keen to stress that God is not a being like other, created beings, but, following Palamas, God is beyond being, *hyperousios*, yet at the same time 'All', in that without God's presence nothing would exist. Participation in God means participation in God's glory or radiance, rather than God's nature. He also suggests that contrasting God's essence/being and energies is not sufficient, for he wants to contrast both with God's *hypostasis* (person). Unity in essence is only possible among the three persons of the Trinity. Hypostatic union occurred at the incarnation, when Christ became human, and the Godhead and humanity were united in a single person, the *Theanthropos*. The third kind of union sought by the saints is that through participation in God's energies, through deification. At the same time the personal life of each remains intact, so that each retains its own personal identity and nature, even though they are united with God's energies. Can such union simply be described in terms of the action of the Holy Spirit in the lives of the saints? Palamas suggests, rather, that *energei* is a necessary concept as it is a shared work of all three persons of the Trinity, rather than just the presence of the Spirit. Other critics have argued that this makes God into a composite figure and it is too complicated; against this charge Palamas states that there is one living God, but God can be understood from different perspectives according to God's *ousia*, *hypostasis* and *energeia*, which expresses the work of God in creation and redemption. The key question in relation to non-human creation is the extent to which creatures other than humans can participate in God. Ware, following Maximus, does allow for this by citing Maximus:

> God, full beyond all fullness, brought creatures into being, not because he has need of anything, but so that they might participate in him *in*

proportion to their capacity and that he himself might rejoice in his works, through seeing them joyful.[21]

Ware also brings to the discussion an important emphasis on the creative acts of God as being not simply an expression of free will, but an act of love for creation, leading to mutual participation and mutual joy. This suggests, further, that human relationship as image-bearer is not simply expressed in freedom, but also through expression of ecstatic, outgoing love.

Divine and creaturely Sophia

Although Ware softens his approach to the God/world relationship as Logos/*logoi* by speaking in terms of God's love and God's energies, Sergii Bulgakov developed another strand in Orthodox theology that is also embedded in the liturgical practice of the Church, namely Sophia (Wisdom). Wisdom was often associated with Logos in the writings of the early Church fathers, such as Maximus the Confessor. However, after the council of Ephesus in 431, where Mary was declared the Mother of God, a tradition of associating wisdom with Mary developed. Popular piety led to a number of different images of wisdom being developed in iconography in addition to that associated with Christ or Mary, ranging from appearance in angelic form, to association with the crucifix. Sergii Bulgakov (b. 1853) developed the poetical and mystical portrayal of Wisdom in the writings of Vladimir Solovyov and Pavel Florensky in a more theological direction, even while admitting that his insights drew from experiences that convinced him of the presence of Sophia in the beauty of the world.[22] Bulgakov used Sophia as a means to connect God and the world, to describe both the immanence and transcendence of God.[23] Although his earlier writing hinted at the possibility of Sophia as a fourth hypostasis, it is important to note that his later works resisted the idea of a quarternity of persons, but rather envisaged Sophia as integral to the life of all three persons of the Trinity. Sophia expresses the yearning love of God, the Eternal Feminine, moving out to all creation, but also the glory of God in a creation transfigured by that love. Traditional Orthodox approaches would resist speaking of God's being, and associate wisdom with God's energies. Bulgakov is less cautious in this respect, and was heavily criticised on account of this, though he does allow for the tradition that speaks of the unknowability of God by acknowledging that God as Absolute cannot be known. In later writings he also distinguishes between creaturely Sophia, as known in the world, and divine Sophia, which once again, puts rather more emphasis on the *diastema* between the world and God.

In the context of the present discussion about the value of creation as such – that is, how far Bulgakov's thinking lends itself to what might be described as a theology that is ecologically friendly – it is necessary to explore more fully what he meant by creaturely Sophia. I will be returning to this theme again in Chapters 9, 10 and 11. He suggests that it is the Father who is the creative origin of the world, but the second and third persons of the Trinity participate in creation through Sophia, since all three persons share divine Sophia. Creaturely Sophia is associated both with the spoken words of the Word in creation, but also with the action of the Spirit, transfiguring creation towards life, beauty and glory.[24] Significantly, perhaps, he also posits the action of the Spirit as being in some sense prior to that of the Word, so that proto-matter emerges from the action of the Spirit, and becomes 'the maternal womb in which the forms of this world are conceived'.[25] Yet he draws back from considering that the Holy Spirit itself is acting here at the dawn of creation, as he wants to retain the idea that the Father alone acts hypostatically in relation to creation. Rather, the Spirit is not so much the hypostatic revelation of the Holy Spirit, but the Spirit of God, the action of the Third person as revealed *through* Sophia. The Son and the Spirit have their hypostases disguised, as it were, by acting through creaturely Sophia in the creation of the world. In this he can claim that 'Three hypostatic flames are lit in a row, one behind the other and therefore they are seen as a single flame; and this single flame is the I of the Father.'[26] Both the hypostasis of the Son and Spirit consent to this action, but they are concealed by the hypostasis of the Father.

The action of creaturely Sophia through the Spirit of God is that which expresses the life of the world according to its own nature, 'the natural energy of the world', 'that life-giving principle which pious paganism, without knowing Him, worshipped as the "Great Pan", as the Mother of the gods, Isis and Gaia'.[27] This is not, he argues, deification of the world in pantheism, but *panentheism*. This, he suggests, needs to be understood in sophianic terms, so that 'God creates the world by and in Sophia, and in its sophianic foundation the world is divine, although at the same time it is extra-divine in its creaturely aseity.'[28] The 'natural grace' of the world is the action of the Holy Spirit in creaturely Sophia, so he is prepared to speak of the Spirit of God as a 'life-giving force' that allows all creation to have being, including an actualisation of divine seeds or logoses which come from the Logos, actualised into forms of creation by the work of the Holy Spirit. Alongside this positive energy we find a struggle with 'creaturely nothing', the 'dark face of Sophia'. This entails a tendency towards non-being, but it is constrained, so that cosmos emerges against a background of chaos. Such chaos is permitted by God, and 'receives its own force of being by a creative act of God'.[29]

In considering the role of humanity, Bulgakov acknowledges the importance of human action, for according to him, nature awaits its 'humanisation', but at the same time it still possesses its own spirit-bearing character independent of humanity. This capacity of the natural world as such to be 'God-bearing' finds expression in the beauty of the world and has the capacity to bring joy to human beings. He sees beauty in the world as a manifestation of the light of divine Sophia, for it is objective, rather than simply subjective. Yet even beauty itself, if considered inappropriately by human beings, can become a source of temptation and occasion for sinful actions. Bulgakov is also keen to stress that the creation of the world is not simply a work of God's power, but a work expressive of divine Love.[30] Furthermore, while creation arose out of 'nothing', it is not nothing before God, since it has its own divinity which it expresses in creaturely Sophia. The correlation between the world and God is in creaturely Sophia. He is also convinced by the idea of divine seeds, planted in creation in the beginning, so that the only residue of evolutionary theory that he retains is that the world is in a state of becoming, resisting the concept of 'absolute randomness'.[31] Leaving this concept aside, his overall theology is significant in an Orthodox context in as much as it allows him to give higher value to the creaturely world as such, rather than simply viewing humanity as the means of linking the salvation of the world and God, as discussed in Zizioulas. Astonishingly, and somewhat unconvincingly, he equates certain distasteful phenomena of the natural world, such as harmful plants and predators – even repulsive insects – with the action of evil spirits that he believes can only be countered by the work of angels acting according to God's providence.[32] Humanity, at the Fall, no longer takes up its proper role of being the 'guide and king' of creation; instead, the animals were originally called to be friends of humanity, 'younger brothers'. He believes that the works of divine providence are properly ascribed to angels, as they are the ideal sophianicity of the natural world, belonging to creation, but being superior to it. Yet another aspect of providence is the gradual convergence of creaturely and divine Sophia, a yearning for God's grace that is never complete, through a process of deification that is at once simultaneous with sophianisation.

Saint Symeon as ascetic and theologian

The hermit tradition needs to be set in the context of the stress on the transfiguration of the world found in Orthodox theology. Saint Symeon the New Theologian's work was characterised by a particular emphasis on the mystical experience, but he also taught extensively on humanity's relationship to the environment in a way that was explicit and practical in orientation. Saint Symeon was an ascetic, but he was also aware of the social dimension of human life. He is particularly critical of those who glean for themselves that which should be held in common.[33] The vice of 'avarice' acts like a tyrant, taking over and appropriating what should be shared. Like other Orthodox theologians, Symeon believed that the reason for existence stemmed from the Logos, expressed in *logoi* or principles of things. As humans sought to discover these principles, they would give creation the respect it deserved, as its existence flowed from the action of a creative God.[34] He also insisted that humanity could not see such principles automatically; rather, it was crucial that humanity repented and became receptive to what he called 'a baptism of tears' in order to experience repentance as a genuine change in their way of thinking. The world as one which 'tells' of the glory of God is only perceived after such spiritual conversion. Once such principles are perceived, then the use of the natural world is that which is in accordance with its nature. Such an attitude requires human beings to approach the natural world with the respect and love it deserves. He also acknowledges the importance of receiving those gifts of the Holy Spirit that will be used for the common good, and also for the purposes of co-creating in the world that God has created and maintains.[35] The idea of co-creation is only possible in the context of a Spirit-filled life – that is, it is not possible to acknowledge this possibility outside a living relationship with God and obedience to God's commandments. Above all, Symeon views a failure in this respect as not just neutral, but as an opening up to sinful satisfaction of egocentric desires, alienating humanity from the rest of creation. Moreover, the keeping of commandments should be viewed in the context of an offering of thanksgiving and praise for all that God has given humanity.

Asceticism, or voluntary renunciation of the demands of the senses, arises because the senses often express unreasonable desires, where pleasure becomes an end in itself. In a state of hedony the true beauty of creation becomes obscured, a fantasy of the original beauty God bestows on creation. An ascetic use of the world is therefore a pre-condition for discovering its true purpose and beauty. Only in matters of 'absolute necessity', including, for example, the food, shelter and clothing needed for survival, is consumption promoted as the 'better way'. Any more than this should be viewed as particular blessings from God. Alongside consumerism, intemperance and hedonism, Symeon notes other passions of egoism and self-love. Asceticism helps to counter these tendencies, regarding all things as resulting from the action of a personal God, rather than objects given economic and utilitarian value. In addition, asceticism points towards a proper appreciation of social justice, so that goods are restored to those to whom they equally belong. Those living in a community of asceticism, as in monastic orders, are not anti-nature or anti-material, but through proper ascetic appreciation and use of the natural world it becomes restored to its original beauty.[36] Symeon extols the monastic life, and was a cenobitic himself, but refuses to restrict salvation to this way of life. Many monks in the hermit tradition resisted ill-treatment of the natural world, while at the same time also resisting friendship with animals, regarded as 'a perversion of the order established by God and contrary to the normal state of man'.[37] There is clearly some divergence here, as Bulgakov, for example, admits to the possibility of friendship with animals. The ascetic monk promotes an ethos that preserves respect in his relationship with the natural world. It is possible to argue that the life of saints expressed in this and other ways is not just an example of a return to a paradisiacal state, but a pointing forward towards a future eschatological age.[38]

Conclusions

In considering the kind of eco-theology that emerges in the context of Eastern Orthodoxy, I have suggested that it is essential to understand the central place of the liturgy in its theological reflection. Western theology has become too accustomed to theorising in the absence of practice, so that it becomes detached from the life of the Church, or in some cases, from the life of faith itself. Orthodox liturgy is less concerned about the particular interpretation of the Bible according to literary criticism, or even reception history. Rather, it follows the example of the way the early Church fathers applied the Hebrew Bible, with its focus on the land and the earth, to the story of salvation as told in the New Testament. The overall result is a liturgy that is much more conscious of participation by the whole of the created order in salvation history. Zizioulas' term 'cosmological propheticism' expresses this combination of an interest in cosmology with history. The particular place of humanity as priest of creation is the subject of some debate. Zizioulas names humanity as the salvific link between creation and God, based on his view that at the Fall humanity failed to use its freedom aright and fulfil its potential for immortality, but is now restored by the coming of Christ. Other writers are more inclined to envisage a more direct relationship between creation and God as being possible through participation in divine energies. The distinction between the transcendence of God and God's living presence or immanence in the world is crucial here. For God's being is not accessible to human minds, rather God is known through God's energies. A similar relation exists in the action of the Logos as expressed in *logoi*, the principles found in the created world. The interplay between *logoi* and Logos is one way of expressing God's transcendence and yet immanence. An alternative is through the notion of divine Sophia, expressed through creaturely Sophia. The latter was developed by the Russian sophiologists of the nineteenth century, especially Sergii Bulgakov. While his ideas are somewhat controversial in terms of Orthodox theology, his stress on the worth of creation through creaturely Sophia, alongside his recognition of the possibility of distortion through a shadow Sophia, lends itself to a high view of creation and appreciation of its true beauty. There are difficulties with his view, such as his use of the language of 'life force', 'seminal seeds', and resistance to all notions of randomness in a way that would alienate him from contemporary evolutionary biologists. Yet appreciation of the actual nature of creation is only really possible, according to Symeon the New Theologian, if we have first undergone a process of deep repentance. In this comes an awareness that the problems of the environment, including the present ones, are not something that can be discussed remotely, but impinge on one's own lifestyle and practices. The life of an ascetic monk was one that bore witness to the power of a life lived in simplicity and prayer, dedicated to thanksgiving and offering up of creation, a refusal to succumb to the temptations of material passions in greed and consumerism. In this the possibility of the future of creation as one that is transfigured by Christ becomes evident. While there are other traditions that would speak of the possibility of a life of simplicity and prayer in a similar manner, the Orthodox tradition lends itself to showing forth this possibility, for it is a theology embedded in life understood in the guise of the divine liturgy and the eucharistic offering of the Church. It seeks to tackle ethical issues indirectly rather than directly, but engendering an ethos enhanced specifically in the liturgical life of the Church. It is concerned less, perhaps, with social analysis and political discussion, and more with the generation of an alternative way of living. I suggest that those in the West may come to appreciate the ethos and mythology that Eastern Orthodox theology inculcates, but modernity has penetrated to the extent that social and political issues necessarily come to the fore in any discussion. Bulgakov was perhaps unusual in the attention he gave to the political economy and in this and other respects he can mediate between Eastern and Western traditions, though his work more often than not takes the form of a sharp critique, rather than constructive alternative proposals.[39]

Further reading

Bulgakov, S., *The Bride of the Lamb*, trans. B. Jakim (Grand Rapids, Eerdmans, 2002)

Bulgakov, S., *Sophia: The Wisdom of God: An Outline of Sophiology* (Hudson, NY, Lindisfarne Press, 1993)

Gregorios, P. mar, *The Human Presence: An Orthodox View of Nature* (Geneva, WCC, 1978)

Keselopoulos, A. G., *Man and the Environment: A Study of St Symeon* (Crestwood, St Vladimir's Seminary Press, 2001)

Rossi, V., 'Christian Ecology is Cosmic Christology', *Epiphany*, 8 (1987), pp. 52–62Theokritoff, E., 'Creation and Priesthood in Modern Orthodox Thinking', *Ecotheology*, 10.3 (2005), pp. 344–63

Theokritoff, E., 'Creation and Salvation in Orthodox Worship', *Ecotheology*, 10 (2001), pp. 97–108

Walker, A. and Carras, C. (eds.), *Living Orthodoxy in the Modern World* (London, SPCK, 1996)

Ware, K., 'God Immanent yet Transcendent: The Divine Energies According to Saint Gregory Palamas', in P. Clayton and A. Peacocke (eds.), *In Whom we Live and Move and Have Our Being: Panentheistic Reflections on God's Presence in a Scientific World* (Grand Rapids/Cambridge, Eerdmans, 2004)

Zizioulas, J., 'Symbolism and Realism in Orthodox Worship', *Sourozh*, 79 (February 2000), pp. 3–17

Zizioulas, J., 'Preserving God's Creation' (Part 3), *Sourozh*, 40 (May 1990), pp. 31–40

Chapter 6

Eco-theology from the West

IT WOULD BE IMPOSSIBLE TO DO JUSTICE TO THE VAST spread of writings on eco-theology by authors who could broadly be considered 'Western' in cultural orientation. Rather than even attempt to survey the full variety here, I will focus this chapter on those writers who have been particularly concerned to address socio-political issues. Later chapters will consider more specific systematic analysis. I will also concentrate the discussion on that agricultural practice that is often regarded as an epitome of Western domination – namely, the use of genetically modified organisms (GMOs). In this case sociological analysis has also had to address an eco-theology of a rather different stripe, namely the implicit theology emerging from field studies that analyse the public response to GMOs through focus-group analysis.

Socio-political currents

The strength of interest in socio-political currents became evident in the earlier discussion of ecological, economic and environmental justice. While Eastern Orthodox writers do comment on the demise, as they see it, of genuine spirituality in the West, alongside consumer culture, the critical voices within the Western tradition have been particularly sharp in their analysis of the social conditions pertaining to present problems.[1] Michael Northcott, for example, is particularly critical of those social trends that he believes have contributed to environmental decline. In particular, he believes that modernity lies at the root of the environmental crisis. Historically, this included the demise of traditional agricultural systems, so that

> the industrial transformation of agricultural systems and land tenure patterns, of economic order, of manufacturing production and household consumption creates a radically re-ordered world. These transformations in the material conditions of human life effect dramatic changes in the natural environment.[2]

He also notes the individualism and consumerism characteristic of modern life, along with a demise of traditional cosmology. His historical analysis includes a swipe at trade and military imperialisms, which he believes brought ecological imperialism in their wake. Historically he believes that more benign models of human partnership with the earth in early monastic communities were destroyed by attraction to new wealth, which seeded the eventual dissolution of the monasteries at the Reformation. Alongside this trend the global mobility of labour and capital contributes to the 'disembedding' of social systems of production and exchange from cultural, moral and ecological limits. He believes that the development of a global market economy independent of land and work was a major factor in the origins of the environmental crisis. Land was now 'commodified' and therefore no longer subject to more traditional relations of kinship and place. He is also sharply critical of modern science and technology, which he believes support the values of domination and progress, set over against nature, which becomes simply available for human exploitation.[3] He also discusses the secular and romantic 'turn to nature' that follows in the wake of this disruption in relationships. His own variety of eco-theology is one that puts emphasis on the created order as that which is given by God and reflecting the goodness, wisdom and ordering of God.[4] Yet he is also anxious to emphasise the covenant ideal in Hebrew thought that sets up a set of relationships that replace those that have broken down and become distorted through the material conditions of modern society. He then develops in a more explicit way an account of soteriology that includes the natural world. The point here is to emphasise the *sequence* of his argument, which begins by consideration of socio-political issues, then subsequently weaves in theological and ethical analyses. This also applies to his more recent book focused specifically on climate, where his theological analysis takes its cues from biblical sources, but only after considerable socio-political and cultural critique of the trends that he believes underlie present global climate problems.[5]

Although Northcott, rather surprisingly perhaps, does not explicitly refer to Murray Bookchin's work, his treatment of ecological themes could be seen in the light of the development of social ecology that Bookchin pioneered.[6] Social ecology contrasts with Deep Ecology (discussed earlier), yet both are political ecologies.[7] Bookchin attacks capitalist economies driven by market goals and statist planned political economies, as both have a view of nature as an object to be used to gain more resources, unaware of the limits to expansion. He is particularly critical of all hierarchical structures of human society, believing that the imbalances in human society give rise to the idea of domination over the natural realm as a deliberate, purposive act. He sees hierarchy implicit in socialism that speaks in terms of class struggle. He is particularly critical of liberal society that promotes the welfare of the minority property owners at the expense of those who lack ownership, restricting their freedom. He also resists hierarchical depictions of nature, believing that these represent anthropomorphisms – that is, reading into nature attributes believed to be present in the human social sphere. Instead of 'environmentalism' he argues for a 'social ecology', where ecology carries political meanings beyond the piecemeal change that he associates with liberal environmentalism. The capitalist system gives the appearance of permanence that is then reinforced by technological forms of production that serve to maintain the order. Technology is used to harness nature. Andrew Light has coined the term 'environmental materialism' to describe Bookchin's position, as the starting point for change is through a critique of the material conditions, such as the ownership and control of technological processes used in the expansion of markets and correlated consumption of resources.[8] Bookchin is also resistant to the idea of moral and spiritual change as being needed in such debates, as he considers that modern capitalism is impervious to moral appeals. He is prepared to emphasise that human reason necessarily entails distinctions between humanity and the rest of the natural world, so that acts of cooperation towards emancipation of the natural world are achieved by *human* acts of will, including humanity's drive towards progress.[9]

Bookchin contrasts the human with the non-human by describing interrelations in the human sphere as social, but interrelations in the non-human sphere as communal. Yet the relationship with the natural world is best corrected by finding harmonious social relationships in the human sphere first of all. This is not achieved so much by a return to pre-hierarchical societies, but by recognising that hierarchy as such is not a 'natural' condition of the social sphere. The unity he proposes between humanity and non-human nature is a unity in diversity, rather than the mergence that he finds problematic in Deep Ecology. The distinctions he finds in the human social sphere are ones that have evolved from non-human ancestors, which allows humanity to recognise itself as also being embedded in the natural world. A failure to acknowledge such diversity amounts to a backward step in evolution. It also follows from this that, unlike Northcott, he is scathing about any attempt to find 'natural laws' as a basis for moral action. But how far does his appeal to humanism radically counter the trends that he is anxious to forestall? Certainly his resistance to the primitive and elevation of rationality in humans also contrasts significantly with Northcott's position discussed above, even though both seek a new vision of social conditions in the present.

Bookchin is best described as an eco-anarchist, in that he combines a rejection of the nation state with a rejection of hierarchy in the non-human and human worlds alongside affirmation of local direct political action and pre-socialist community.[10] Bookchin's social ecology is in dialectic relationship, where nature and society form a unity in diversity linked through differentiation, rather than nature providing a template to which humanity must conform. Bookchin's ecology has a keen sense of subjectivity and agency throughout nature, along with non-human precursors to human freedom, reason and consciousness. But there are two strands in Bookchin's thinking that seem incompatible. On the one hand he argues that human domination is always prior to its domination of nature; while on the other hand he suggests that human society has necessarily evolved from natural roots in dialectical relationship. In addition, he traces the historical growth of hierarchies through the emergence of gerontocracy, when ageing humans found it necessary to compensate for their increasing biological frailty by proving indispensable in social realms. Bookchin's insistence that hierarchy in the human realm is always prior to domination of the natural world makes no sense even by his own standards, as he links gerontocracy with ageing bodies.

Bookchin's favouring of eco-communities is also inconsistent, even though he initially sets up a contrast between communities in animals and institutionalised communities as human societies. Most likely this is a way of privileging the anarchist turn to community, but it would make more sense to speak of the relationship between society and nature in social, rather than communal categories. Instead of the standard rendition of evolution as competitive, he prefers to emphasise more collaborative, symbiotic elements. This organic link with natural evolution engenders a form of naturalism that parts company with other social scientists who would insist that human society has no connection with evolved nature. Human freedom fulfils a latent potential in the natural world; the ecological is an organising principle of human social development. He detects germinal aspects of human freedom, subjectivity and mutuality in the non-human realm, and thus it serves to set the particular conditions for the development of human society. The relationship between what he calls 'first nature' (that is, the natural world as such) and 'second nature' (that is, human society) is always a dialectical one. So we can find, for example, indeterminacy in nature compared with autonomy in humanity, openness in nature compared with freedom in humanity, and so on.

In more specifically political terms Bookchin argues for a political realm that is distinct from the social and the state. Rather like the Athenian *polis*, the political is engendered by municipal face-to-face democracy in a way that is harmoniously tailored to the natural surroundings. This amounts to a confederal municipalism that affirms diversity and freedom, and opposes state hierarchy. The goal of such a dialectical society is one that privileges richness, diversity, complexity and rationality in human societies. The local, regional nature of this political model allows for particular regional concerns about the natural world to be taken into account. Local communities also interact with each other, hence avoiding the possible charge of parochialism. Bookchin's separation of the social, the state and the political is too sharp, since opposition to the state could just as easily emerge from the social.[11] While the idea of a municipality conveniently allows Bookchin to critique the state as emerging from hierarchical tendencies in community, the basis for grounding society in its political organisation, its *polis*, seems unjustified. It is also not clear how the political relationships between the natural world and the municipality are worked out, given that he rejects the idea of political representation as a valid form of political governance. But how can voiceless nature be taken into account in ways other than representative ones? Just as non-human nature can be recipients, rather than agents of justice, so duties of citizenship can be exercised towards beings who are not citizens.

Peter Scott draws on Bookchin's ideas in the development of his eco-theology that is overtly political in orientation.[12] He believes that Bookchin provides a secular counterpart to his construal of a common realm of God, nature and humanity, where there is not only holistic unity, but also diversity and difference. He also believes that a politics of nature needs to be more concerned with a perceived stinginess of nature, that is, its lack of appropriate fruitfulness, rather than Bookchin's focus on the way nature has been erroneously projected into Stalinism or Nazism. Accordingly, a liberal state will seek to both distance itself from the natural realm and correct this stinginess and lack of fecundity by technical means and through state control of nature's goods. Scott challenges this view in as much as he doubts that these are merely technical matters or that the state has sufficient insight to arbitrate for nature's goods. He also believes that we need to scrutinise which hierarchies are being served in the liberal view, and, importantly, he follows Bookchin by affirming that nature is also important for the development of humanity, not just its emergence. Nature, in other words, can be thought of as having agency that is in dynamic relationship with human society. He draws back from affirming the particular form of political organisation through confederal municipality, as it overlooks his own themes of sociality in nature. He also correctly sees Bookchin's understanding of nature in terms of local communities as far too restrictive; nature surpasses community in that effects on the natural realm move beyond the natural to the global.

Scott's theological input relates to his perception of God as the activity, ground and force permeating the natural and human realms interpreted in non-hierarchical ways. Unlike Northcott, and following Bookchin, Scott resists naming the continuity between the natural and the human in terms of natural laws. Like Northcott, he recognises that the relationship between humanity and nature needs to resist mastery. Scott also resists Bookchin's tendency to portray humanity as that which completes the natural in some way – as nature made self-conscious. He also affirms the idea of dialectical relationships between God and the world in Trinitarian categories. Both humanity and non-human nature orient towards God as both social and natural in dialectical relationship. Yet it seems that such sociality arises as a transcendental – that is, it is theologically situated first and foremost, rather than deriving from nature as such.

He also, significantly, wishes to stress the sufficiency of the liberation of nature in Christ, so that there is no Christian imperative to 'save the world'.[13] The spiritual realm in which Scott envisages such activity is eschatological but also an ecological fellowship of openness. Such a dynamic relationality leads, he suggests, to an idealised peaceable kingdom. The way forward, he suggests, is through a democratisation of non-human nature, thereby enlarging the fellowship that has arisen through the expansion of Trinitarian social relationships. He draws back from the notion of attributing subjectivity to nature, which such a view might logically imply, but in this respect Scott is suggesting a representative democracy, rather than a participatory one. Instead of a re-enchantment of nature Scott prefers to speak of a eucharistic participation in the united common sociality of God, humanity and nature.

Genetically modified crops – a case study[14]

Controversies, both socio-political and theological, continue to rage over the merit or otherwise of introducing genetically modified organisms into agriculture. It provides an excellent example of the technical manipulation of nature, alongside contested discussion about how far and to what extent it is possible to re-order the natural realm.[15] The theological and ethical responses to GMOs are often interwoven, and this is characteristic of eco-theological responses in general emerging in a Western context – namely, that there has been more attention paid to ethics and practices compared with specific doctrinal considerations. The intention in this short section is to draw out as far as possible some of the key theological ideas emerging from public debate on this practice, rather than discuss the ethical issues in any detail.

There has been a gradual realization in recent years that the public's perception of risk has its own value and can contribute to the overall assessment of particular technologies. The acceptance or otherwise of a particular technology is ultimately dependent on public approval. Hence the public response to genetic engineering is a vital ingredient in its further development. The Centre of the Study of Environmental Change based at Lancaster University investigated public perceptions of risks associated with technologies such as the genetic modification of organisms. Unilever and a number of non-government organisations sponsored one of the more recent reports, *Uncertain World*. The research is significant in and of itself as it demonstrates the way *some* large companies may be starting to show a more responsible attitude to the impact of new technologies. A research method known as *focus groups* involved guided discussions with nine small groups of people from different parts of the UK and with different social characteristics. The results overall showed very little public enthusiasm for biotechnology. Public perception identified commercial interest as lying behind many of the new proposed products, especially those related to food. Their concern seemed to be exacerbated by certain kinds of information, rather than reduced. A similar finding arose out of the results of the more recent GM Nation debate that covered an even wider range of different groups, and used different methods in order to collate the results of the survey.

The most relevant aspect that concerns us here is the implicit theology that emerges from this social scientific analysis, even though the original researchers did not apparently notice it in the first survey. Almost all respondents were anxious or worried about the idea that genetic engineering amounted to a 'messing about with nature'. Their sense of risk arising from such 'tampering' was related to possible effects on both their own health and damage to the environment. Furthermore, a strong sense of order in the natural world prevails: 'I don't think we should mess with nature. Nature was designed for specific reasons. We mess with it. We have no right'; 'It's actually broken the natural order.' A deep sense of order in the natural world, with humanity having a special place, followed by animals and then plants, has its basis in the theological doctrine of creation. While the idea of the Creator as the divine Designer has gone out of fashion ever since the demise of natural theology, a sense of design in the natural world does seem to prevail in the public mind. In some cases a more explicit reference to theism surfaces. For example, one respondent believed that interference with nature goes beyond permissible boundaries, for 'I'm not sure whether man should play God and change things for the better, for the lucre, at the end of the day.' For many, the idea of God *as such* is hidden, but the sense of ordering prevails.

Another theme that surfaced is the idea that what is present in nature and untouched by human interference is good. Overall the *reason* for changing the natural to something else was questioned. While a form of biotechnology has been going on for centuries in cheese-making, beer-making and so on, any attempt to try and persuade us that this is the same as genetic engineering was dismissed. The irreversible nature of genetic change is such that the original 'natural' form may be lost, and this seems threatening. Most philosophers argue that equating the natural with value – that is, what is natural is automatically good – is a weak philosophical argument. It has been dubbed the 'naturalistic fallacy'.

However, it is more likely that the public insistence on the natural is less a philosophical premise than a theological one. By this we mean that there is an implicit *religious* concept that what is created is good. Again, God's blessing of creation in Genesis and affirmation of the natural order in other scriptural texts, especially the wisdom literature, affirm this as a core element of the Christian tradition. Nonetheless, a romantic affiliation with the natural world is unnecessary and at times unhelpful in view of the realities of the harshness of the natural world. Yet it would be odd to regard diseases themselves as 'sinful' in any sense. Overall there is in the public mind a 'yes' to creation as a gift from God. This sense of affirmation prevails as an implicit, rather than an explicit, theology.

What was somewhat surprising was a tendency in all groups to look at the wider environmental consequences of genetic modification. The long-term and latent effects of BSE served as an example of how hidden dangers could surface much later. When soap powder was modified, for example, the immediate thought in many minds was: what about the effect on the ecosystems? Furthermore, questions surfaced regularly about the Third World, and possible effects on poorer communities. Such global and broad ecological concerns perhaps reflect an implicit eco-theology and ethics which is holistic and integrates human need with the wider interests of the environment.

While the notion of 'sin' was never mentioned, another clear theme was an underlying sense of mistrust of the motives of those involved. There were strong statements like 'It's all for human greed', 'It's for profit'. BSE again served as an example that reinforced the suspicion that the full story is never really made explicit. One participant commented: 'I think if I'd read that before BSE my thoughts might have been more positive … Sometimes we meddle too much … You can never be sure what the effects are going to be at the end of the day.' There was little belief in the underlying values of the organisations, especially supermarkets and the government. While the former were suspected of encouraging such developments for pure self-interest and profit – for 'filthy lucre' – the government was viewed with suspicion as being out of touch with the needs of ordinary people.

Are there any signs of hope in this somewhat negative assessment? There are certainly signs that hope is still present, but it does not seem to be the lot of the Church to be bearers of this hope. One group mentioned the idea that the Church *might* be able to become bearers of moral and ethical values – in other words, somehow act as a 'moral voice'. However, this was undermined by the perception that the Church was also a landowner, which would compromise its impartiality. Groups that did come over very strongly as bearers of an alternative vision were Greenpeace, Friends of the Earth and other non-government consumer organisations such as Watchdog. They were seen as those who could balance the discussion by presenting an alternative view that was unsullied by desire for profit. This is a somewhat naïve view, since the political agenda of campaign organisations is far from neutral, hence it sets up polarities that may or may not be helpful in reaching decisions. Since the survey was written, the Church of England has made the decision not to facilitate the commercial testing of GM crops by banning such testing on their own land.

Given the implicit theology emerging from public discussions of genetic engineering, it is relevant to ask: How far does the above pose a specific challenge to theology – in particular, to an adequate eco-theology? Public religious intuitions need to be taken into account in developing an adequate theology. We could ask ourselves which models of the God/world relationship are adequate in the light of the rapid changes taking place in our social fabric and our creaturely environment brought about by biotechnology.

Process-theological models tend to liken the world to an 'organism', rather than a 'machine'. There are also numerous instances of eco-theologians drawing on process thought as a basis for their valuation of the whole of the natural order as such.[16] At first sight, then, any idea of the natural world as a mechanism, which is presupposed in biotechnology, is rejected. Process theology would reject the reductionism at the heart of biotechnology. Another concept in process thought is the notion that everything has a *telos* or goal, which is directed towards greater enrichment. Biotechnology suppresses this goal at the heart of all living things.

However, there are other strands in process thinking that might suggest a more positive appraisal. For example, the drive towards human enrichment and creativity is a strong element. Some theologians suggest that the ability of humans to manipulate genes is just one more example of human creativity.[17] Indeed, some leading exponents of biotechnology have suggested as much, that such a science is the flowering of our human potential. On this view the new genetics should be seen less as a threat than as an opportunity to exercise our freedom. Any moratorium on genetic engineering assumes that genetic determinism is in control, rather than humanity. However, we suggest that human freedom needs to include the *capacity* to reject, as well as affirm, the latest developments in science. In general it is the positive appraisal of our human abilities that seems to win through in process thought. The increase in novelty possible through genetic engineering would also suggest that, in some contexts, process thinking would favour this approach. We might ask ourselves how the God who lures all of creation towards its fullness could respond to the radical shifts in genetic make-up induced by transgenic transformations. In other words, the positive assumption that seems to be behind process thinking does not seem to deal adequately with drastic genetic changes that are radically different from the 'natural' evolutionary process. It also does not consider adequately the social and political contexts in which genetic engineering is situated.

It would be inappropriate to lay the blame for the abuse of genetic engineering on the scientists alone. We are all implicated in the social and political web of which scientists are a part, and as became clear in Chapter 2, it is the way transgenic crops have been aggressively introduced in vulnerable societies, often completely disrupting traditional ways of life that is particularly offensive in that it represents more extreme examples of environmental injustice. In seeking for a change in attitude amongst those more directly involved, a wider transformation of heart and mind, or *metanoia*, or conversion and acknowledgement of breakdown in relationships is arguably needed which incorporates sensitivity to creation in every aspect of our lives. This *metanoia* includes an attitude of humility and respect for all members of the human and non-human community. A Christian theological perspective would insist on examining the long-term consequences to poorer nations and communities and the environment – in other words, a commitment to the public political good. It is this broader view that is essential to keep in mind when dealing with decisions about the validity of particular biotechnology and genetic engineering projects.

The controversies over GMOs also highlight the fact that while in many cases they originate from Western societies, their social and political impact is far wider than this; it is played out on an international canvas. This challenges the co-federal municipal system of governance suggested by Bookchin. The question now arises: How can we link concern for the earth with solidarity amongst all people, including those from different communities? Are the international legal frameworks, such as the Cartagena protocol on Biosafety developed out of the Convention on Biological Diversity (CBD), sufficient to protect those who are affected by the proliferation of GMOs?[18] For example, when conflicts arise in relation to the World Trade Organisation's agreement on Trade Related Intellectual Property Rights (TRIPS), it is the economic imperative that takes precedence.[19] A critique of unjust systems of trade is therefore appropriate in such contexts.

In this context it is instructive to consider how Peter Scott develops his own socio-political theology in the light of issues raised by genetic engineering of crops. He situates his discussion in the immediate aftermath of the political shambles arising out of the GM Nation debate in the UK. In this context the UK government gave permission for the commercial growing of GM maize, even though the majority of public opinion in the public consultation was against the commercial planting of GM crops and virtually all stated that they would not consume GM products. In the end the company decided against planting because of legal stringency in protection of organic farm crops, but the basic issue of legitimacy remains – that is, how far it was legitimate use of political authority to make such a decision.[20] He is particularly exercised by the political suspicions in the lay public response to GMOs,[21] so that 'people regard GM foods as remarkable, partisan and domineering on account of their suspicions regarding the transparency of the political process, the robustness of regulatory frameworks and the nearness of commercial interests that accompany this new technology.'[22] Yet the anxiety about GMOs may also be related to what is feared as a contingency and un-recallable agency through the new technologies. In other words, the new technologies cannot avoid a contingency that is built into biological processes as such or remove a sense that such events, once they happen, are irreversible. In addition, the blurred boundaries prey on a liberal understanding of nature as other than human. Further, the liberal sense that competing interests undermine reasonableness leads to a loss in trust of political authorities. He concludes that political challenge, a 'rioting', in common with that of the Spirit of God, is the only authentic Christian response. Accordingly he concludes that:

> It is not clear which decision participants in such pedagogy of insurrection might arrive at regarding the farming of GM crops. However, it is clear that such a community would find troubling a decision taken for administrative reasons, without reference to nature, and employing 'reason' in coercive fashion. Indeed, it might be argued that in operating with such an 'administered authoritarianism', the UK government operates within the law but against 'rule': a realm of anti-rule and disorderedness. In theological perspective, Christian worshipping communities seek a more enacted form of authority: the political act is always a plural act

of rioting, an act of blessing which is within the law but beyond 'rule': a realm of disorder and no-rule.[23]

In a European context, it is clear that eco-theology evolves not so much in isolation from secular discourses, such as that found in social anthropology, but in dialogue with them. Hence, we find the self-professed humanist Nina Witoszek writing for the journal *Ecotheology*.[24] The challenge is also not one way, for now previously respected models for globalisation in post-religious, secular societies are reassessed in the light of an upsurge in interest in spirituality. Provocatively she suggests that the stories that most capture our imagination are those that speak of excess or profusion, rather than coldly calculating accounts of how to live sustainable lives in relationship with the earth. Perhaps in this sense, Scott is correct to speak of a 'rioting' of God, for it points to profusion and excess as sourced in theology. Moreover, she notes that a new carnival global *multitudino* appears on the global stage, one that is less taken with representative democracy as a global anarchy. Her essay, and others in this collection, speak of a widening agenda for eco-theology, stretching further than the socio-political to previously largely uncharted waters. Sigurd Bergmann's contribution is a good example in this direction, for he maps out a new study of the significance of the spatial dimension in the interactions between religion, nature and culture.[25] His particular concern is the environmental space in which human and non-human beings are situated. He also includes a discussion of the Holy Spirit as a way of interpreting such experience in Christian terms; the Holy Spirit is one that imbibed all life spheres, including spaces and environments. Drawing on the classic theologian Gregory of Nazianzus, where God and creature cooperate together in synergy, he sets the tone for theological development. His use of Patristics illustrates too the eclectic mix of theological sources used by Western eco-theologians, reflecting a paradoxical attention to the political, social and economic restraints of the present alongside incorporation of classical ideas.

Conclusions

The primary concern of this chapter has been to illustrate the ways in which the social and political aspects of human life have become woven into eco-theologies emerging in a Western context. Such concerns include a discussion of social theory, such as the social ecology of Murray Bookchin, alongside more practical discussions of sociological analysis of public responses to genetic engineering of crops. Although Bookchin is resistant to the religious dimension as having any relevance, there are insights in his work concerning the dialectical relationship between nature and society that are worth careful consideration. Peter Scott's work, in particular, illustrates a concerted effort to bring political discussion into theology that evolves in dialogue with current political and social disputes. Even secular analysis of public attitudes to genetic technology in the United Kingdom reveal an implicit theological response to biotechnology. Such a response is significant in that it highlights the fact that theology is more deeply embedded in cultural attitudes than some scholars are prepared to acknowledge. Social scientists are less interested in the validity of such a religious response, than the fact that it exists, latent in the human community. Theologians engaging in this field need to be aware of this discourse, especially if they are concerned with political and social deliberations, while also acknowledging insights from other cross-disciplinary perspectives. Above all, perhaps, there is a sense in which theological traditions do not flourish in a cultural vacuum, so those insights from other religious traditions and secular traditions all help to uncover important dimensions in the relationship between humanity, God and nature.[26] Yet, perhaps the most enduring source for eco-theologians has been and still is the biblical text, informing all but the most liberal interpretations of eco-theology. It is therefore to this tradition that we turn in the chapter that follows.

Further reading

Bookchin, M., *The Philosophy of Social Ecology: Essays on Dialectical Naturalism* (2nd edn, London, Black Rose Books, 1996)

Bruce, D. and Bruce, A. (eds.), *Engineering Genesis: The Ethics of Genetic Engineering in Non-Human Species* (London, Earthscan, 1998)

Deane-Drummond, C. and Szerszynski, B., *Re-Ordering Nature: Theology, Society and Genetics* (London, Continuum, 2003)

Deane-Drummond, C., 'Biotechnology: A New Challenge to Theology and Ethics', in C. B. Southgate (ed.), *God, Humanity and the Cosmos: A Companion to the Science and Religion Debate* (2nd edn, London, Continuum, 2005), pp. 361–90.

Hefner, Philip, *Technology and Human Becoming* (Minneapolis, Fortress Press, 2003)

Light, A. (ed.), *Social Ecology After Bookchin* (London, The Guildford Press, 1998)

Northcott, M., *The Environment and Christian Ethics* (Cambridge, Cambridge University Press, 1996)

Northcott, M., *A Moral Climate* (London, DLT, 2007)

Scott, Peter, *A Political Theology of Nature* (Cambridge, Cambridge University Press, 2003)

Chapter 7

Biblical eco-theology

THE VAST LITERATURE THAT HAS MUSHROOMED in both popular and academic texts on eco-theology commonly includes some reference or other to biblical literature, most often from the Hebrew Bible, but also from New Testament texts. It may be used as a way of emphasising particular theological strands previously neglected in contemporary theological discussion – for example, theologies that deal more specifically with creation, rather than human history as such. Alternatively, it may be used to highlight a particular apologetic for active environmental care – in other words, to provide a foundation for environmental ethics. The latter is particularly popular among evangelical Christians – that is, those more inclined towards seeing biblical literature as a primary source of authority for Christian faith and practice. Unlike the discussion highlighted in the previous chapter, authors writing in this vein are more likely to speak about 'creation', rather than 'nature'. There are a number of reasons for this; most important perhaps, is that the audience is the Christian community, where speech about creation makes sense, as it puts more emphasis on God as the Creator of all that is, while 'nature', though it has multiple meanings, engages more specifically with secular discourse. Those outside the Christian community would not readily appreciate a presupposed understanding of the world as that created by God. Of course, some authors will be inclined to bridge both discussions, but in as much as their discussion is orientated towards Christian theology understood as that emerging in the light of faith, then biblical themes come into view. The purpose of this chapter is to provide an illustrative overview of the key areas in which biblical discussion serves in the development of eco-theological themes.

The Bible and creation care

The theme that the Bible provides impetus for human care of the earth is one of the most well-rehearsed themes in the literature, more often than not used in the context of particular statements by churches or affiliations in order to support particular practices.[1] It provides, for many, biblical and thereby theological endorsement of particular ethical practices. Evangelicals in particular are likely to be attracted to this form of reasoning, given the high status of the Bible in evangelical traditions. At least one reason for this profusion stems from reactions to the accusation by the American historian Lynn White, writing in 1967, early on in the environmental movement, that the Judaeo/Christian tradition was responsible for causing the environmental crisis. He regarded the biblical mandate of domination of the earth read from the book of Genesis to be vitally important in this respect.[2] More bluntly, he pointed to the way Christian natural theology endorsed the rise of science and technology that then, he suggested, subsequently became out of control in terms of ecological restraint. It thus led to Christianity's 'huge burden of guilt' as causative of the environmental crisis. He is critical, in particular, of the development of attitudes that separated the divine and human from the natural world through their emphasis on human and divine power and transcendence, and the natural world's desacralisation and subsequent exploitation. He has, arguably, influenced a generation of both secular and Christian scholars, with many of the former dismissing Christianity as a valid resource for responsible ecological action. From a historical perspective, blaming Christianity alone for the rise in science and technology and linking this with ecological stress is far too simplistic, though in this respect at least, some Christian scholars are prepared to be critical of those attitudes of mastery that were fostered by early experimental scientists such as Francis Bacon. In as much as Christians share in the global guilt of the human community by their consumerist habits, especially but not exclusively, in the richer, Northern societies, the burden of guilt remains. This, arguably, can begin to be addressed by appropriate attention to more traditional Christian teachings on the reconciling work of Christ and the grace of God experienced through forgiveness.[3] Other secular historians also pointed the finger at the biblical account. British historian Arnold Toynbee claimed that the command in Genesis 1:28 to have dominion and subdue the earth both permitted and directed humanity in exploitative attitudes to the environment. While White recommended a return to Fransciscan traditions, Toynbee argued for a recovery of pantheism.[4]

It is the biblical aspect of White's and Toynbee's thesis that most concerns us here, for Christian and Jewish scholars have, accordingly, leapt to the defence of the biblical story in most cases, arguing that dominion does not mean domination, rather it means humans taking responsibility for the earth as stewards and viceroys of that creation.[5] While it is true that the biblical account speaks of human distinctiveness from other creatures, for only humans are made in the image of God (Gen. 1:26) and only humans are called to name the animals (2:19–20), there are also considerable lines of continuity expressed in the biblical account. For example, God created humans on the same day as the other animals, and Adam means quite literally 'of the earth'. The particular vocation of humans is to 'subdue' and 'have dominion over' the earth, but if this is seen in the light of humanity's role as divine image-bearers, then such terms could not mean 'exploitation', but rather, careful service for the earth. In addition, the dualism between humanity and the earth that White wished to emphasise is far too simplistic an interpretation of biblical anthropology. The actual account states that humanity became a living being through the breath of God (Gen. 2:7); hence, ensoulment emerged from material earth, rather than being 'added to' that material in a dualistic way. Admittedly, some strands of Christian tradition have not always adhered to this particular interpretation and have been influenced by Plato's dualistic philosophy. However, as Paul Santmire elegantly demonstrated, alongside more dualistic trends, many Christian traditions have stressed more ecologically affirming attitudes to the natural world.[6]

Many authors are not content with just defending biblical Christian faith in the wake of accusations that it is exploitative, but rather wish to go further and affirm its value as a source of positive directives for care for the earth. This aligns with a strategy in hermeneutics recognised by contemporary biblical scholars to *recover* the interpretation of a particular text for a particular purpose.[7] Just as God's care is reflected in divine Providence over all, so human care reflects that care-giving. The Christian environmentalist Calvin B. de Witt is one of the most articulate authors in this vein, speaking as one who has scientific acumen, but who is also deeply committed to realising his vision through appropriation of biblical arguments for the stewardship of creation. He identifies the following seven principles[8] as emerging from this general theme:

- *We must keep the creation as God keeps us.* Human *earth-keeping* (Gen. 2:15) mirrors the providence of God in keeping human beings (Num. 6:24–26). Dominion is exercised after the pattern of Christ, so that humanity joins with the Creator in caring for the land (Deut. 11:11–12; 17:18–20).
- *We must be disciples of the Last Adam, not the first Adam.* Just as in Christ all things are reconciled (Col. 1:19–20), so the human vocation is to participate in the restoration and reconciliation of all things.
- *We must not press creation relentlessly, but provide for its Sabbath.* Exodus 20:8–11 and 23:10–12 show that Sabbath rest applies to the land as well as animals and human beings.
- *We may enjoy, but not destroy, the grace of God's good creation.* The tendency for human greed to destroy the *fruitfulness* of the earth is documented in the biblical accounts of human behaviour (e.g. Ezek. 34:18; Deut. 20:19; 22:6).
- *We must seek first the kingdom, not self-interest.* The mandate for this comes from the Gospels, as in Matthew 6:33.
- *We must seek contentment as our great gain.* This means being content with the gifts that creation brings, rather than always grasping after more. There are therefore *limits* placed on humanity's role within creation. Paul's letters here give some encouragement, as in Hebrews 13:5 and 1 Timothy 6:6–21.

- *We must not fail to act on what we know is right.* The marriage between belief and action needs to be fulfilled in stewardship practices. The need for a link between belief and action is a strong biblical theme, as in Ezekiel 33:30–32.

Certainly, drawing out general principles of careful stewardship rooted in biblical practice rules out the legitimacy of White's thesis that Christian biblical teaching is exploitative in its attitude towards the natural world. R. J. Berry also warms to the ideal of stewardship and its biblical precedents.[9] Yet there are two questions that are worth raising here. In the first place, is the general theme of stewardship adequate as a basis for environmental ethics? Stewardship has connotations of management and, arguably, implicit exploitative attitudes that principles of stewardship when used in an ecological context are aiming to correct. Secondly, can a theology of stewardship respond to the reality of human sinfulness – that is, is it adequate to describe human responsibilities on earth?[10] Ernst Conradie argues, correctly in my view, that human responsibility cannot be derived simply from the dominion verses in Genesis 1 and 2. Rather,

> [human] responsibility is best understood as a grateful response to the story of God's salvific grace epitomised in the life, ministry, death and resurrection of Jesus Christ, a story of grace which is cosmic in scope and which is yet to reach its narrative completion. The thrust of this story is not towards the restoration of a lost paradise, but towards an eschatological transformation and consummation.[11]

While I would certainly concur with the basic argument here, I also believe that the Hebrew Bible may have rather more to say about human responsibility than Conradie allows for in this case. Other relevant traditions include, for example, the wisdom tradition and the apocalyptic traditions.[12] Thirdly, is stewardship, any more than domination, an appropriate reading of the biblical text? Biblical scholar and historian Richard Bauckham, for example, finds the term 'stewardship' alien as a biblical term. It is used for the first time in the seventeenth century with the rise of modern experimental science.[13] Historically, human dominion in Genesis was not interpreted as either stewardship or exploitation, but rather, up until the modern period, 'dominion' merely meant the limited use of the environment. Matthew Hale began to use the term 'stewardship' in the seventeenth century, as he wanted to supplement the view of Francis Bacon that nature is simply there for human benefit, with the view that humanity also has a responsibility to care for the earth. The stress here was on the management of the earth for its own good by responsible human subjects; human control was inevitably beneficial rather than detrimental. In this sense human supremacy was unquestioned and unchallenged as an ideal. Although Bauckham sees stewardship used in the sense of preservation and protection in the contemporary evangelical discussion, the notion that humanity might be capable of *improving* nature is also implicit in de Witt's principle of restoration and reconciliation. Given the history of the use of 'stewardship' and its managerial connotations, it may be worth considering using alternative terms to describe those practices that both de Witt and Berry are keen to endorse. Its advantage, of course, is that it makes sense to scientists, and perhaps it is significant that R. J. Berry and de Witt are both practising scientists first and foremost, ones who are keen to put more emphasis on the responsibilities of that science. Whether or not we choose to use stewardship as an adequate summary of idealised ecological practices may depend on our sensitivity to history; practising scientists are less likely to be swayed by historical concern, and more likely to be convinced by its practical effectiveness. Certainly, ecclesiastical statements, whether denominational or from a particular tradition, have frequently used stewardship as the concept which best describes human responsibility for creation care.[14]

Biblical precedents for creation care set in the context of concerns about justice in the community are more likely to be emphasised by Roman Catholic writers, since their church has a strong tradition of social teaching. In this instance, care for the earth complements social care of the poor and marginalised; sin is seen as damaging to human social relationships, whether they be between peoples or with the earth. Inspiration for such a linkage comes from the prophetic biblical tradition. Isaiah 24:4–5, for example, speaks of a polluted earth that follows directly from human transgression of God's laws. Hosea 4:2–3 is similar in tone: the languishing earth is a mirror of God's displeasure at human wrongdoing. Mary Grey believes that a more inspired eco-theology needs to begin from the prophetic tradition, as it begins by acknowledging the brokenness of a creation ravaged by human sin.[15] She argues that the vision of *Shalom*, the future reconciliation of all created reality, is one to which humanity needs to aspire.

In this context it is worth mentioning that while some church groups may draw on the biblical text of Genesis as a foundation for creation care, their statements on responsibility often extend wider than this to include not only environmental justice issues, but also concern for future generations. An example of this is found in the most recent resolution on climate change adopted at the 2007 Triennial National Conference of the South African Council of Churches, which includes 26 member churches, as well as the Roman Catholic Bishop's Conference. The text of Genesis 2:15, to 'keep the earth', was used as a basis for care for the earth for the benefit of future generations. This mandate was set in the context of a strong call for justice.[16]

The Bible and the status of creation

Increasingly, many authors have become unsatisfied with the theme that human stewardship is demanded by the Genesis account. It leaves, for example, untouched the question of *why* we should care for creation, other than that humanity is commanded so to do by having dominion over the earth as in imitation of God's providential care. In other words, while this may be a consequence of a deeper understanding of the significance of creation, we need to appreciate that theological significance first and foremost. It is only then that it becomes possible to act appropriately. Genesis speaks of all creation as good, as all creation is loved by God and gains its worth through this love. Yet if we turn to the book of Job (38—41) we find another picture of the relationship between humanity and the earth. Here the natural world in all its wildness is presented alongside humanity, who remains humbled before its savagery and ambiguity. Here God's knowledge outstrips human ingenuity and domestication of animals. Here God's authority reigns to support wildlife in and of itself, rather than just for the needs of human beings. While there are hints at this in Genesis in as much as God blesses all of creation even prior to the arrival of humans, it makes more explicit the theme that God blesses all of creation even after humans have appeared. It highlights an important strand that runs through the literature of the Hebrew Bible, namely that of *blessing*, one that stresses the fecundity of God's creative activity, with an emphasis on celebration/joy in creation.[17] Of course, authors such as Matthew Fox have isolated this theme of blessing from the rest of the biblical witness that puts more emphasis on deliverance/redemption, but this is a misreading, for the deliverance theme, also discussed in the section below, needs to be seen as interwoven with that of cosmic blessing.[18]

Yet alongside this affirmation of creation's worth, there is a responsive theme to that blessing, namely creation's praise of God. The theme of creation's praise of God finds its way into biblical writings in both the Hebrew Bible and the New Testament (e.g. Isa. 42:10; Pss. 19:1–4; 69:34; 96:11–12; 98:7–8; 103:22; 150:6; Phil. 2:10; Rev. 5:13). While these passages are metaphorical in that they claim that non-human creatures praise God in human language, they are certainly not expressions of 'animism' or some kind of panpsychism that accords rationality to all living things, or even just poetic decoration.[19] The most likely explanation is that in most cases the praise stems from creation's acknowledgement of being created the way it is. There are also some texts that celebrate salvific themes, and in this non-human creation joins with humanity in a participatory way. It is also worth noting in this context that theologians have often failed to appreciate the full significance of the biblical account of the involvement of the earth in the act of creation. Genesis 1:11 and 1:24 claim that in the initial act of creation the earth brings forth plants, and in turn, animals of the earth in response to the divine command. While commentators initially interpreted these verses to mean natural life cycles, the use of Hebrew term 'create' is a reference to new creation, rather than simply regeneration.[20] While the concept of 'Mother earth' may be in the background,[21] the Hebrew writer wanted to emphasise something different, that the creative response of the earth to God's will and Word is one that is *participa-*

tory in the creative process – in other words, it is *empowered* by God to act in an intermediary way in order to bring forth particular creatures. Not only does this cohere with an evolutionary account of the generation of life on earth, but, more important in this context, it also suggests that non-human life from the beginning participates with the divine in creativity.

Given the above, the Noahic covenant after the flood (Gen. 9:8–17) seems entirely reasonable, for it is a *cosmic covenant* between God and all living creatures. Robert Murray suggests that this is a realistic account of the relationship between humans and other creatures, while pointers in the prophetic tradition to an idealised peace between all creatures and wild animals are metaphors for cosmic and social peace.[22] He also notes links in the Hebrew Bible between royal imagery, ritual practice and the promise of cosmic stability. A common interpretation of human image-bearing relates to this royal function, where the ideal king was called upon to maintain peace and security. The ideal king is also one who expresses the virtue of justice. It is, indeed, justice that serves to link the theme of blessing with that of God's liberating activity. A prophetic stream emerges, one that envisions a future of the land which expresses fecundity and where justice reigns.[23] While the image of kingship may not be appealing to many contemporary readers, metaphorically speaking, kingship applies to Christ and can be used in more democratic ways as applied to the human community.[24] A connection with kingship expresses the dignity of human oversight in a way that is somewhat lacking in the term 'stewardship'. The royal metaphor also speaks of wisdom, justice, compassion and responsibility in a way that gives a fuller account of the status of human beings in relation to that of non-human creatures. Moreover, the link with ritual is also important, for humanity needs to find ways of expressing ideas imaginatively in liturgical settings. Indeed, human acknowledgement of the status of creation is perhaps best experienced through renewed liturgical expression, for this is how the biblical witness was intended to function in the human community.

The Bible and the future of creation

The possibility of deliverance or redemption emerges from a theology of blessing, even though both are in some sense distinct from each other. The Deuteronomic texts point to a future of a promised land, one which is inclusive of the human and earth community. The book of Exodus recounts a deliverance from a land of oppression to one that is 'flowing with milk and honey', a figurative portrait of fecundity, but also where justice reigns on earth. Land is, moreover, not owned as much as given by divine gift. The prophetic tradition highlighted those instances where monarchy ruled in the absence of justice. The option for the poor and the land becomes clearly visible. The theology of blessing can be thought of as emerging after a theology of deliverance, in the particular context of festivals of worship in the Jerusalem Temple. Yet the ordering of the creation story in Genesis as prior to that of the Exodus account is significant, as it points theologically to the universal creative activity of God as grounding more particular accounts of redemption, which only later widened in scope.

The link between justice in the land and human community is an important facet of the prophetic tradition. The post-exilic prophets declared that the restoration of the land required a return to integrity and justice. The future promised such restoration where human relationships to the wider cosmic community would be restored. Isaiah's vision of *Shalom* is one replete with accounts of ecological harmony that are more obviously metaphorical, but it is a vision that encourages change in the direction of that harmony.

In the New Testament Paul's letter to the Colossians speaks of Christ as having redeemed all things; it is through Christ that the future can be secured. Romans 8:19–23 also speaks of all of creation awaiting its time of deliverance, along with the children of Israel. Creation is groaning now, but this groaning will not last indefinitely, for there will come a time when this groaning will be heard. This passage also links the suffering of creation with humanity's failure to act, so that the corollary is that appropriate human behaviour is required for creation's flourishing. Where humanity has failed to act according to divine command, the future of the whole universe is at stake. Yet human action is action that is empowered by God's grace in service, rather than through inordinate exercise of power over creation. The royal figure of Christ paradoxically expresses the humility of the servant king.

Reading the Bible from an earth perspective

While biblical interpretation or hermeneutics at one time attempted to distance itself from the presuppositions of the scholar, contemporary biblical scholars are more likely to admit that such a stance is virtually impossible, even if unacknowledged or unconscious. Indeed, rather than making any claim for neutrality, we need to read the Bible through particular lenses in order to highlight different facets of its meaning. Much the same can be said of feminist readings of the Bible, that in the past have been ignored, as interpretation remained focused on a particular culture, namely Western, male and historical. The Earth Bible project invites a particular reading of the Bible in the light of particular principles; moreover, it claims that its readings open up horizons that have been ignored or unnoticed in the past.[25]

This is not the same as reading *into* the text particular meanings – an approach that is disparaged among biblical scholars – but rather, literary and cultural analysis is emphasised alongside ecological hermeneutics. Hermeneutical strategies of both recovery and resistance (or reconstruction) can be used in such a context – that is, recovery and affirmation of those texts that are in alignment with particular eco-justice principles – as well as resistance to, that is, arguments against, those texts that seem to suggest an alternative, such as a focus on humanity or anthropocentrism, for example.

Some critics have argued that the principles used are not open enough to allow alternative interpretations, but it is also apparent that this strategy is a corrective one, for earlier scholars brought their own particular cultural biases. The principles themselves were arrived at in consultation with ecologists as well as biblical scholars; it therefore represents a listening to the natural world that is in tune with the biblical wisdom tradition. Of course, it is possible to criticise this approach by suggesting that the principles are deliberately biased towards ecology in a way that does not necessarily emerge from the religious tradition as such. While this is an obvious danger, I suggest that there is also another interpretation, namely, that these principles form a useful heuristic tool in order to uncover important facets in the biblical text that would otherwise be ignored. It is also possible to argue that it is never possible to completely free oneself from particular cultural values. Each principle does, I suggest, need to be thoroughly scrutinised by reference to other religious traditions and biblical texts, but this does not necessarily mean that this form of hermeneutics is unhelpful. Some principles may situate more readily within Christian traditions compared with others. I offer such an appraisal in what follows.

There are, in all, six eco-justice principles, all of which have significance in relation to interpretation of the Bible:

- The first principle of *intrinsic worth* relates to the importance of the status of creation mentioned above. The worth of creatures is not just a simple fact of moral value; rather it arises out of God's word.
- The second principle of *interconnectedness* is one that is universally familiar to ecologists and environmentalists. Yet the kind of interconnectedness of biological life is not that expressed by the vision of Isaiah, for some elements will always have more strength than others, and the food chain shows that life is dependent on other life for its survival. Some ecologists speak of hierarchies in the chain, though the Earth Bible team wants to strongly resist the idea that hierarchy is an adequate description of such relationships. Moreover, it implies a hierarchy of rights that they would want to actively resist.
- The third principle of *voice* claims that the earth is capable of raising its voice in celebration and against injustice. This is not the same as the human voice, for if so, it would be an anthropocentrism that is contrary to the other principles. Rather, it is seeking to pay attention to what the earth might have to say, to viewing the Earth in *kinship* with rather than in alienation from humanity.
- The fourth principle of *purpose* claims that the universe, the earth and all its components are part of a dynamic cosmic design, where each contributes to that purpose. This design is taken to be theocentric in orientation; that is, the God-given purpose to which the cosmos inclines is one of renewal rather than replacement.

- The fifth principle of mutual *custodianship* reflects on the role of humans in relation to the earth. Instead of being masters over the earth, humans should think of themselves as guests on it, custodians of their host planet. This does not deny responsibility, but it includes respect for the bonds between humanity and other creatures.
- The sixth principle of *resistance* claims that the earth and its components actively resist those injustices imposed by humans. This does not divorce eco-justice from social justice, but recognises its claim on human lives by identification and being with the earth in a way that has some parallels with indigenous perspectives.

Such principles become more comprehensible once we see how they are used in the interpretation of the Bible. The first principle of intrinsic worth is relevant to an interpretation of 1 Timothy 4:1–5 that asserts the goodness of the earth over against others who might claim otherwise. This pastoral letter was addressing the claims of gnostic opponents advocating ascetic practices such as forbidding marriage and abstinence from food, based on the belief that the material world was tainted in some way. They also believed that the general resurrection had already happened. It seems that this was possible through a spiritualisation of the claims of the resurrection, which rendered more worldly concerns obsolete (2 Tim. 2:18). The response to this claim by the author of the letter to Timothy is that food is to be received with thanksgiving, and everything that God has created is good (1 Tim. 4:3–4).[26] This verse echoes the Genesis text, with its affirmation of all creaturely being alongside a command to be fruitful. Moreover, thankfulness is a reminder that the food we receive is a gift of God. In addition, the author of 1 Timothy claims in 4:5 that *all of creation* is sanctified or consecrated – that is, made holy. This contrasts with more traditional uses of sanctification as applicable to the human community. This implies that creation is more than just made fit for human use; rather, it is *holy*, reaching even beyond the simple declaration of goodness in Genesis. Violation of what is made holy by God warrants the penalty of death. The affirmation of creaturely being would also come from the author's strong belief in the incarnation of Christ as human, material reality; God's very appearance in human, fleshly form affirms the material reality that the opponents are trying to reject.

The principle of interconnectedness becomes relevant for the interpretation of the narrative in Genesis 4. Gunther Wittenburg takes a close look at this narrative and finds that scholars have overlooked the third player in the well-known story of Cain and Yahweh – namely, the earth itself.[27] Cain wanted a blessing from Yahweh for his labour of the land, but he failed to secure this blessing. His response to his brother Abel, who kept sheep, was to murder him. Yahweh then claims that the voice of Abel's blood cries out from the ground (Gen. 4:10). The curse of the earth that follows is such that Cain can no longer live off the soil. He becomes totally alienated from the earth and is forced to be a wanderer, driven away from the land. Eventually Cain establishes a city where he finds a new form of security, but this is predicated on violence towards the peasant population to supply its food needs. Historically the city depended on violence, war and aggression on a scale unknown to palaeo-neolithic village communities. Lamech, descended from Cain, even boasts of his murderous activities towards children (Gen. 4:23). Of course, vengeance is delivered eventually through the flood narrative, with Noah, named as a man of the soil, one who had a right relationship with the earth, being singled out for deliverance. Noah was the first to plant a vineyard after the flood, again affirming the crucial importance of right relationship with the land.

The principle of voice is also illustrated in the above account, where the earth is spoken of as metaphorically 'crying out' to Yahweh for the blood of Abel. There are other passages that more explicitly speak of the lament of the land, such as Jeremiah 12.[28] The climax of the lament is expressed in 12:4, with an appeal on behalf of all creatures. The desolate land mourns to God (12:11) and God responds (16:19), which shows that the land has a relationship to God beyond simply that mediated by human beings. This need not necessarily imply 'vitalism' or pan-psychism, rather simply that a relationship exists. The message of Jeremiah is that moral order affects the order in creation, but not in an inevitable way. Divine emotion is expressed as both sorrow and anger, and that anger is also made partly responsible for environmental degradation in Jeremiah 4:23–26. Such anger is provoked by Israel's infidelity, but alongside this anger is also grief. Violation of the moral order leads to breakdown that is experienced as God's anger. The lament of the land touches God's heart (Jer. 12:7, 11). God's own possession or 'heritage', which links both people and land, is forsaken and therefore no longer the subject of God's blessing. Although the land belongs to God, God gives responsibility for it to others, revealing a divine vulnerability. The withdrawal of God arises because the people have forsaken God. God now calls upon wild animals to be instruments of judgement, hinting at the eco-justice principle of resistance (12:9). The final vision that Jeremiah presents is one of hope of salvation that is universally inclusive of both all peoples and the land.

The principle of purpose is illustrated well by a discussion of Romans 8:18–22.[29] An interpretation of this passage presupposes the concept of a common fate between people and the earth, as indicated above, and also as alluded to in the book of Genesis. Creation is subject to futility against its will, so it retained a hope of reversal where human beings would once again find favour with God, leading to positive effects on creation itself. This passage arguably assumes Paul believed in a traditional interpretation of Genesis 1, where humanity is set over against the rest of the created order in relation to God. Byrne suggests that Romans 8 softens this approach in that it sets forth another possibility for human behaviour that is less exploitative. Indeed, the subjugation of the earth spoken of in Romans 8 could be viewed as connected with the sin of Adam discussed in Romans 5. As a result, a more positive view of human relationships ensues, once they are regarded in the light of Christ, where human beings respond to God's grace and act accordingly. The depiction of creation suffering is that of birth pangs, promising a positive future for the earth. Byrne suggests that there is no mention of resurrection here because Paul wishes to emphasise a sense of continuity and transformation rather than destruction and rebirth, so that the cosmos would evolve into an age of salvation, rather than being destroyed first.

The fifth principle of custodianship has proved rather more difficult to discern in the biblical texts. Keith Carley, for example, finds in Psalm 8 an apology for human (particularly male) domination of the earth.[30] This is also illustrated by Norman Habel's interpretation of Genesis 1.[31] He finds in this text reference to a shift in emphasis, from a story predominantly about the earth and its flourishing, to one where the earth takes a secondary role under *adam*, a creature that has power over all life that has emanated from the earth. The earth is thus devalued by being portrayed as a force that humans are expected to subdue (*kabash*) – a term used in other contexts to express forceful subjugation. Habel believes that we cannot escape the fact that the story ends with a negation of the earth as a force to be overcome by humanity. However, scholars have failed more generally to notice that the first part of the story is highly affirming for the earth: it serves to reveal God in a geophany. In this the earth becomes a genuine counterpart to the story as told through human lenses. Hence, rather than attempting rehabilitations of difficult texts which speak of human domination, or reinterpretations in terms of stewardship, Habel is suggesting something far more radical – namely, giving the story about the earth greater prominence. The consequence of such a reading would be a deeper sense of custodianship and kinship with the earth, even if the principle of custodianship rarely finds its expression in the biblical text as such.

The principle of resistance relates to the possibility that the earth may also have a voice that counters injustices imposed upon it. Illustrations of biblical interpretation where this came into view are illustrated in the discussion of Romans 8 and Jeremiah 12 above.

Overall the Earth Bible project represents a highly creative and imaginative recasting of biblical interpretation from the perspective of current environmental concerns. It also allows for a deeper appreciation of the importance of this theme in biblical literature that has so far remained largely unnoticed, but in such a way as to acknowledge the difficulties associated with some texts that seem to tell a story of human domination. Yet even in these cases, such domination is set within limits that, if broken, have dire consequences. As in all forms of biblical interpretation, there may be tendencies to over-emphasise some aspects. For example, I am less convinced by the argument for some of the ways in which forms of subjectivity in creation seem to go beyond the metaphorical – for what exactly does this subjectivity mean? Claiming that we need to be more sensitive to aboriginal perspectives where this seems more 'natural' does not help those of us who have little or no contact with such traditions, even while we can try in an empathetic sense to understand different starting points. Of course, process theology would cohere with such a stance, but any hints at vitalism would be resisted by the majority of the scientific community. There is also a clash with scientific renditions of evolution in as much as hints at final purpose for the earth are counter to current interpretations. Of course, this also applies to any theological interpretation as well, namely the difficulty of announcing the possibility of purpose within the natural order. Of the six principles, other sources could be used to support the idea of justice, though applying this specifically to ecological justice presents a greater risk. Clearly, however, if we take for granted the principle of intrinsic worth, in theological terms reflected in the goodness of creation, which cannot be disputed, then it follows from this that eco-justice is valid. The difficulty, of course, is the extent to which eco-justice might detract from justice in the human community. The principle of interconnectedness is also a premise of a created world, as are principles of purpose and custodianship. The only principles that are more problematic are those of voice and resistance, yet the idea of God being on the side of the marginalised and oppressed is a strong theme throughout the Bible. The difficulty here, as I have alluded to earlier, is how far subjectivity might be applied to the creaturely world in general. Such a premise does not seem to emerge from either ecology or the Bible, but stems from prior philosophical commitments.

The significance of biblical wisdom traditions[32]

There has been a resurgence of interest in biblical wisdom traditions in contemporary scholarship. Wisdom literature is significant for the development of a biblical eco-theology for a number of reasons. There can be no argument about its place in biblical literature, compared with, for example, the eco-justice principles discussed above. There is also little danger, compared with the notion of stewardship, for example, that it can be seen as imported from the cultural milieu and then used to mediate between text and reader. It is also, like some of the eco-justice principles, grounded in a doctrine of creation. It opens up interpretation by serving to generate a way of thinking that links cosmic, social and human concerns, illustrative of the interconnectedness principle as elaborated above. Thirdly, wisdom is important as it provides a link between vertical and horizontal strands in theology: in a vertical sense it speaks of wisdom as artificer in creation (Proverbs 8), and wisdom is personified as divine Wisdom; but in a horizontal sense wisdom is also more generally concerned with ethical conduct, based on cumulative human experiences, including experiences in relationship to the earth. It therefore has a constructive theological task that goes beyond a recovery of ideals such as that of creation care, for it points to the basis from which such care must emanate. Moreover, wisdom as character formation is vitally needed if principles such as human custodianship of the earth are going to be consistently applied.

Yet we should also note that while scholars have found that wisdom carries an implicit creation theology, the earliest wisdom literature seemed to be more concerned with justice in the human community, rather than centred on creation as such.[33] Yet, observation of the natural world is included as a basis for reflection in some proverbs, such as Proverbs 6:6–9. Here humans are exhorted to notice the 'way of the ant' – this could imply just a way of finding truths in the natural order, a kind of implicit natural science, but it could also be the exemplar of a different kind of social order that is non-hierarchical. This seems to be subversive to much of the wisdom literature that attributes wisdom to elite, royal functions. In addition, in Proverbs 30 we find Agur comparing the world of nature and that of humanity: the way (*derek*) of an eagle in the sky, a snake on a rock, a ship on the high seas, and a man with a woman. He also recognises wisdom in the smallest and most insignificant of creatures who apparently lack rulers – the ants, badgers, locusts and lizards. In this sense the 'voice' of the earth alluded to above makes perfect sense, for it is by paying attention to the quiet witness of such creatures that human beings learn of the possibility of a different form of society.

Proverbs 1—9 also speaks of the way of wisdom and Woman Wisdom, which are apparently two different styles of wisdom. The first is to follow tried and tested paths to success, including prosperity and honour, and eventual crowning by Woman Wisdom herself, though there seems to be little explicit reference to the earth apart from the exceptions noted above. In Woman Wisdom we find a move beyond wisdom as a means for success in human society, for she claims in Proverbs 8 to have been there in the primordial creation of the world. Woman Wisdom is one who is portrayed as co-creator with the earth, playfully engaged with creation, but she also acts as the 'voice' of the earth as she knows the key to the vast interconnected web of the universe.

The book of Job provides further insights. In the context of suffering, Job cries to God for explanation, and turns to listen to the suppressed voice of the earth (12:7–9). Yet God's reply is one that expresses care for all of creation, in that God has planted wisdom in all wild creatures in a way that is quite independent of human society and its needs. Furthermore, while God, humans and earth creatures search for wisdom, God seemingly finds such wisdom while searching the depths of the earth – measuring the waters, weighing the wind, and ordering the storm (28:23–27). It is not completely clear if God finds wisdom in the earth by accident or through a deliberate search, but it happened when God was creating the domains of the earth. It seems more likely, from the context of the passage, that this followed from a deliberate search, but it is not akin to human discovery, for God acquires such wisdom in the process of creating.[34] Here, the table seems to be turned; God is now the *discoverer* of wisdom and looks to earth for this wisdom. Everything seems to have its *derek* or way, including light (38:19), lightning (38:24) and thunderstorms (38:25). This seems to point to an ancient ecology that speaks of a belief that the earth is governed by regulated systems, whose principles follow natural wisdom, rather than through divine intervention as such.[35] Yet even after God has discovered wisdom in the natural ordering of things, such wisdom is then 'seen' by God, which is most likely to imply a form of assessment, which is then established and confirmed.[36] This would challenge more Platonic views of wisdom in God that suggest wisdom exists prior to creation of the world as ideas in the divine mind. Wisdom dwells in the earth in the sense that it resides in its ordering principles, and likewise, humanity can also gain in wisdom through searching creation as long as they are prepared to give due respect and honour to God. Yet are we necessarily forced to choose between wisdom in creation, as suggested by Habel, or divine wisdom as being in some sense prior to the creation of the world?[37] Certainly, from the perspective of the book of Job, it seems to make more sense to speak primarily of creaturely wisdom as being that which God discovers in creation, rather than that which is imposed by God.[38] Yet, God's ability to create in the first place according to a 'design' and purpose, and then assess that wisdom and confirm it, implies wisdom in God that is *beyond* that which God discovers as existing in the world that God creates. How far and to what extent these different strands set the agenda for a theology of wisdom needs to await a discussion of New Testament texts which speak of wisdom Christology.

The apocryphal book of Wisdom declares wisdom to be the Spirit of God who fills the whole earth (Wisd. 1:6), emanates from God's glory as the breath of God (7.25), but also is the divine artisan at work in creation (8:6), guiding the history of Israel according to divine intentions. Wisdom teaches about the systems of the earth that are more commonly described today as botany, zoology, pharmacology and astronomy.[39] There is a sense in which wisdom is divine in origin, but also speaks for the earth.

The argument emerging from this discussion is that the wisdom tradition represents a vital ingredient in any biblical eco-theology. It resists too facile an attempt to go straight from biblical text to ecological practices by alerting the reader's attention to a way of being with the text that is more conscious of a poetic appreciation of the created world, rather than narrative accounts about human history. Its task is one of both enhancing a sense of beauty in the natural world, as well as more practical everyday environmental decision-making, as expressed through the tradition of practical wisdom or prudence.[40]

Fostering a biblical ethos through the Sabbath

In this section I would like to explore the idea that the biblical Sabbath theme has particular significance for the development of what I would term an *ethos* for eco-theology. By this I mean that it encourages a particular way of relating to God and to the natural world that is less about following certain rules, and more about encouraging a way of *being with* the world that is conducive to many of the eco-justice principles elaborated above. Importantly, living from the Sabbath is a reminder to the human community to live according to covenant responsibilities that may be expressed in concrete ways.[41]

The Sabbath rest on the seventh day is the ultimate goal of the creative process in Genesis, so that humanity is less the 'crown of creation' than has perhaps been assumed. The rest of God in creation stands in stark contrast to the empty waste and brooding uncertainty that was there before the first creative acts. The state of the earth before the creative acts of God described in Genesis 1:2 is bare and uninhabited – and it seems that there is no need to assume that some kind of 'chaos' reigned prior to these acts.[42] The rest enjoyed by God following active creation is not so much passive rest as active appreciation, and it puts the creative work of the previous six days in perspective, but now the holy is attributed to time, rather than space. It points to the ultimate purpose that God intends for all creation, namely to give glory to God by being what God has intended it to be through God's wisdom. Perhaps the greatest challenge in the development of eco-practice is that sense of setting apart of a particular time for being with the natural world and with God, joining with God in active rest understood as appreciation of the intrinsic worth of creation; moreover, creation itself is not just 'good', but also declared holy. It is in such contexts that we can, perhaps, begin to hear the 'voice' of creation and its demands.

The link in Genesis between making time holy and reflecting on the works of creation suggests that holy time is also a time to celebrate the earth – the earth story needs to be woven into liturgical celebrations if it is to express the spirit of the meaning of the Sabbath. The Jewish institution of the Sabbath was a reminder of covenant relationships between God, the people and the land. The rest enjoyed by the people also applies to the land and creatures as well, and became integral to Jewish legal requirements (Lev. 25:1–22). Keeping the covenant aligned with the Sabbath resulted in fertility of the land. In a Christian context the Sabbath ideals were taken over by celebration of the eighth day. While the seventh day begins with creation, but looks to a future redeemed creation, the eighth day begins with a transfigured creation, but points back to its roots in material creation. The way in which the theme of redemption applies specifically to creatures of earth awaits further development in later chapters. For the moment it is enough to suggest that the Sabbath theme is one that reminds humanity to take stock of its place with the rest of creation, to appreciate what custodianship might mean, to understand interrelatedness, to search for ways of taking steps that promote active resistance to the ecological and social injustices in which we are all implicated.

Conclusions

Although the Bible has been castigated in the history of environmentalism as a source of inappropriate attitudes to the environment, it is clear from this all-too-brief survey that the story is far more complex than this assessment implies. Certainly, scholars have sought to defend eco-practice by revisiting the story in Genesis, particularly the role of humans as image-bearers of God in the light of their responsibility for earth keeping. While this seems to many scientists to be a satisfactory way of responding to an ever-deepening environmental crisis, others are less certain that this is sufficient. It is one thing to know theoretically what one *ought* to do, and quite another to have the inclination to follow through with specific actions. In this sense an awareness of the created world as having supreme worth for God, that violation of the earth amounts to an affront to God's holiness, may give more pause for thought. Creation, too, can join with humanity in giving praise to the Creator for its existence and flourishing. The metaphor of kingship gives a royal dignity to human relationships with the earth, and traditional wisdom associates kingly rule with wisdom that issues in justice, peace and *Shalom* for creaturely being. Yet the prophetic traditions challenged the monarchic rendering of ordered existence, especially where that tradition issued in injustice for the land. A more radical approach is one that argues for a re-reading of the Bible from the perspective of the earth – in this case hermeneutics is itself shaped by ecological concerns. Principles of intrinsic value, interconnectedness, custodianship, voice, resistance and purpose serve to promote eco-justice. As well as the book of Genesis, the biblical wisdom traditions are also important to consider in this context. Finally, biblical themes such as that of the Sabbath are instructive in providing a way of shaping theological commitments to give space and time for creation and for liturgical celebration in building up an ethos that fosters ecological sensitivity.

Further reading
Bauckham, Richard, 'Joining Creation's Praise of God', *Ecotheology*, 7.1 (2002), pp. 45–59

Bernstein, Ellen, *The Splendour of Creation: A Biblical Ecology* (Cleveland, The Pilgrim Press, 2005)

Berry, R. J. (ed.), *The Care of Creation: Fostering Concern and Action* (Leicester, Inter-Varsity Press, 2000)

Berry, R. J. (ed.), *Environmental Stewardship: Critical Perspectives: Past and Present* (London, Continuum, 2006)

Berry, R. J. (ed.), *When Enough is Enough: A Christian Framework for Environmental Sustainability* (Nottingham, Apollos/IVP, 2007)

Habel, Norman C. (ed.), *Readings from the Perspective of Earth, The Earth Bible 1*, (Sheffield, Sheffield Academic Press, 2000)

Habel, Norman and Wurst, Shirley (eds.), *The Earth Story in Genesis, The Earth Bible 2* (Sheffield, Sheffield Academic Press, 2000)

Habel, Norman and Wurst, Shirley (eds.), *The Earth Story in Wisdom Traditions, The Earth Bible 3* (Sheffield, Sheffield Academic Press, 2001)

Murray, Robert, *The Cosmic Covenant* (London, Sheed and Ward, 1992)

Santmire, H. Paul, *Nature Reborn: The Ecological and Cosmic Promise of Christian Theology* (Minneapolis, Fortress Press, 2000)

Westermann, C., *Genesis 1—11, A Commentary*, trans. John J. Scullion (London, SPCK, 1984)

White, Lynn, 'The Historical Roots of Our Ecologic Crisis', *Science*, 155 (10 March 1967), pp. 1203–7.

Chapter 8

Ecology and Christology

IT IS SURPRISING, PERHAPS, THAT WHILE THE LITERATURE on eco-
theology has proliferated in the last half century, there is a relative lack of
sustained focus on the relationship between ecology (or evolution more
generally, for that matter) and Christology. Given the central importance of
Christ for Christian belief and practice, this might seem odd, especially given
both the varied cultural interpretations of the significance of Christ and the
preoccupation of present culture with environmental issues. This chapter sets
out to address ways in which different facets of christological reflection might
engage with ecological concerns. This is of relevance in making ecology
crucial to core elements of Christian belief, rather than simply through vaguer
references to a worldview affirming God as Creator that could (albeit mistakenly) be pushed to the margins of discussion. Different aspects of Christology
will be considered here as a way of setting a framework for further discussion
in later chapters on eschatology and theodicy. What is the meaning, for
example, of the incarnation of Christ in the flesh? In what sense might we
understand Christ as involved in the creation and redemption of the world as
hinted at in the cosmic Christology found in the epistles to the Colossians and
Ephesians? What might be the relationship between Christ and the land as
such? What insights on the doctrine of redemption emerge from an analysis of
wisdom in the New Testament?

John Hall is perhaps the most successful at constructing an ecological
reading of Jesus as that which bears on the Jesus of history.[1] He argues that
Christ is the image of God, and in this sense carries the *imago Dei* through to
responsibility for caring for creation.[2] More specifically, he suggests that
Christ gives humanity a model for stewardship, which itself is paradigmatic
for how to treat the earth. Of course, the particular version of stewardship that
Hall advocates puts emphasis on Christ as one who comes to serve all of creation in humility. Yet, as I indicated in the last chapter, the term 'stewardship'
per se is somewhat ambiguous in providing a model for human behaviour.
More important, perhaps, stewardship leaves intact interpretations of
Christology that emphasise Christ's historical nature, while not addressing the

sense in which Christ's incarnation *as such* might be deeply significant for an ecological reading of who Christ is and his significance. In other words, in this model Christ is still one whom we should emulate as a man who expresses his divinity through stewardship interpreted as servanthood.

Perhaps one of the disadvantages of any Christology 'from below' – that is, one that focuses on the significance of the *human* personhood of Jesus – is that it tends to address the *human* nature of Jesus in a way that could detract from the wider significance of the incarnation as being embodied 'in the flesh' (John 1:14).[3] The separation of Jesus of Nazareth, the human Jesus, from cosmic renditions of his significance has been a tendency among theologians focused on historical accounts of Jesus who have dismissed the cosmic significance of Christ in Colossians as unwarranted speculation. Cosmic Christology has proved unpopular among Western authors, as it has seemed to them to be either irrelevant or pointing to a metaphysics which is difficult to understand in a contemporary context.[4] While at first sight a focus on the Jesus of history might seem to make Jesus more understandable, as his human presence and his cultural embeddedness is emphasised, it leads to highly unfortunate consequences. Humanity understood in terms of history alone becomes 'unfleshed' – that is, humanity is no longer situated in the overall concept of 'all flesh' as that which includes all living things, and the 'flesh' is subordinated to the human, with deleterious ecological results. John's Gospel is a reminder that in the form of the Logos, Christ exists in relationship with all created things, but at the incarnation Christ becomes one with all flesh – that is, exists in kinship with all created beings. Although there are biblical texts which appear to render 'flesh' as that which is specific to animals (such as 1 Cor. 15:39), there are other traditions which point to a wider usage which is more inclusive in scope. Also, given an understanding of humanity as emerging from the dust of the earth (*ha adamah*) in the Genesis account, it makes sense to see the incarnation as similarly being thoroughly identified with the earth as such – that is, a wider meaning than identification with humans alone, or even humans in companionship with animals, for example.[5] Christ came as an expression of God's love for all of creation, following the tradition of John Scotus, not simply as a way of dealing with human sinfulness. Such a move runs counter to a trend in theology that amounts to a revolt against the fleshliness or bodiliness of humanity, which Paul Santmire has called 'a metaphor of ascent'.[6]

Cosmic Christology in Colossians 1

Those who have developed a cosmic Christology have almost always drawn inspiration from the hymn in Colossians 1:15–20, so it is worth recounting it below:

[15]He is the icon of God, the invisible one, first born of all creation, [16]because in/by him were created all things in the heaven and upon the earth, things visible and invisible, whether thrones or dominions, whether sovereignties or authorities, all things through him and for/to him were created. [17]And he is before all, and all things in/by him cohere, [18]and he is the head of the body, the church. He is the beginning, first born from the dead, in order that he might be in/among all things pre-eminent [19]because in him all the fullness was pleased to dwell, [20]and through him to reconcile all things unto himself, bringing peace through the blood of his cross [through him], whether things upon the earth or things in the heavens.[7]

The context of this hymn is one where the author addresses a situation where the person of Jesus was depreciated and his ordinary humanness stressed so that his divinity was obscured. In addition, they sought to separate the cosmic from the anthropological world in a form of world-denying asceticism. Paul[8] countered this view by celebrating the extent and scope of Christ's significance in cosmic terms. The first part of this hymn expresses a cosmic Christology as that which encompasses the whole creation: Jesus Christ is the one through whom and for whom the whole creation was made. The second half of the hymn points to cosmic redemption: *all things* will be reconciled in Christ.

Jesus as the 'icon' of God (verse 15), normally translated 'image' of God, does not mean 'image' in the physical sense, but rather the pre-incarnate Christ or Christ in his glory, having the connotation of *manifestation* of God.[9] In this reading it is more likely to be drawn from wisdom traditions, such as Wisdom 7:26 that speaks of wisdom as the image of God's goodness, rather than Genesis 1:28 that speaks of humanity as the image of God. The 'first born' (verse 15) could mean the priority in time or rank, though most commentators prefer the latter since temporal priority is hardly what the author is trying to emphasise here. In pre-existent form the image could hardly reveal God in the way suggested. The creation of all things 'through' him (verse 16) has the sense of Christ as a mediating agent, while in other contexts the term is often used to express Christ as mediator between humanity and God. Of course, some interpreters have given this passage a thoroughgoing anthropocentric reading, so G. B. Caird writes that the framing of the hymn in redemptive categories is crucial, 'since man was destined by God to be Lord of the universe, this is the secret also of the whole creation'[10] and 'only in union with the "proper man" could the universe be brought to its proper coherence'.[11] Yet this interpretation assumes that redemption is necessarily confined to humans, restricting the meaning of 'all things' to those principalities and powers that are of importance in the cohesion of the human world, and thus Christ's scope is limited in this respect. Given the challenge that this writer is addressing, namely a reduction in Christ's authority, it seems far more likely to be broader in scope and include creation as such. Other biblical scholars have been quite prepared to concede that 'all things' does refer to all creatures, as such an idea was already in prophetic literature such as Isaiah and Jeremiah.[12]

What are the origins of this magnificent hymn? Many scholars have adhered to the theory that the first stanza (verses 15–17) is an ancient hymn to wisdom/divine Word that was then adapted by the author in order to celebrate the status of Christ. An alternative, ingenious theory is that Paul is adapting to Christian use a rabbinic interpretation or *midrash* on Genesis 1:1, 'in the beginning (*be-reshith*) God created', and Proverbs 8:22, 'the Lord begat me as the beginning (*reshith*) of his way'. The three meanings of the Hebrew word *be* are 'in', 'by', 'for', and the three meanings of *reshith* are 'beginning', 'sum-total' and 'first fruits', so from this it followed that God created the world in, by and for wisdom, and wisdom was the first born of all creation, its sum-total, head and source. The equation of wisdom and the Law or Torah in the Jewish tradition meant that Paul could now also claim that this applies to Christ, as the fulfilment of the Torah, as he seems to have done in other passages such as 1 Corinthians 10:1–4 and Ephesians 4:7–11. The second stanza then moves to a focus on the human community; Christ is named as the one who is capable of reconciliation in both the cosmic community and the human community, with authority over all imaginable powers.[13] The universe, according to the hymn, is revelatory of the presence of Jesus, and as he is the manifestation of God, so at the same time Jesus reveals God. Some commentators have suggested that the 'fullness' in verse 19a refers to the fullness of God. Yet an equally plausible interpretation is that this refers to the creation, so that Jesus is the fullest expression of creation as well as being an icon of God. Michael Trainor writes:

> What creation is about is revealed in him, in his relationship to God. In Jesus the cosmos is taken to a new height; it is sanctified and revelatory of God's own being. This insight leads to the final verse of the hymn, 1:20, affirming Jesus' agency of reconciliation that is global and total. Jesus' power, being about peace and reconciliation, permeates every place and thing – even in the potentially annihilating powers, agencies and principalities.[14]

Such a view interprets the text so that we can view the world as the writer did in a way that still has fresh relevance for contemporary theological reflection on ecology. In this sense it does not matter if the biblical writer had no knowledge of ecosystems or of present environmental problems; rather, it is through coming to the text with certain questions that fresh insights bear fruit.[15] The hymn also reflects what Ernst Conradie has reminded us of from the Reformed tradition, namely, the importance of holding together themes of the creation alongside the recognition that the witness of the Gospel in Christ's death and resurrection responds to the devastation caused by human sin.[16] In this way, widening the scope of the reconciling work of the cross to include creation should not detract from the deeper meaning of the cross as that which enables reconciliation to take place between humanity and the rest of creation and God. In the contemporary context of what might be called anthropogenic sins against the cosmos and environmental injustices committed against vulnerable human beings, atonement of human beings for their individual and structural sins against God, other human communities and the wider community of creation become particularly relevant. Perhaps only humans can suffer the kind of deep guilt that follows a failure to reflect the responsibilities towards earth-keeping that are a common mantra in different church traditions and official statements. However, this does not necessarily mean that there is a sharp split between humans and other non-human animals, who, in a certain sense, can be said to share in moral agency, and therefore in a limited sense can also be recipients of the atoning, as well as the reconciling or redemptive work of Christ.[17] I would also add that a theological response to evil is even wider than this, as I will discuss in the next chapter.

Varieties of cosmic Christology

Joseph Sittler[18] and Jürgen Moltmann[19] are examples of two key theologians who have widened the scope of Christology to include cosmic dimensions as relevant for ecological concern, though the starting point for their reflection on the breadth of Christology is God's grace and the risen Christ respectively. Matthew Fox has also responded to an almost exclusive focus on historical accounts in theology by building a spiritualised cosmic Christology, and while he draws on the figure of Wisdom, he uses other sources to build a picture of the cosmic Christ.[20] Fox's particular interpretation of cosmic Christology is one that is now completely shorn from the historical Jesus, a reaction to the tendency to 'humanise' Jesus noted above, and also an incarnate Christ that has no relationship to Christ the redeemer understood in classical terms of Fall and redemption. For Fox, the incarnate Christ *is* the redeemer, for Christ as the cosmic one serves as the example or teacher for all to follow, opening up the possibility of finding Christ as the eternal ground of creation. Redemption also means a return to the original blessing found in the Garden of Eden, pointing to a transformed future that is turned back on itself.[21] It is a theology of blessing in excess, and may be one reason why among mainstream Western theologians there seems to be a continued failure to include portrayals of Christ in cosmic terms, for they would be suspicious of any tendencies towards such a truncated development of Christology, in effect missing out all due consideration of redemption as a response to human sinfulness.[22]

Joseph Sittler, in using Colossians 1 as the starting point for his reflection on the cosmic Christ, succeeds in bringing redemption within the larger orbit of creation, and thus avoiding those dualistic tendencies separating the material and spiritual, nature and grace, which Fox has also sought to overcome in his own particular way. Sittler urged a return to Irenaeus' view of nature and grace working together, so that nothing was outside that grace, the promise of grace held out to the whole of the natural order.[23] The split between nature and grace reached its zenith in the Enlightenment period, so the response must now be, Sittler urges, 'to claim the world of nature for God's Christ', in a manner analogous to the claim for history in Augustine's *City of God*.[24] Moreover, he argues that the wide scope for Christ's work is not a minor key in the epistles, since it appears in prominent places such as Romans 8:37–39. He also draws on Ephesians 1:2–14 in order to argue for a Christology imbibed by grace; grace is embodied in Jesus Christ and through him points to a future unity of the universe.[25] Such a Christology of grace means that there is no longer a split between natural and revealed theology, for 'it is a theology for nature in the inevitable sense that the hand of God the Creator, which is the hand of the Son, should be seen, following the Incarnation, also in nature'.[26]

Sittler acknowledges his debt to Eastern Orthodox approaches to Christ and their cosmic vision. The contemporary Orthodox theologian Vincent Rossi has stressed the importance of this tradition in his claim that Christian ecology *is* cosmic Christology.[27] He argues that the cosmic covenant between God and all living creatures in Genesis was not abolished either by the Mosaic covenant or by the New Covenant in the coming of Christ, for it is set in place until the end of time. Drawing on Colossians, he interprets the passage in terms of the Logos, so that 'Reconciliation of order and harmony is reconciliation with the Source, the Logos.' He advocates, then, a Logos Christology, but lest we think of this in too-remote categories, he marries this with Philippians 2:10, 'that at the name of Jesus every knee should bow, of things in heaven and things in earth and things under the earth'.[28] This means that reconciliation with the Logos restores order and harmony. Taking Ephesians 1:15–23 and 3:8–19 as his cue, he names the Church as the place where the Logos dwells in bodily form through a eucharistic marriage of heaven and earth. The Church in this way *becomes* the cosmos made new. The naming of the life of the Church as central is typical of Eastern Orthodox reflection, where liturgical celebration becomes the means through which all of creation is gathered up to God. This is perhaps the meaning of the Church becoming the cosmos made new, though giving the Church such a central place might sound somewhat triumphalistic to those outside the community of faith. Rossi is also prepared to stress the 'supernatural' in countering what he believes is a dangerous cultural biocentrism that has attracted some Christians, so that for him the 'new creation story' with its reference to psychic dimensions falls dangerously short of the true revelation in Christ. Instead, the natural world cannot be considered apart from the incarnation, so that it is only fully 'natural' in Christ, as he is the one by whom all things consist. His elevated view of Christology means that both theocentricity and Christocentricity are equivalent and necessary in order to approach ecology aright.[29]

Rossi's particular condemnation of the value of finding in nature a psychic dimension is also of interest in relation to the cosmic Christology developed by the mystic priest and palaeontologist Pierre Teilhard de Chardin. Teilhard was also inspired by Colossians and Ephesians, but he was more prepared than Rossi to weave in an evolutionary story that was synthetic with his view of Christology.[30] He claimed that evolution was not simply a process; it was holy, 'a light illuminating all facts', by which he meant that it was God's way of creating.[31] For him Christ makes evolution possible, but equally and importantly, evolution makes Christ possible as well.[32] Christ incarnate was, in an important sense for Teilhard, the *evolved Christ*. God incarnate is more than just a once-for-all appearing, but an embedding in the whole evolutionary process. Teilhard envisaged an evolution that was purposeful and went through different stages of *orthogenesis*, including eventually hominisation and *Christogenesis* – that is, the emergence not just of a cosmic Christ on earth, but a resurrected, exalted Christ of the Second Coming or Parousia as the one Omega to which the universe points in its fulfilment. Christ, through divine love, becomes the organising magnet that attracts all aspects of the universe and eventually leads to its unification in him. The direction of movement in this case is broadly towards the spiritualisation of the universe. Some interpreters have found, for this reason, an implicit world-denying anti-materialism in Teilhard's thinking.[33] While this is understandable, it does not really do sufficient justice to the influence of Eastern traditions in his thought, according to the Logos tradition of Christ as immersed in the created world. Teilhard claims, therefore, that there can be for him 'No God (up to a certain point) without creative union. No creation without incarnational immersion. No incarnation without redemptive repayment.'[34] His 'Hymn to Eternal Feminine' makes the remarkable suggestion that the Virgin in her purity and love actually seemed to provoke the incarnation, so that he claims: 'Without the lure of my purity, think you, would God ever have come down as flesh, to dwell in his creation.'[35]

It is, then, a Christology that is shaped by an understanding of love as both relationship and energy in the universe. Love is creative, saving and redemptive, and it is through love that Jesus Christ acts as the world's loving and animating centre. Most importantly, perhaps, Teilhard sees creation not so much as an act in world history, but a loving process in the heart of Christ risen that is still ongoing, drawing it towards the future.[36] Yet this process should not, in my view, be seen as anti-materialist, for this would oppose his spirituality. His vision was one where the love of the risen Christ was vividly present to all creatures and the whole creation, rather than in any way detached from material reality.[37] Moreover, he also included as a minor key the idea of suffering and death in his understanding of Christ, but it was seemingly an inevitable part of the overall hope-filled process towards a future that is hidden in Christ.[38] Teilhard did not write at the time when ecological concerns had come to the fore. His theology does present some difficulties for eco-theology, such as his elevation of the human person through his linear hominising evolutionary axis. His cosmological vision of Christ is ambiguous in that while it affirms reality by making Christ author of creation in a continuous sense, it also tends to detract from Christ's human nature, and it is hard to identify with Christ as the one who lures the world process to completion. He also does not give sufficient attention to those aspects of evolution that lead to endless suffering, death and extinction of species. It would also have been more helpful if Teilhard had managed to find more critical distance between evolutionary ideas and his vision of Christ. His tight synthesis leaves much to be desired, for it seems to baptise a particular theory of human origins, that itself has been superseded by subsequent scientific discussion of evolutionary processes.

Jürgen Moltmann develops a cosmic Christology that is also orientated towards the future, but it is one that is grounded more firmly in the idea of the historical Christ as one who suffers, as developed in his earlier account, *The Crucified God*.[39] Moltmann believes that a recovery of cosmic Christology is essential in relation to ecological concern, but it also needs to draw in those elements of historical Christology as well. Exactly how this might take place seems to be through a thoroughgoing eschatological interpretation of Christology. He insisted that Christology that was not also cosmic in scope was incomplete, though the inspiration for the cosmic christological dimension is Easter, so the significance of Christ in cosmic terms is only appreciated in the light of faith in the resurrection.[40] In this sense the parousia is not just a historical moment of Christ's final appearing, but the final unveiling of Christ as Lord of Creation, Pantocrator hidden in the cosmos and 'of the hidden subject nature in reconciled, redeemed and hence newly created cosmos'.[41] Christ's coming, then, reveals the natural world as that which is God's creation. He is also prepared to name this as a profoundly Wisdom Christology, where wisdom is the creative ground and sustainer of cosmic history.[42] The death of Christ is also significant in building a cosmic Christology, for now his death takes on a universal significance. He argues for a threefold movement to Christ's mediation in creation. First, Christ is the ground of the creation of all things. Second, Christ is the moving power in the evolution of creation, and third, Christ is the redeemer of the whole creation process. In this way Moltmann's cosmic Christology weaves together creation and redemption. Christ as the ground of creation appears in the form of God's Wisdom, Spirit or Word. Moltmann thinks of the Word acting in creation as being like a song of creation, rather than command and response; while the Word names, the breath binds the words together, so the Creator acts through the Word and Spirit. The Word is the one who specifies and differentiates. Word and the Spirit act as mediators in God's work of securing and preserving creation, since that work is not just a continuous watching over the created world to preserve it from chaos, but all of creation is also included in the kingdom of grace. This means that the renewal of creation is anticipated already, so that the historical human movement from creation to redemption 'has its hidden correspondences in the world of nature'.[43] How is this evident? Moltmann suggests that it is through evolution that we see the works of God as innovator, but these are like 'symbols' or 'parables' of the perfected world to come. Yet he is also aware of the ambiguity of evolution itself, its tragic dimension and loss, that Teilhard failed to appreciate. In this Moltmann believes that Christ needs to be seen as a victim, along with all the other victims of evolution. Christ, on this basis, needs to be viewed as the redeemer of evolution, set in the light of Christ's future coming in glory. Yet how can Christ be both victim and the ground of the creation of all things and the redeemer of all things? This raises the issue of whether the entanglement of Christ in the suffering of the world is such that God's suffering and that of the world become indistinguishable. The problem of theodicy looms large, and will be addressed in the next chapter. Another problematic aspect is Moltmann's particular interpretation of kenosis as a spatial withdrawal in the Trinity prior to the development of a kenotic Christology, in an attempt to keep the distance between God and creation preserved, while embedding Christ as the crucified God. While he affirms the cosmic incarnation of God, he also interprets this under the guise of redemption themes, so that creation and redemption are interlaced together towards a future messianic age where God will be all in all.

Christ and the land

Theological descriptions of cosmic Christology have the advantage of bringing all of the created universe into the orbit of Christ's role as Word in creation and Christ's redemptive work, but suffer the disadvantage of detaching Christ from the historical Jesus as understood according to the Gospel accounts. We need, therefore, in working through the implications of Christ for ecology, to look once again at the historical Jesus and seek ways in which his perception of the earth might be important.[44] If the earth has been cursed by Adam's disobedience, then Christ, as the second Adam, must be in a position to care about what happens on earth. Moreover, since in the Hebrew tradition hope for the creation was bound up with that of humanity, so with the coming of Jesus there would have been expectations for such hope to be fulfilled, since both Jesus and his followers believed that the kingdom was coming already in their presence.[45] One aspect of this restoration of created order came through Jesus' ministry of exorcism of demons, showing to his followers that he had authority over Satan, and in this sense, bore witness to his cosmic authority. In addition, his healing ministry demonstrated that he cared about the physical, material condition of humanity, but more widely it could be viewed as a healing of the created order as such. Accounts of more direct interventions in the natural order, such as the stilling of the storm, also bear witness to his capacity for redeeming creation. In addition, the standards that Jesus seems to have set for his followers go beyond the law of Moses to an earlier creation mandate. For example, he strictly forbade divorce (Mark 10:1–12), based on the account of God's creation of man and woman, and he also forbade oaths, for these represented a compromise position. Also, his teaching about cleanness and uncleanness is somewhat remarkable given his Jewish background, for by this he seemed to override the food laws, cleansing all foods. He does not give a rationale for this position, though given the tradition in 1 Timothy 4:4 which refers to the goodness of all created things, it is quite possible that he had the creation ordinance in view. In addition, it is likely that he was deliberately seeking to challenge those laws and practices that served to separate off Israel from its neighbours through its designation of certain things as profane. Instead, he taught a universal inclusive love that opened up to other nations and peoples.

More controversial, perhaps, is the idea that in designating himself 'the Son of Man' in the Gospel accounts – which means, literally, 'the human being' – he is making a claim that has cosmic relevance.[46] The Hebrew phrase for 'Son of Man' is *ben adam*. Is he referring to himself in relation to Adam? Or does he intend a reference to Daniel 7 that speaks about 'one like a son of man'? Daniel's vision of a new kingdom fits in well with the context, but an alternative is that the book of Ezekiel is the background, where 'son of man' is the way the prophet is addressed. Psalm 8 also speaks of the 'son of man' and human dominion over the earth, as then alluded to in Hebrews 1:6–9 and 1 Corinthians 15:27. This latter interpretation may have been overlooked as a background to Jesus' self-designation, but it is plausible for the following reasons. In the first place, Jesus understood his mission as eschatological fulfilment that is presented in the Psalm. Secondly, there is a close verbal parallel between the way Jesus uses 'the son of man' and that found in Psalm 8 compared with either Daniel or Ezekiel. Thirdly, the idea of authority associated with 'the son of man', including that of the Sabbath, finds its parallel in the Psalm. Fourthly, the Psalm was used as a reference to Christ early on in the Christian tradition, as exemplified in Hebrews and 1 Corinthians. Of course, it is possible to refer to many different backgrounds to this expression simultaneously, where Psalms such as 80:17 provide the link with more explicit messianic texts found in Daniel.

The Psalm itself speaks of humanity in a way that puts emphasis on the importance of humanity understood as in hierarchical relationship to the natural order.[47] If this is the case, then this might imply an endorsement of such attitudes by Jesus, identified with the 'son of man' in this Psalm. On the other hand, however, it could equally be the case that Christ intended to *subvert* the kind of kingship portrayed in this Psalm and interpret it in a different way, for his view of kingship was one marked by suffering and servanthood. The naming of the cross as 'the king of the Jews' speaks of his kingship in a radical way that is the very opposite of the mastery portrayed in the Psalm. Given this, however, such kingship is necessarily one to be exercised not through domination, but through the humility of a suffering servant.

Such an attitude is reinforced by Jesus' teaching itself, which speaks of God's providential care of all creatures (Matt. 6:26–30). This care of creation was an integral aspect of Jewish teaching on the treatment of non-human creatures that shows love and respect for the natural world. For example, the non-human creation shared in the sabbatical ordinance, so that animals were expected to have rest on the Sabbath day (Exod. 23:12), and the land was to be left uncultivated every sabbatical year (Lev. 25). But restrictions also applied to certain practices, such as cutting down trees (Deut. 20:19–20), and taking away a bird with eggs or muzzling a threshing ox was prohibited. Jesus' sayings go further in that humanity is invited to learn about the providential care of God by close attention to the non-human world. Jesus' vision of a future kingdom of God is one that includes all creatures. Mark describes Jesus as being with the wild animals in the temptation account (Mark 1:13), and this may possibly be an allusion to such a future kingdom. Hence, the vision of Colossians is not as speculative as it might appear, for the Jesus of the Gospels seemed to have in mind the future restoration of a community of creation.

Reflection on the Gospel of Luke also uncovers further insights about the relationship between Jesus and the land.[48] Luke was writing to a mixed audience of city-dwellers and landowners alongside country peasants without wealth and social influence. His birth narrative emphasises Jesus' birth outside the conventional place of hospitality, finding a welcome among those peasants whose livelihood is drawn from the earth. The announcement of the birth of Jesus to shepherds is also significant in relation to the land. While shepherds shared the same utilitarian attitude to the land as the peasants, they often acted on behalf of a powerful elite in that the animals commonly belonged to others, so that they had a different attitude to inherited land compared with the peasants, allowing their flocks to stray onto this land and leading to tensions and conflicts. There was often considerable violence between shepherds and the peasant farmers who regarded the land as rightfully theirs to protect. Their attitude to the land was rapacious rather than one that expressed its intrinsic worth.

In Luke's account the birth is announced to all, those dwelling in the city, the peasants and the landless shepherds, but importantly it also brings together heaven and earth, bringing peace on earth. The earth, which has been a context for division and enmity, now is blessed with peace, so that with the coming of Jesus' birth the possibility of its transformation from a place of rivalry and competition to one where humanity can live in peace now exists. That peace is one that is characteristic of heaven, as echoed in Luke 19:38, showing Luke's understanding of a cosmic duality between heaven and earth.[49] As Trainor says, Luke therefore 'presents in the birth story a vision of social harmony linked to a renewal of the land. Rather than being the stage on which economic and political battles were waged, the land could become the place of divine blessing and grace for all people.'[50] We need to be wary, however, of the cosmological hierarchy that Luke assumes, for this could work against what seems at first sight a land-affirming Gospel. Against this, there is the possibility that heaven could be thought of in a way that is less hierarchical and more integral to creation as such. The Lord's Prayer, which assumes a background dualism of heaven and earth, points to a future where distinctions between heaven and earth would no longer exist.[51]

Christ as incarnate Wisdom

A further way of developing the cosmic dimensions of Christology is through a recovery of the Wisdom Christology alluded to in Colossians 1. But what might this Wisdom Christology mean? Given that authors as diverse as Matthew Fox and Jürgen Moltmann have claimed to find inspiration from the idea of Christ as Wisdom, how can it be used to good effect in developing a Christology relevant for ecological concern? In the first place, wisdom is effective in marrying the historical Jesus with cosmological renditions of his significance. Wisdom as operative in the human social realm and the universal creaturely realm also brings creation within the orbit of Christology. In the Gospel traditions the relationship between Jesus and wisdom is portrayed as either the teacher of wisdom, as in the Synoptics, or as God's wisdom, as in John's Gospel. The way Jesus drew on the proverbial and parabolic traditions of wisdom is familiar, and like the Hebrew Bible, most are maxims for living based on human experience. Yet he also draws on everyday events from the natural world in order to reinforce his teaching, such as the lost sheep or the sower. Luke compares him favourably in relation to Solomon as a teacher of wisdom (Luke 11:31).

There is also good evidence that in the earliest texts of the Gospel accounts known as Q, the wisdom categories were ascribed to the person of Jesus and his message.[52] There are some passages in Matthew that point to Jesus as not simply the teacher of wisdom, but also wisdom incarnate. James Dunn has consistently argued that one of the earliest Christologies to emerge in the New Testament period was a Wisdom Christology which finds its full flowering in the Gospel of John.[53] While Proverbs 8 reflects the immanence of God in creation by personification of wisdom, in Ben Sira wisdom is identified with the Torah, and in the Gospels Jesus is identified with both the Torah and Wisdom. John 1:1 echoes Genesis 1:1, but John 1:3 echoes the idea of wisdom as the agent of creation found in Proverbs 8:22–23, and John 1:4 echoes the thought of Proverbs 8:35. Yet the analogy between wisdom and Christ goes further than this in that the pattern of descent and ascent is similar to that of wisdom found in Proverbs 8, Sirach 24 and 1 Enoch 42. There are also other parallels later in the Gospel – for example, that between Jesus as the bread of life (John 6:27) and Proverbs 9:1–26. The most striking transformation of wisdom in John is his portrayal of Christ's death as an example of wisdom. Wisdom as a feminine personification of the divine means that a tension exists between a Logos Christology and a Wisdom Christology, and the eclipse of the latter by the former may be one reason why Wisdom Christology ceased to have such influence in the historical development of Christology.

I have suggested so far that the gathering up of Jewish wisdom sayings as pointing to the person of Christ allows for a cosmic Christology that is inclusive of all of creation. But the transformation of wisdom through Christ's death allows for an equivalent inclusiveness for the redemptive work of Christ as well. 1 Corinthians was written in the context of a community engaged in bitter rivalry about their own or their leader's superiority and rhetorical performance.[54] Against this, Paul pitches the wisdom of the cross, quoting Isaiah 29:14 in 1 Corinthians 1:19 – the Jewish people were mistaken in trusting their own wisdom in forming an alliance with Egypt. He is pointing to the dangers of too much trust in human wisdom, rather than dismissing the whole of the Jewish wisdom tradition. Instead, at the moment of his shameful humiliation, Christ demonstrates the power of God and the wisdom of God. How might this be the case? Paul links wisdom with righteousness, sanctification and redemption – that is, the cross points to the means through which God enacts a plan of salvation. The foolishness of God's wisdom is the foolishness of divine love and vulnerability. In John's Gospel we find a further theological development, for now the cross becomes a manifestation of the glory of God. He portrays Jesus' death as a self-offering of love. While the Jewish tradition looked to Wisdom or the Torah as bread from heaven, now Jesus is portrayed as one who offers up his own flesh of blood as an offering of life for all who believe.

In the context of ecological theology, we can ask in what ways is a wisdom reading of Christology helpful? In the first place, it is significant for the development of an anthropology that focuses on the humility of Christ as an example to those who believe that human wisdom is all-sufficient in meeting the complex demands of ecology today. Secondly, it provides a way of thinking about Christ's incarnation as that which is affirmative for the whole of the created order – Christ's incarnation as Wisdom was not simply to restore humanity from sin, but an expression of divine Wisdom now manifest fully in the flesh. But in the third place, it assists in helping to tease out the way creation might be included in the canvas of redemption. If we follow the universal claim in Colossians 1, then all things are caught up in both the creative and the redemptive work of Christ, who died on the cross and was then raised from the dead, pointing to a future restoration of all things. The difficulty, of course, is how the traditional language of atonement, which is Christ's work on the cross, might be made relevant and appropriate to non-human creatures. One way to respond might be to divorce accounts of atonement and redemption, so that in relation to creation as such there is no need for atonement; rather, it is redemption *for* future glory, rather than salvation *from* sin.[55] Nonetheless, my preference would be to resist making too sharp a divide between categories of atonement and redemption as applied to human and non-human species, and to retain the notion of atonement as that which is relevant for the wider community of creation in that the breakdown of relationships epitomised by the mythical account of the Fall is also anticipated in the evolutionary account of the emergence of humans.[56] Moreover, as far as ecological impact is concerned, human beings are culpable, and so in need of atonement understood in a more traditional sense of human sinfulness, though now expanded to include not just sins against God and one another, but also the wider community of creation. In other words, an emphasis on the breadth of reconciliation wrought in Christ should not detract from the wisdom of the cross in atoning for human sinfulness, including ecological sin.

In addition, a Wisdom Christology is significant in that it allows for an understanding of the second person of the Trinity in Wisdom categories, while also retaining an emphasis on Christ's full human personhood.[57] Arguably, Wisdom, as a feminine term, is a reminder of Christ's significance for all humanity, male and female. Just as the goal of wisdom is righteousness and justice, so Wisdom Christology is one that points to liberating right praxis, a seeking of right action in daily life, a way of knowing informed by love.[58]

Conclusions

Reflection on the significance of Christ in an ecological context challenges exclusively anthropocentric interpretations of his significance, either by a focus on Jesus' human nature, or by more classical claims that the incarnation simply followed from human sinfulness. Instead cosmic interpretations of Christology lend themselves to an ecological interpretation. This may be through perceptions of Christ as the divine Logos who became incarnate in the flesh, thus affirming material being as such. The hymn to wisdom in Colossians has also inspired many theologians to develop cosmic interpretations of Christology. The author includes the vast sweep of the universe in the orbit of Christ's work in creation and redemption, thus hinting at the close relationship of nature and grace found in Joseph Sittler, or eschatological interpretations of Christ's significance in evolution, as found in Jürgen Moltmann. Identification of Logos Christology in John with the Jewish wisdom traditions permits a Wisdom Christology to emerge. Wisdom, when due account is taken of the wisdom of the cross, reinforces the link between creation and redemption, while offering the possibility of more historical reflection on Jesus the sage, grounded in his life and ministry. Wisdom, as that which relates specifically to life in the community and family, is a reminder of the implications of Christology as praxis. The way of wisdom is the way of imitating Christ in his concern for what happens here on earth; more specifically, challenging those who believe that following him leads to a rarefied escape into heavenly realms. But how can the God of love also be involved in the creative process understood in evolutionary terms, if it is also wrecked by so much suffering and death? How might Christ be significant in developing an adequate theodicy that takes account of evolutionary and ecological suffering? We turn to these questions in the chapter that follows.

Further reading

Barth, Markus and Blanke, Helmut, *Colossians: A New Translation with Introduction and Commentary* (The Anchor Bible), trans. Ashid B. Beck (New York, Doubleday, 1994)

Bouma-Prediger, S. and Bakken, P. (eds.), *Evocations of Grace: Joseph Sittler's Writings on Ecology, Theology and Ethics* (Grand Rapids, Eerdmans, 2000)

Deane-Drummond, C. (ed.), *Teilhard de Chardin on People and Planet* (London, Equinox, 2006)

Deane-Drummond, C., *Creation through Wisdom: Theology and the New Biology* (Edinburgh, T. & T. Clark, 2000)

Dunn, J., *Christology in the Making* (London, SCM Press, 1989)

Edwards, D., *Jesus, the Wisdom of God: An Ecological Theology* (Homebush, St Pauls, 1995)

Edwards D. (ed.), *Earth Revealing, Earth Healing* (Collegeville, The Liturgical Press, 2001)

Edwards, Denis and Worthing, Mark (eds.), *Biodiversity and Ecology* (Adelaide, ATF Press, 2004)

Moltmann, J., *The Way of Jesus Christ* (London, SCM Press, 1990)

Rossi, V., 'Christian Ecology is Cosmic Christology', *Epiphany*, 8 (1987), pp. 52–62

Teilhard de Chardin, P., *The Human Phenomenon*, trans. Sarah Appleton Weber (Brighton, Sussex Academic Press, 1999)

Chapter 9

Ecology and theodicy

THE QUESTION OF THEODICY UNDERSTOOD IN philosophical terms is the question of how it is possible to maintain the goodness of God in the face of evils that we experience or witness in the natural world. A question that has exercised the minds of theologians more recently is whether we need more specific evolutionary theodicy(ies), or whether existing formulations of theodicy that have more commonly concentrated on moral evil, understood as restricted to the human realm, are sufficient to deal with suffering in the non-human world. Another question is how far purely philosophical analyses, sometimes dubbed 'thin' descriptions, deal adequately with complex questions of suffering, leading to broader, 'thicker' theological analyses. This chapter will explore the different varieties of theodicy and question their adequacy in the light of what we know of ecology in both its evolutionary and present dimensions.

Introduction

Evil can be broadly categorised as 'natural evil' or 'moral evil'.[1] 'Natural' evil means that suffering which comes about through 'natural' causes, such as earthquakes, or through 'natural' processes of evolution and predation. 'Evolutionary evil' is a sub-branch of natural evil and stems from evolutionary processes, and some prefer to term this 'biophysical evil' – that is, non-human suffering arising out of non-human causes.[2] Moral evil, on the other hand, arises through the deliberate evil choices of human beings, leading to suffering in self and others. Of course, the line between 'natural' and 'moral' is blurred in two senses. In the first sense it may be that choices made by humans enable 'natural evils' to occur, such as, for example, sexually transmitted diseases. In the second sense, higher animals may also be capable of choices within their own worlds that would be broadly analogous to human morality.[3] Historically philosophers, following Descartes, took the view that non-human animals do not suffer, but this is a very uncommon view today. A less extreme view is to say that while non-human creatures do suffer physical pain, they do not suffer psychologically in the same way as humans. Brian Davies, for example, argues that 'they cannot, for example, be pained because their colleagues do not value them enough, or because they have been rejected by people with whom they have fallen in love, or because they endure deep remorse for something they did'.[4] However, this view is also possible to challenge, for it seems that the kind of social suffering that Davies believes is unique to humans finds some parallels in primates, and possibly other intelligent mammals as well.[5] One of the ways in which both evolutionary and non-human suffering has been dealt with by philosophical theologians and ethicists is to dismiss the issue and suggest that suffering and pain in the non-human world are just the way the world is, and should not lead to moral difficulties for human beings. This rejection of any consideration of creatures other than humans seems remarkable in the light of both an evolutionary and ecological understanding of the world where humans are embedded in nature, and in the light of a theological understanding of the world as created by God, and as created out of the goodness of God. Well-established philosophers may still be liable to pay insufficient attention to the problem that this poses for belief in a Creator.[6]

One does not need to spend a long time studying natural history in order to find grotesque and, to our sensibilities at least, disturbing narratives of what we perceive as cruelty in the natural realm. Stephen Jay Gould has described the natural world as 'amoral' for this reason. He recounts in graphic terms how ichneumon wasps eat live caterpillars from the inside, but in this instance perhaps it is less horrifying once we stop to reflect on the level of pain likely to be suffered by these simple creatures.[7] Yet suffering in the natural world is often rather more complex than this. There are plenty of examples where the victim is advanced in terms of its levels of consciousness and intelligence. What about the case of the Komodo dragon that lies in wait for pregnant animals to give birth, then plunging its poisonous fangs into the newborn infant, proceeds to consume the young, beginning with the intestines? Their prey are not simple organisms lacking sentience, but intelligent mammals, quite capable of both intense physical suffering and psychological pain. Biologist David Hull suggests that evolutionary processes are 'rife with happenstance, contingency, incredible waste, death, pain and horror … The God of Galapagos is careless, wasteful, indifferent almost diabolical.'[8, 9] Certainly what comes through in his account is a shocking recognition of the extent and level of suffering and cruelty in nature. His comments are not just relevant to evolutionary history either; examples could be found of equally horrifying (to us) cruelty and indifference. Christopher Southgate believes that the pain that we witness is necessary in order for sentient beings to be able to avoid difficulty.[10] Death and mortality is also a thermodynamic necessity and without it life would be impossible to envisage. But he argues that what really is challenging is the *level and extent* of pain for those creatures that are caught up at an early stage in their life in the processes of predation and parasitism. What about the 'insurance chick' that is hatched by birds of prey, but doomed to a life cut short, except on rare occasions?

Holmes Rolston, whom many regard as the 'father' of environmental ethics, also describes in a number of places what he terms the 'life struggle' that is embedded in natural processes – that is, in ecology. The wastage and cruelty here will dent any accounts of divine design, as Hume recognised some years earlier. He suggests that just as emptiness and vastness is the challenge in physics, so 'the timespan of ceaseless struggle is the challenge to interpret in biology'.[11] He believes that this aspect has been uncomfortable even for those without religious belief, so modern biologists will prefer to re-phrase processes as 'adaptation', or 'fitness', hence taking away the sting of what is implied.[12]

I suggest that in addition to the categories of moral evil and natural/ biophysical evil, in the light of current ecological issues we face a *third* category of evil that bridges moral and natural evil in that it is caused by human beings but leads to evils in the non-human world. I suggest that we can name this as *anthropogenic evil*. This is evil that arises indirectly through the growth in human populations, industrialisation and the economy, leading to the production of pollutant wastes which then have devastating impacts on other species and on human populations through processes such as climate change and habitat destruction.[13] It is associated with moral choices made by humans in that if we chose to live more 'lightly' on the earth, human impacts would be reduced, but because these choices are not as visible or obvious compared with most moral dilemmas, it is worth assigning this kind of evil a particular category for special consideration as a way of highlighting its importance. In a sense it links the categories of moral and natural evil, for these anthropogenic evils emerge indirectly through the moral ethos of human societies and lifestyles. In addition, because extinctions of other species is far more severe now as a result of the impact of human activities compared with the basal extinction rate in the course of evolutionary history, this contributes to the instability of the climate, which then reverberates in additional threats to both human and non-human survival. With Ernst Conradie I believe that we need to confess guilt in the context of climate change, but, more broadly still, we all need to confess more generally to anthropogenic evils wrought through habitat destruction and loss of biodiversity, more often than not either unacknowledged or pushed away from more traditional categories of moral concern.[14]

Holmes Rolston suggests that while life may seem 'cruel' to us, premature life for one is a good from the perspective of the one predating and consuming. The fecundity of life is needed to ensure that variation that leads to further development of forms, so he can say that 'the cougar's fang has carved the limbs of the fleet-footed deer'.[15] Also, as one moves up the phylogenetic scale, the amount of 'wastage' in terms of offspring shrinks, so premature dying goes down in proportion to the capacity to suffer. Rolston is offering here a form of theodicy, so it is worth teasing out elements of what this might entail. One of the classic theodicies is the suggestion that even though things may seem painful or difficult, *overall the goal of the process is a good*. This is explicit in Rolston's account, that while there is suffering in the natural world, it is fundamentally 'pro-life', and not just any old form of life – it is life that is increasing in complexity and sophistication, leading ultimately to the emergence of human beings. This is a *means and ends* argument, one that supports the overall process because the final result is a good one. Hence, for him the evil found here cannot prove that God no longer exists.

Another dimension to this argument is the *free will defence* – that is, the good of freedom will only exist where there is the possibility of its opposite occurring. The argument runs something like this. If there were no evil, there could be no genuine choices, and therefore no genuine free will, exercised by free human beings. Alvin Plantinga believes that it is logically impossible for God to create creatures whose actions are determined by God, yet also free.[16] Related to the free will defence is an argument for *soul-making* that John Hick makes for suffering, that through suffering we mature and grow as individuals. Although this might seem to be specific to the human sphere, the idea of progress achieved through suffering is also embedded in Rolston's account, for he stresses the increase in complexity through different phylogenetic systems, leading to an overall gain in the level of consciousness, so that eventually the number of offspring that are subject to death and suffering is lower compared with levels further back, but the intensity of that suffering is increased. There is also a third possibility implicit in Rolston's account, namely that *evil is unreal*. Early classic writers such as Augustine and Aquinas used this account of evil. They did not mean that evil did not exist or was illusory; rather, they meant that something is wicked or bad because it lacks, in some sense, something of the good. In other words, evil appears where there is a gap between what is and what could be the case. This neatly gets round any idea that evil is produced by the creativity of God; rather, evil appears where God's creativity is not found – it is a privation of the good. It is worth taking each of the strategies in turn and asking how far and to what extent they are sufficient to meet the demand placed on them by ecological evils, understood under the categories of moral, natural and anthropogenic evils.

Eco-theodicy

Although some scholars have commented on the extent of suffering embedded in the evolutionary processes through which life as we know it has come into being, rather less attention has been paid to ecological suffering itself. The two are clearly related in that if we find a way of coming to terms with suffering in the evolutionary processes, then it is likely that we will also be able to deal with that non-human suffering in our present world. Of course, some theologians argue that we do not need a special category of theodicy, for the way theodicy has traditionally dealt with this issue is sufficient. There are two elements to this argument. In the first place, we can ask ourselves whether the theodicies that have been discussed in relation to human beings are adequate to meet those kinds of suffering that we find in the non-human sphere. In the second place, we can ask if there is a need for any further reflection that is unique to the specific situation in hand, namely, non-human suffering. By considering the adequacies of traditional formulations of theodicy in the light of ecological ills, this should put us in a good position to ask if any more is required or not.

Of course, one approach to theodicy in the human sphere is to say that it is itself far too theoretical to really deal properly with the devastation that suffering brings. In other words, theodicy itself has connotations of *immorality*; it is immoral because it does not help us know how to behave, and can even seem cruelly theoretical to those in desperate need who are suffering terrible pain.[17] It might even seem to alleviate the need to face up to moral responsibility and guilt. I suggest that it is still worth making the *attempt* to consider theodicy, even though at the end of the analysis we may find it wanting. Also, arguably, theoretical discussions about suffering should not have a negative impact on non-human species in that, unlike our human companions, they would have no conception at all of the more theoretical debates taking place among humans. It would have a negative impact, of course, if as a result of such theoretical reflection humanity became complacent towards non-human suffering. This is particularly important when dealing with what I have called anthropogenic evil.

Process arguments

In the first place consider the view that the overall *process* is a good, and therefore suffering that is the means to achieve this can be accepted as part of that process. Southgate and Robinson name this kind of argument 'developmental good harm analysis' (GHA).[18] Within this category there will be those who argue that the process of development of the good includes the harm, and those who argue that the harm arises indirectly as a by-product of the good. Where analysis is restricted to the human sphere it is human GHA; where it broadens to include non-humans, but is focused on human goods, it is anthropocentric GHA; and where it widens out to the non-human community, it is termed biotic GHA. I suggest that these categories are most useful as ways of analysing different *ethical* approaches to decision-making using consequentialist arguments. In terms of theodicy as such, it is a justification that seems to depend on defending a God who must act as a moral agent, according to our own particular rules for what goodness might entail. The idea that some harms are *inevitably* part of the process of the development of the good comes into play in John Hick's understanding of the world as a training ground for the emergence of the soul. Analogous are those who argue that the suffering embedded in the natural world is necessary in order to allow self-aware human beings to emerge as an end product of the process.[19] Holmes Rolston's portrayal of evolutionary and ecological suffering as that which leads eventually to a good outcome is also similar, but he broadens out the analysis to include the good of the biotic community, not just restricting a concept of good to human beings. Arthur Peacocke has also written of the inevitability of suffering as part of the overall process of evolution.[20] A variation on this theme is that suffering is an unfortunate 'by-product' of the evolutionary process that leads to increasing complexity and intelligence. The difference between 'by-product' and 'instrumental' suffering is that in the latter case the suffering or harm seems to be embedded in the process of change and growth, whereas in the former it may arise as a secondary effect. Southgate suggests, correctly in my view, that the idea that life might be possible through the pain and suffering of another creature does not in itself 'redeem' that suffering, and extinction could not be justified on this basis either.[21] However, *one* of his strategies is that being the victim of predators 'is a necessary cost of selving' – this seems inconsistent, for now such suffering is reconciled on the basis that self-transcendence emerges.[22]

Theologians who perhaps hesitate to enter the territory of more theoretical discussions of theodicy draw heavily on eschatology – that is, envisaging an ultimate future goal where suffering and pain are no more.[23] The use of eschatology has also become more popular with the realisation that philosophical arguments alone are too 'thin' a description of reality.[24] Jürgen Moltmann, for example, has dedicated his whole theological project to writing in an eschatological vein, arguably in response to the lack of hope occasioned by suffering. The question for theodicy, of course, is how far this is really convincing as an argument, especially if used in isolation or instead of confronting the realities of evil, for it might leave one open to the charge of Gnostic escapism from the harsh realities of the sufferings of this world. Any teleological theodicy bears this burden, for it seems to justify the suffering in this world based on the good outcome, if not now, then in some perfected future beyond death. Of course, Moltmann pays considerable attention to the idea of a suffering God on the cross; hence he confronts the problem of pain, but does so through ontological arguments about God as one who co-suffers with creation.[25] I suggest, therefore, that eschatology is an important theological element, but it needs to be more conscious of inherent difficulties.[26]

Possibility arguments

According to this argument, good that arises includes the *possibility* that evil *may* also be present. The classic definition of this kind of argument is known as the 'free will defence'.[27] This is not so much a by-product of the process, or an inevitable aspect of the process itself, as suggested above, but related to the particular characteristic in view. Hence, in order to exercise free will there must inevitably be the possibility of alternatives, which include choices that harm. Some philosophers have argued that just because free will exists, does not inevitably mean that evil must follow, for humans might always have chosen freely for the good, not evil. However, this argument becomes clearer if we consider the idea of sentience, or the ability to feel. The ability to feel leads to the good of that experience, and the possibility of suffering. One might ask: how can a free will defence be applied to the non-human world? Of course, in the most general sense some of the suffering in the non-human world would be the result of the exercise of human free will. Any move towards a minimisation of this impact is mistaken, as it seems to relativise human impacts, which I term anthropogenic evils, by comparing them with the total suffering of cosmic history in a way that might soften their seriousness. Attempts have also been made in this direction by arguing for an extension of the argument to non-human creatures in what might be termed a 'free process' defence.[28] This position has been defended by Thomas Tracy who argues not so much for a personal freedom for relationship with God for non-human creatures, but for the acquisition of particular characteristics of life that also entail the possibility of an opposite.[29] All attempts to justify evil on the basis of the possibility of freedom, either of processes or moral action, are problematic in that they do not deal adequately with innocent suffering or where humans or other creatures are unable to either express their freedom or their flourishing. Those process philosophers who have argued for the possibility of subjectivity throughout the cosmos would seek to extend the possibility of good or its opposite in the material conditions of the cosmos.

A rather different position on the idea of the possibility of freedom and love is one where God's involvement is thought to be minimal in the process. Ruth Page, for example, argues that God's desire for freedom and love are such that it would be impossible to conceive of God as having a direct involvement in the creative processes of the world, imbibed as they are with so much waste and suffering. Hence, for Page, God companions the world in its suffering, without being directly responsible for that suffering. For her, God 'gives creation freedom to respond to possibility', so that 'tectonic plates that developed in one time in that freedom will later cause earthquakes, and probable suffering'.[30] She is unconvinced by process theologians' suggestions that the positive outcomes of eventual enrichment in evolutionary terms somehow justify the intense suffering along the way, so the 'divine lure' of process theology leaves much to be desired. I suggest that her work can be broadly considered under the category of the 'free process defence', for it is the freedom for possibilities inherent in creation that seem to allow her to admit to the possibility of evil. The difference in her case is that she can no longer conceive of God as being involved in this process in a direct way; rather, God just 'companions' the sufferers in the present. Underlying her understanding of creation is one that stresses freedom; for her, 'the fundamental freedom to use possibility … is the gift of creation'.[31] The difficulty, of course, is how far an understanding of God as merely 'companioning' the world is an adequate rendition of God as Creator of all that is. It seems that in facing theodicy, Page has emptied the idea of the Creator of its meaning, for God is no longer Creator except in a thin deistic sense, but fellow sufferer. Also, if in the name of freedom and love God has allowed for such suffering, then even if God is not directly responsible, God would still be accountable. In this way is the idea of a suffering, 'companioning' God sufficient or even helpful? This brings us to more ontological arguments.

Ontological arguments

This view states that the existence of good is inherently inseparable from the experience of harm or evil.[32] This differs from the second category in that the evil in question does not arise through processes leading to the good or as a consequence of the good, as discussed in the above two cases, but as a result of an inherent property of that good. The existence of the evil in question is not just a possibility, but inherent to the existence of the good. Examples in this case could be drawn from aesthetics, where arguments are put forward that beauty is inseparable from ugliness, or the value of life only appears in the face of death, and so on.[33] Philosophers have defended this view on the basis that it is logically possible to argue for the constitutive existence of evil and good in a world created by a benevolent God. The harm is there in order to highlight what constitutes the good – as, for example, silence serves to highlight the musical notes that follow.

One advantage of the ontological approach is that it allows for more practical responses to the problem of evil and suffering. Marilyn McCord Adams, for example, argues that 'horrendous evils require defeat by nothing less than the goodness of God'.[34] In the first place she argues that trying to ask why God does not prevent such ills or provide reasoning for this is mistaken, for we can never think of *sufficient* reasons, and there is a danger of presenting these as solutions to the problem of evil, which they are clearly not. She is therefore ruling out the kind of arguments that rely on processes or possibilities discussed above. She also discusses different types of constitutive suffering, where love is fulfilled or expressed through suffering. According to this view, 'Because God suffers, created suffering has positive value as a dimension of Godlikeness.'[35] God also feels compassion with those who suffer, giving that suffering a positive meaning in relation to the whole, and in this sense it has redemptive value.

An alternative might be that suffering is integral to a vision of God, not because God suffers in the sense that God is passible, but because it is paradigmatic for mystical and divine presence that associates the mystical vision of God with horrendous suffering. Simone Weil, for example, believed that affliction was a means of expression of the Divine embrace, even in the face of concrete ruin.[36] Adams believes that such expressions of suffering as constitutive ultimately only make sense if combined with the idea of perfection in the afterlife. This brings in a process element, but it is still constitutive in that the participant eventually perceives how participation in horrors were actual occasions for intimacy with God.[37]

The question we can address now is in what sense are such views applicable, if at all, to the non-human sphere? In the first place it is possible to argue that God comes alongside those who suffer, be they human or non-human; this is Page's notion of a companioned world. Yet does this necessarily need to involve actual suffering on the part of God? It strikes me that an *empathetic God* is not necessarily the same as a *suffering God*; rather, taken to its limit, the latter might imply an impoverishment of God's power to provide support in times of need. Certainly, the ability of God to suffer with other creatures would be of a different order entirely compared with human companioning. But perhaps the pain that humanity experiences in witnessing the suffering of other species is in a sense a sharing in Divine compassion. A God who through love is involved in such suffering is not, therefore, necessarily 'passible' in the sense that God's experience bears some *resemblance* to human suffering, but rather makes sense only through further reflection on the Passion narrative. Existential accounts of suffering as constitutive to a vision of God are most appropriate to consider in the light of reflection on human experiences. However, if, as has been argued by some theologians, humanity's task is to act as in some way as priest of creation, then, human creatures can take up the sufferings of the non-human world into an experience of a vision of God. Such a vision would not be a means of justifying that suffering or horrendous evil, but a way of sharing in the burden and opening up the possibility of redemption, not just for human creatures, but for non-human creatures as well.

Unreality arguments

The argument takes two forms. The first is that evil is illusory and so does not need to be considered. The second form is that evil reflects an absence, and so is unreal in the sense that it is not a positive, creative quality. This argument was developed by Thomas Aquinas, and has since been taken up by authors indebted to his position, such as Brian Davies.[38] The argument allows for the presence of evil as an absence or privation of the good. Hence, what we experience as evil is really the gap that exists between what could be and what is actually the case. Aquinas developed this idea because he could not conceive of God as having actual causative involvement in the evils of the world, while wishing to affirm God as the Creator of all that is. Southgate dismisses this view rather too quickly on the basis that it does not deal adequately with evolutionary and other harms.[39] It is worth contrasting this view that pits the difference between God and creaturely being more sharply compared with many of the ontological views discussed above.

Davies rejects the view that God suffers, as he suggests that this provides too close an identity between God and God's creatures. If God suffers *like* us, why does that make God more admirable? On the other hand, if God's suffering is unlike that of humans, as Marilyn McCord Adams suggests, in that the kind of emotional suffering that human beings experience would be impossible for God, then what is the point of that suffering? A classical solution to the problem is that Christ's human nature suffers like ours in representative ways, whereas Christ in his divine nature could not suffer. Aquinas' view of evil as the privation of the good takes a further step in the direction of guarding a distance between God and creaturely being, which is subject to vicissitudes and changes occasioned by the failure to fulfil its potential in the good. However, this does not mean that God is not involved or concerned with what happens in the world, for God loves the world from the beginning and desires its flourishing and good. In particular, Davies roundly rejects the idea that suffering and loving are synonymous. He is incorrect, though, in his view that the suffering God is simply 'passive' in the face of suffering; rather, the vulnerability of God, such as it exists, is one that is deliberately *chosen* in the name of that love. Moltmann and others use the idea of divine *kenosis* to describe the deliberate withholding of power in order to make room for the other in love; hence omnipotence is reinterpreted, rather than abandoned.[40] Davies affirms that God is involved in and cares about the sufferings of creatures, for he holds that 'he is with us in our suffering as nothing else is'.[41] But given this possibility, could we also enlarge on the idea of God suffering with those who suffer evil, be they human or non-human creatures? And what would such intimacy mean if we do not use the language of passibility? In other words, do we need the language of passibility in order to express the intimate love of God for vulnerable, suffering creaturely beings or not?

Mystery arguments
In the light of the above discussion I suggest that all attempts at providing an adequate theodicy, even those that draw in richer theological concepts of God's passivity from Christology or redemption through eschatology fall somewhat short. In such cases we need to remind ourselves of the apophatic tradition, one that admits that there is an understanding of God such that the workings of God are unknown or unknowable. Denis Edwards makes much the same point when he suggests that:

> suffering does not find any kind of full explanation in the Christian tradition, but is understood as a critical memory that calls for liberating and healing praxis and that opens in hope to a future in God; God is not subject to our limited human concepts but confronts us as incomprehensible and uncontrollable Mystery.[42]

Of course, as Edwards is well aware, too quickly resorting to this kind of argument would fail to grapple seriously with the issues in hand. An attempt, at least, needs to be made in the direction of ecological theodicy. Importantly, perhaps, theodicies that deal with the non-human realm invite a refocus on praxis, on theory informed by practices, as a way of mediating between more theoretical reflections and practical outcomes. He does this by employing a combination of arguments, particularly drawing on the work of Rahner, even while using the Mystery of God as the 'base' within which such arguments need to be framed. I believe he is correct to use mystery in this way as both the first and last word – he speaks more commonly of 'suffering', rather than 'evil' or 'harm'. Edwards also includes what I have termed the 'process' argument – that is, for the sake of the overall good of freedom in the creature, God's power is held back. So he suggests that:

> God's nature, as lovingly respectful of both human freedom and the finite limits of creation, sets limits on what God can do at any one stage in the history of the universe. The love that defines the divine nature is a love that lives with the process, a love that accompanies creation, sometimes suffering with it, promising healing and liberation.[43]

Yet it is hard to discern in here any sense of constitutive or ontological evil or suffering; rather, he, with Rahner, appears to name the resurrection as that which has ontological significance, rather than suffering as such.[44] It seems, then, that what he terms 'failures of creaturely processes' are unfortunate side-effects of creaturely processes of coming into being, rather than integral to that being.

Ethical (praxis) arguments

Perhaps in order to avoid the difficulties associated with too strong a focus on eschatological themes of redemption, and the uncomfortable split between theoretical and pastoral treatment of evil, Christopher Southgate has proposed that humanity needs to be actively engaged in prevention of extinctions.[45] By this he seems to mean active interventions by humans in the 'natural' processes leading to extinction that are found in the 'wild'.[46] He proposes that the vocation of humanity is not simply to be the 'priest' of creation in offering up the natural world, but as an intermediary in the process of redemption, humanity is actively involved in 'saving' those lives that otherwise would be lost. This gives an important ethical dimension to theodicy, in that evil is countered through pro-active human choices. One of the interesting aspects of this proposal is that the idea that humanity might actively intervene in the natural world for its good has historical precedents in accounts of the purpose of science in Francis Bacon and other writers of the seventeenth century. In this case, however, humanity was called to counter some of the negative effects of the Fall of humanity, becoming a 'co-redeemer'. The difference in Southgate's proposal is that he rejects the Fall as an adequate description of evil in the non-human sphere, and widens the basis for human activity so that the good sought is not just the good for humans. Taking inspiration from Romans 8, Southgate argues that humanity needs to relieve extinctions that he sees are intrinsic to Darwinian evolution. In this sense he is suggesting that we interfere with evolutionary processes. But how do we decide which extinctions to prevent and which to permit? Also, it strikes me that the rate of extinctions that are caused by anthropogenic evil is far higher than that caused by natural evil.

Hence, in order to tackle anthropogenic evil, we need to do far more than simply tinker at the edges of the process using our technology and science. Of course, programmes in zoos that attract much publicity to help 'save' those unfortunate species that are becoming endangered or extinct in the wild do offer some good. But we deceive ourselves if we think that we have the necessary wisdom and knowledge to intervene correctly for the good of the biosphere. Such has been the problem of models of 'stewardship' of the natural environment that presumes human management will be all-sufficient. I would therefore be more cautious about recommending such a strategy as integral to reflection on theodicy, for it seems to me to forfeit our responsibilities to face wider issues and problems in human lifestyles that are responsible for mass extinctions of species. In other words, too close attention to solutions through human endeavour can anaesthetise our sensibility to that suffering and dampen any sense of responsibility and guilt following from actions caused by human negligence and greed. In this respect, the link that Denis Edwards makes to practices in the light of suffering calls for a rather different interpretation of Romans 8.[47] For him the cross is a reminder of the suffering of the poor and resurrection hope is still informed by the memory of the wounds of the risen one. Above all he suggests that forms of liberating praxis develop following suffering, that is, they emerge in the context of a solidarity in suffering.

Shadow sophia

As a contribution to this debate, I suggest that all the above arguments need to be synthesised in a way that draws out the advantages of each position, while recognising their limitations. Many of those defending their particular view will argue against alternatives as a way of reinforcing their own position. Might it be possible to approach this issue more synthetically, rather in an analogous manner to the way wisdom draws together different perspectives and positions? Is there a theological way of expressing paradoxical statements, such as evil being both ontological and expressive of unreality, presenting an account of creaturely freedom, yet looking to the future? Theological antimony is not uncommon, and perhaps this also applies to consideration of evil. I suggest that one way of doing this is through reflection on 'shadow sophia', though this is intended to be a contribution through poetic symbol-making, or a cipher, rather than suggesting that such language amounts to any kind of meta-narrative about evil. What follows will also necessarily be somewhat speculative, though arguably no more so than other attempts at theodicy from a theological perspective. Although there is insufficient space to develop this to the full here, shadow Sophia is what the Russian writer Sergii Bulgakov calls the 'dark face of fallen Sophia'.[48] It is also important to emphasise the distinction between shadow sophia and Divine Wisdom. Shadow Sophia is an aspect of creaturely Sophia, not divine Sophia.[49] In fact, it serves to reinforce the contrast between divine Sophiaand creaturely sophia discussed in an earlier chapter. I would not wish to tie in the idea of shadow sophia specifically to the Fall, if by doing so this implies either that suffering in non-human creation is unimportant or that humans are directly responsible for *all* suffering in the natural world.[50] Literalistic interpretations of the Fall are not what Bulgakov intends either; rather, the Fall is a cosmic event that has repercussions both prior to and after the appearance of humanity. While human beings epitomised disobedience (sin) in the garden in a self-conscious way, the tendencies towards immorality were present long before, and seem to be constitutive of the possibility of creaturely sophia. It is only in this sense that shadow sophia has an ontological quality in that it is inherent in the nature of created being as creaturely sophia to have the opposite possibility present. Yet I would also draw back from an account of shadow sophia that implies that it was in any way *necessary* for creaturely sophia: the horror of evil must not be overlooked.

I propose that there are different facets of shadow sophia, just as there are different facets of creaturely sophia. The latter has a creative dimension, in that it is through the operation of creaturely sophia that the world comes into being, as recounted in Proverbs 8.[51] The biblical counterfoil to Lady Wisdom is Dame Folly, who epitomises shadow sophia as that which lacks the positive quality of Sophia. In the sense that shadow sophia is a lack in the positive quality of Sophia, it is a privation of the good, or expressive of the unreality of evil, as according to Aquinas. It is a lack of following the path towards goodness, understood in relation to the goodness of God and the needs of the global commons. On the other hand, it is also an expression of the freedom and free will inherent in creaturely sophia in that when sophia as practical wisdom or prudence chooses aright, there is always the possibility of the opposite, imprudence. With respect to more developmental models, the teleological goal in creaturely Sophia is one that hopes for eventual participation in divine Sophia; the goal is participation in the Wisdom of God, even if expectation for complete participation lies beyond the grave. Is the process of development also inclusive of shadow sophia? Certainly, if we see the meanderings of evolution as encompassing mistakes that lead to the possibility of 'higher' or more complex forms of creaturely sophia, then there is also the possibility of more intense expressions of shadow sophia in its wake. In some cases this might be the 'by-product' of growth in wisdom – the deeper the wisdom, the deeper the possibility for evil – and this is certainly evident in the human community, but it may also be a by-product of evolutionary change. Characteristics of humans or hominids, for example, that were perhaps useful in one context in early Neolithic times (such as consuming sugar) are now expressive of more negative characteristics of folly later on in human history. Human wisdom as such also needs to be viewed in its cultural context as that which expresses social reflection on learning, rather than as emergent directly from adaptive evolved capacities in the manner implied by evolutionary psychology. On the other hand, in other cases shadow sophia may express those tendencies that arise out of the process of development of creaturely sophia, and be an inherent part of this process, in that the learning of creaturely sophia understood as practical wisdom is always through experience, some of which may include mistakes.

Shadow sophia offers an account of evil that takes up, then, the different dimensions of theodicy, and gives them appropriate expression in both the non-human and human worlds. Since it is embedded in creaturely being as such, it is present to all creaturely being, not just humanity, even though its eventual expression in the human community can be viewed in moral and ethical terms. Is shadow sophia helpful if it encompasses so many different dimensions of evil? I suggest that here is its particular strength, for it reminds us of the limitations of all types of theodicy, and seeks to offer a synthetic account of what evil might entail, while remaining qualified as to precisely what it represents – shadow sophia, like wisdom more generally, is deliberately elusive as far as clear definition is concerned – for it cannot be tied down to one particular form of reasoning.

As a counterpart to the cipher of Sophia, shadow sophia is a dark cipher of the opposite tendencies latent in all facets of creaturely being and becoming. The difference between this and some other ontological models is that shadow sophia, while in one sense created by God, it is not inherent in divine Sophia and exists as a latent possibility in creaturely sophia. It represents, perhaps, the depth of kenosis expressed in creaturely sophia; as Word and Spirit it both allows for creaturely becoming, and gives free space to creaturely being.[52] The enigma of the sense in which God as Spirit and Word is both involved in evolutionary and ecological process, yet remains distinct from them, finds expression in kenotic categories. In the eschatological future, shadow sophia will be revealed as such, one that is no longer included in the eschaton. Yet ultimately the role of shadow sophia, the why of its existence, remains unknown, just as full knowledge of divine Wisdom is outside the boundary of human knowing. It is here that words reach their limit and human language is reduced to silence. In the face of the countless slaughtering of the innocents, as some have described mass extinctions of species, shadow sophia only goes so far. It is less a rationale than a way of coming to terms with the presence of evil.

Moreover, the weight of shadow sophia is born by Christ on the cross, the wisdom of God, so an explanation of its meaning needs to take on christological dimensions. Christ's creating, atoning and reconciling work discussed in the last chapter in cosmic categories now includes that which has gone awry in the creation of the world and finds expression in shadow sophia. Rational agents, in as much as they exercise moral choice, can choose to walk the way of creaturely sophia or shadow sophia, so that human responsibility for sin remains. In as much as the Christian community enters into the suffering of Christ, it also takes on the suffering that is included in shadow sophia and bears its burden along with that of the Redeemer. In as much as the Christian community shares in the creative work of creaturely sophia it points the way towards an eschatological future. Yet we need to tread very carefully here, in full recognition of the inadequacies of human wisdom to meet these challenges.

Conclusions

How far can it be said that theodicy is adequately conceived in the light of evolutionary and ecological suffering? Certainly, given the complex relation between moral, natural and anthropogenic evils, finding appropriate strategies to deal with such evil has proved particularly difficult and in many respects ultimately unsatisfying. Nonetheless, clarity about the different strategies that might or could be used in developing arguments are helpful in as much as they show why some scholars are drawn to particular ways of dealing with evil. Process arguments merge with theological discussions of eschatology, though both have the danger that present suffering may not be properly acknowledged. Possibility arguments permit evil in order to make something good allowable, and while this works reasonably well for free will choice in humans, it does not deal adequately with many practical cases of innocent suffering, and it is even less satisfying in the non-human realm. Classical arguments that speak of the unreality of evil do not seem to acknowledge the full negativity that evil entails; in other words, there is more to it than simply the absence of the good. Ontological arguments also do not really justify evil as much as simply describe its presence as a fact of the natural world. Ethical arguments may be more positive about the role of humans, but ultimately can slip into hubris or a lack of adequate appreciation of the anthropogenic harms caused by human beings and the capacity for human sinfulness. I have suggested that while all these explanations are ultimately unsatisfactory, the cipher of shadow Sophia as a means of theological symbol-making at least has the advantage of taking up threads from the different approaches to theodicy and offering a way of seeing evil so that it is both a created reality, but is distinct from the Wisdom of God, who acts through creaturely sophia in the creation of all that is. Moreover, knowing that shadow sophia penetrates right to the heart of the human condition means that approaches to ethics will be suitably modest.

Further reading

Adams, Marilyn McCord, *Horrendous Evils and the Goodness of God* (Ithaca, Cornell University Press, 1999)
Bulgakov, S., *The Bride of the Lamb* (Grand Rapids, Eerdmans, 2002)

Davies, Brian, *The Reality of God and the Problem of Evil* (London, Continuum, 2006)

Edwards, Denis, 'Why is God Doing This? Suffering, the Universe, and Christian Eschatology' in *Physics and Cosmology: Scientific Perspectives on the Problem of Natural Evil*, Nancey Murphy, Robert J. Russell and William Stoeger (eds.) (Berkeley, CA, CTNS/Vatican City, Vatican Observatory, 2008)

Hull, David, 'The God of the Galapagos', *Nature*, 352, pp. 485–6

Page, R., *God and the Web of Creation* (London, SCM Press, 1996)

Peters, Ted and Bennett, Gaymon, Hewlett, Martinez and Russell, Robert John, *The Evolution of Evil* (Dordrecht, Vandenhoek and Ruprecht, 2008)

Polkinghorne, J. (ed.), *The Work of Love: Creation as Kenosis* (London, SPCK, 2001)

Rolston, Holmes, *Science and Religion: A Critical Survey* (2nd edn, Philadelphia, Templeton Foundation Press, 2007)

Russell, Robert J., Murphy, Nancey and Stoeger, William (eds.), *Physics and Cosmology: Scientific Perspectives on the Problem of Natural Evil* (Berkeley, CA, CTNS/Vatican City, Vatican Observatory, 2007)

Southgate, C., 'God and Evolutionary Evil: Theodicy in the Light of Darwinism', *Zygon* (2002), pp. 803–21

Surin, K., *Theology and the Problem of Evil* (Oxford, Blackwell, 1986)

Ward, K., *Pascal's Fire* (Oxford, One World, 2006)

Chapter 10

Ecology and Spirit

REFLECTION ON THE ROLE AND PLACE OF THE SPIRIT in ecological terms is perhaps one of the most difficult areas of Christian theological reflection, but also potentially one of the areas that are most fruitful for discussion. It is difficult because the traditional restriction of the work of the Spirit, understood as the Holy Spirit working exclusively in the human community, has engendered a counter-reaction through attempts at recovery of animist notions of the Spirit as being equally and universally identified with creation itself. Some authors believe that we need to resist any doctrinal claims for the work of the Spirit, and speak instead of the task of theology as rhetorical performance; hence only those versions of the Spirit that serve to promote such change are appropriate today. Yet it is hard to maintain such a position consistently, and others have turned instead to pre-modern, classical modes of thought in order to develop their understanding of the Spirit. Above all, especially in the context of the Christian community, it is important to perceive the work of the Spirit in Trinitarian perspective. This chapter will seek to review some of these alternatives, and also argue that figuring the Spirit as the Wisdom of God relieves at least some of the difficulties encountered.

The Creator Spirit

Traditional discussion of the Holy Spirit perceived the work of the Spirit as that involved in redemptive activity – most particularly, the redemption of humankind. Yet such notions of redemption tend to be world-denying, and lead to unhelpful detachment from the concrete history of nature that ecological theology tries to redress. In the light of the discussion of a wider appreciation of the cosmic Christ discussed earlier, a cosmic rendition of the work of the Holy Spirit is equally in order.

The involvement of the Spirit in the creation of the universe takes its cue from Genesis 1:2, which speaks of the Spirit as hovering over the waters. Other passages also speak of the importance of the Spirit as life-giving, including that given to human beings in Genesis 2:7. The view that life is sustained only by the presence of God's Spirit comes through in passages such as Job 33:4 and Psalm 104:29–30. Jürgen Moltmann describes creation as 'a fabric woven by the Spirit' and 'a reality to which the Spirit gives form'.[1] Yet he believes that in order to distinguish this view from animist notions of the Spirit in all created beings, the starting point for understanding the Spirit must first come from theological reflection on the experience of the Holy Spirit in the Christian Church.[2] For this he names three modes of the Spirit's action, namely the mode of being born again in the person of faith (2 Cor. 5:17); the overcoming of natural and social divisions in the community (Gal. 3:28); and the individual vocation of each person through the Spirit's endowment of gifts (1 Cor. 12). Moreover, all such actions of the Spirit point to eschatological fulfilment, which is one that includes the cosmos as a whole. Moltmann extends these modes of the Spirit's action in the human community to that in the creation as such. First, he argues that the Spirit is the 'principle of creativity on all levels of matter and life. He creates new possibilities ... In this sense the Spirit is the principle of evolution.'[3] Secondly, the Spirit is the 'holistic principle', creating harmony and cooperation and community. Thirdly, the Spirit is the 'principle of individuation', bringing together the apparent opposites of self-assertion and integration along with self-preservation and self-transcendence. Fourthly, the creation is one that is open to the future.

The link between the experience of the Spirit, or *pneuma*, in the human community and the Spirit of life and creation serves another purpose in Moltmann's argument, for he believes that this reveals the common structure of the Spirit in creation, so that 'What believers experience in the Holy Spirit leads them into solidarity with all other created things.'[4] Moreover, the idea of the self-emptying and self-withdrawal of God through *kenosis* is crucial for his understanding of the Spirit as one who identifies with the suffering in both the human and creaturely communities. Hence, in some way the suffering history of the created world is bound up with the suffering Spirit, but it is the same Spirit who is able to transform such suffering into what he terms 'a history of hope'. He believes that this link to shared suffering prevents this understanding of the Spirit becoming too romanticised. Moreover, he argues for *panentheism*, God containing the world, which is a view that for him is capable of distinguishing different degrees of manifestation of the Spirit of God in different created beings.

Moltmann also holds to the traditional notion of God as Creator of all that is *ex nihilo* – that is, out of nothing. Such creative power of God is achieved through the work of the Spirit; the Spirit is not created, but emanated or 'breathed forth' by the Creator. The Spirit's work is not over after this initial creative phase, for Moltmann insists that the Spirit continues to indwell creation, likening this to the Jewish experience of *Shekinah*, the empathetic and loving indwelling presence of God in God's suffering people.[5] He also argues that the Spirit is more than simply energy, for the Holy Spirit is a divine subject, alongside the other divine subjects, the Father and the Son. Yet such indwelling presence of God in creation is not, according to Moltmann, simply the sustaining of a creation that was brought into being at the beginning. This classical doctrine, he suggests, needs to be revised in the light of the prophetic tradition that allows for the new, that allows for the possibility of liberation. Hence, it is both *creatio continua* and *creatio nova*, and, in anticipation of the final glorification of creation, *creatio anticipativa*. In this sense God's action through the Spirit is one that both preserves and innovates. The Spirit is also involved not just in the work of creation, but in the work of redemption as well. The two movements are distinguishable in as much as the first could be seen as the Spirit at work primarily in relation to the Father, while the second could be seen as the work of the Spirit primarily in relation to the Son. In other words, just as the immanence and transcendence of God can be appreciated through an acknowledgement of God as Trinity, both the creation and redemption of the cosmos are joined through an understanding of the Spirit in a Trinitarian way.[6]

Moltmann has succeeded where other theologians have failed in widening out the scope of discussion on the Spirit to include creaturely existence that is other than human. Ruth Page, among others, speaks of the relationship between God and creation, referring to a world companioned by God, in pan-*syn*theism, but describing what have traditionally been attributes of the Spirit to God. She suggests that this is necessary in order to get round the problem of a distant God having to 'send' the Holy Spirit in order to be present to the world.[7] However, such an image of a distant God sending the Spirit is unnecessary if we think of the Spirit in a Trinitarian way. Moltmann's work is pioneering in this sense, and has served to inspire a generation of scholars in both ecological theology and liberation theology. By beginning with what is known of the work of the Spirit in the human community, he warms the reader to his approach, for such discussion is relatively uncontroversial. His extension of the Spirit's work in creation as the source of creativity, as the source of cooperation, as the source of individuation and as the source of openness to the future, reflects a common experience of the natural world by human beings. The question that needs to be addressed, however, is how far his writing actually deals effectively with creation as such. His starting point for discussion of the work of the Spirit in the human community opens up a bridge with more traditional narrowly conceived views of the Spirit as acting in the human community, but it tends to limit the attention paid to the created world. His major book, *God in Creation*, subtitled *An Ecological Doctrine of Creation*, seems to focus more on questions about God and origins of the universe, rather than ecological existence.

Describing the work of the Spirit as the 'principle of evolution' noted above also lands him in some difficulties, given the propensity for suffering through Darwinian interpretations of evolutionary processes. Moreover, his idea of the Spirit as the source of cooperation could usefully have engaged with com-

plementary views about evolutionary change that stress symbiosis and cooperation among living things, rather than Darwinian notions of competition
and survival of the fittest. He does approve of Gaian imagery in this respect,
but how this fits with Darwinian views of nature is left vague. He seems to
shift away from a close identification of the Spirit's work with Darwinian
process in his later book, *The Way of Jesus Christ*.[8] Here he criticises
Teilhard's identification with evolution by naming evolution as not just
creative, but also 'cruel'. His solution, and one that he also hinted at in his earlier work, is to identify both Christ and the *Shekinah* with the suffering of the
natural and human communities. He still acknowledges the work of the Spirit
in the creative movement of evolution, but he speaks of it in the following way,
by suggesting that 'Here the creative energy of the ground of the whole
cosmos can also be theologically perceived. The process of creation is not yet
finished.'[9] But then, he acknowledges that evolutionary progress also comes
with its victims, and the only identification that Christ can have is with its
victims, so he can claim that 'Not even the best of all possible stages of
evolution justifies acquiescence in evolution's victims, as the unavoidable
fertilizers of the future – not even the Omega point, with its divine fulness.'[10]
He therefore speaks of the 'ambiguity' of evolution.

The question left unanswered is how the Spirit of God is *both* a principle of
creation, presumably through evolutionary processes, and united with Christ
in the suffering victims of evolution. A hint at a way through this dilemma
seems to be Moltmann's understanding of the creativity of God as being related to the final redemptive history of the universe, where the future impinges
on the present rather than emerging from evolutionary history. The final future
of the universe is cosmic incarnation, and it is in this light that he can name
the Spirit as the Spirit of Creation. He argues, then, that evolutionary processes stand in need of redemption, but then this raises once more the question
of what is meant by the creative work of God's Spirit in creation or how
evolution is connected, if at all, with this work.

The difficulties raised above may be one reason why some other authors
strongly object to the close connection between Trinitarian theology and ecology.[11] Günter Altner, for example, unlike Moltmann, puts much more weight
on the evolutionary and ecological aspects of the created world. In a manner
somewhat similar to Moltmann, he describes the natural world as an open
system, but the common evolutionary origin impinges on his valuation of the
natural world. For him, as in Schweitzer, all life has equal value, but humanity is placed in a particular position in relation to the world because of its
capacity for knowledge.[12] Instead of Trinitarian sociality, which he regards as
having little meaning for secular reason, he prefers to focus instead on the
eschatological interpretation of the cross.[13]

The Spirit of creation

A question that is worth asking is, going further than Altner, how far *any* doctrinal formulations of the Holy Spirit are tenable today in the cultural climate of postmodernity. Such a climate will resist doctrinal formulas and argue that greater account needs to be taken of the context in which human communities develop their understanding of God. Mark Wallace argues that all we can hope for are 'fragments' of what the Spirit might mean, and such fragments are useful in as much as they deliver a performative dimension, one that actually seeks to change and transform positively for another's good the way people think about themselves in relation to each other and the natural world.[14] His work bears some resemblance to Moltmann in drawing parallels between human violence and that in nature, and the need to view the Spirit as identified with victims, leading to liberating praxis. The difference is that he sees no need to adjust his understanding of the Spirit in creation based on the way he perceives the Spirit acting in the human community; in other words, the action of the Spirit in the latter seems equivalent to that in the former.

Wallace suggests that the Spirit is best thought of as a wild bird of the mountain wilderness, one who challenges the domestication of earlier concepts and brings healing in its wings. He believes that in the light of our lack of awareness of dependence on all other creatures and the interconnectedness of biological existence, we need to part company with any theology that seems to distance human beings from the natural world. Hence, rather than the differentiation that Moltmann accepts, he stresses the need for radical identification of the Spirit with all life forms. He suggests that we need to recover a sense of the 'Holy Spirit as a natural, living being who indwells and sustains all life-forms', so that the 'Spirit is a natural being who leads all creation into a peaceful relationship with itself'.[15] How is earth distinguished from the Spirit? He answers this question by viewing the Spirit as 'the unseen power who vivifies and sustains all living things, while the earth is the visible agent of the life that pulsates throughout creation'.[16] He accepts Gaia as the visible agent of the earth, while the Spirit is her inner, unseen power.[17]

Like Moltmann, he views the suffering of the earth in mutual relationship with that of the Spirit; the difference lies in his more positive affirmation of animist nature spiritualities. He believes, in other words, that we need to shed all traces of anthropocentrism from our understanding of nature, making a 'full turn to a biophilic earth spirituality that figures all life, including the divine life, as interdependent'.[18] This means that ecocide, the death of nature, brings not just suffering to the Spirit, but *deicide*, the death of God. He believes that the alternative to this view is a mechanistic one, with no inner spiritual life. Such a contrast strikes me as far too stark. While his revisionary paganism[19] is bold in its transformation of traditional categories of the Spirit, we might question if such a shift really represents what he terms a 'viable biblical and theological response to the prospect of present and future environmental collapse'.[20] It is certainly possible to love the natural world and befriend it without necessarily removing the distinctions between living things, or viewing the Spirit's presence in the natural world as 'a natural living being', which implies ontological identity between the personhood of the Spirit and that of living creatures.

Wallace, like Moltmann, views the Spirit in Trinitarian terms, but is more inclined towards the Augustinian understanding of the Spirit as the bond of love (*vinculum caritatis*) between Father and Son. He then extends this concept of *vinculum caritatis* to the community of creation. Yet, given the status he wishes to give to the work of the Spirit, it is doubtful if the idea of the Spirit as the bond of love is really sufficient as a means of defining who the Spirit is, for such a view renders the Spirit as a more shadowy form, one that seems only to exist in relationship to the other persons of the Trinity. An alternative approach to Trinitarian relationships, and one that Moltmann favours, is to begin with the three persons prior to expressing their interrelationship and unity through the notion of mutual indwelling or *perichoresis*. Wallace argues that we need to view the Spirit as a healing, liberative force in such a way that it leads to mutual respect, friendship, and unity in creation. However, this view stems more readily from considering Eastern models of the Spirit, compared with a dyadic understanding of the Spirit emerging from the interrelationship between Father and Son.

Wallace reasons that unless we remove all distinctions between human beings and other living creatures, then those creatures remain ripe for exploitation.[21] But surely if we do not consider other creatures as in some sense 'other' or 'different', then we are failing to do justice to their own worlds and respect creatures in their own terms. I suggest, contrary to Wallace, that all creatures do need to be considered valuable in their differences, and that this difference should not become a means for exploitation, but rather a way of regarding the creatures in the natural world as mutual 'others', worthy of respect for their own inner life and *telos* that is different from that of humanity. Such a statement is based on careful study and acknowledgement of ecological relationships and distinctive behavioural attributes of different living beings. Certainly it would be inappropriate to name certain characteristics of humans as unique to our species, apart, perhaps, from our destructive tendencies that by far exceed those of any other living creature.

But real respect comes, I suggest, from paying attention to the way things are and acknowledging points of contact and dissimilarity. The Spirit is, in other words, expressed differently in different creatures, and the luminosity of that same Spirit is more obvious in some creatures than others. This is why I am able to use disinfectant with a clear conscience, while taking the trouble to pay special attention to the particular needs of my pet dog. Moreover, such distinctions do not mean that we need to erect barriers between peoples, or between persons and animals in the manner that Wallace fears. Rather, as in feminist thought, a greater mutual respect between men and women, and other

creatures who are different, comes from knowing and acknowledging difference, while respecting that difference as valuable, rather than conforming to
previous negative stereotypes. Can the Spirit necessarily be addressed as both
'thou' and 'it' in the manner that Wallace suggests, signifying a distinction
between personal and creaturely modes of being?[22] While I would agree that
the Spirit is in all life, and not all of that life is personal, identifying the
personhood of creatures with that of the Spirit seems odd, and is related to his
own sense that the Spirit seems to be tied into the individual and mutual relationships of different life forms. If instead, the first way of thinking about the
Spirit is as the third person of the Trinity, then the life of the Spirit is always
personal, but that life is expressed in different ways in different creatures.

Finally, Wallace sees the Spirit of creation as being not just that involved in
the creative life of the world, but also through suffering, so that such suffering
is interpreted through the Spirit as a cruciform Spirit.[23] For him, the suffering
of Jesus is related to the suffering of the sinful world, but the suffering of the
Spirit is related to the suffering of nature. For him, the Spirit is fully enfleshed
in the world of nature, even incarnate, just as the Word is incarnate in the Son,
Jesus. The consequences of this are twofold. In the first place, the incarnation
of God in Jesus is not a unique event, for all creatures are incarnations of God
through the Spirit. In the second place, the idea of the cosmic Christ loses its
force, so that Christ's suffering is that of the Spirit, and the Spirit is also one
who suffers in the world. This gives greater importance to the place of the
Spirit in theology over and above Christology. This comes through even
clearer by his adaptation of christological formulations of the two natures of
Christ to his understanding of the Spirit, only this time it concerns the relation
of the Spirit to the earth and the divine, rather than, in the case of Christology,
divine and human natures. In other words, just as in the case of the incarnation, the Spirit indwells the earth, and the earth enfleshes the Spirit.[24] This
view, attractive as it might be in reinstating the importance of the Spirit, seems
to separate the person of Jesus from creation, for the Spirit, rather than Christ,
seems to identify with the life and the suffering of creation, and the person of
Christ is separated from the work of the Spirit of Christ in the renewal of
creation.[25]

The Spirit of communion

Wallace's rediscovery of what he terms the 'pagan roots' of Christian faith is
a bold turning towards uncharted territory, at least within the claims of what
is termed Christian theology. Are there alternatives to this vision that are
equally sensitive to ecology? Other scholars have also looked back, but rather
than enter the world of paganism and its defence of the sacredness of all life,
they have instead sought to recover some of the earliest Christian teachings
prior to post-Enlightenment mechanistic interpretations of nature. Denis
Edwards draws on the fourth-century Cappadocian Father, Basil of Caesarea,

for his inspiration in reawakening the notion of the Spirit as the Breath of God who always accompanies the Word.[26] The fruitfulness of such a turn also relates to its potential for dialogue with Eastern churches, for Basil's writings pre-date the split between the Roman Catholic and Orthodox Church traditions. His views were grounded in the community life of the Church and his pastoral and practical responsibilities in it.

Basil developed his understanding of the Spirit at a time when many doubted the possibility that the Spirit could be thought of as divine and personal in a manner akin to the Father and Son in the Trinity. For him, the unity of the divine nature is the *unity of communion* between all persons of the Trinity. It is also a unity without hierarchical distinction, so that all three persons of the Trinity are honoured equally. The Spirit, as breath of God, draws creatures into communion with God. The Spirit gives life and also perfects all things, so that all things dwell in the Spirit and the Spirit dwells in all things. Such dwelling is not individualistic, but social, leading to empathy between persons. Edwards argues that the aspect of the Spirit as bringer of communion is vitally important, for it makes interrelatedness the essence of the way things are, rather than merely a trivial characteristic.[27]

Edwards uses Basil's conception as a basis for his own re-working of the idea of the Spirit as the breath of life in the natural world that echoes the Trinitarian communion in God. He includes the idea of the Spirit working through evolutionary processes and chaotic structures, so that 'the zone of the Spirit embraces the chanciness of random mutations and the chaotic conditions of open systems'.[28] He engages more thoroughly with evolutionary aspects of existence compared with Wallace, but similarly views the Spirit as 'wild and unpredictable'. For Edwards the Spirit is 'the immanent divine principle that enables an emergent universe to be and to evolve'.[29] Drawing on Basil, and in a manner analogous to Moltmann, he suggests that experiences of the Spirit in the human community point to authentic patterns of communion in all creation, leading into an open future. The dynamic, open ways in which the Spirit works are not according to traditional concepts of a pre-planned God-given 'design', but rather, 'Charles Darwin's evolution through natural selection and Ilya Prigogine's concept of new forms of order emerging at the edge of chaos in open "dissipative" systems'.[30]

Of course, the difficulty here is portraying *exactly* how the Spirit is working with evolutionary events, so that on the one hand the Spirit is thought of as in some way 'creatively empowering a world in process', but on the other hand it is a world that 'has its own integrity and proper autonomy'.[31] In what sense can we think of the Spirit as both energising events in the world, and yet giving the world its proper autonomy, unless, with Wallace, we assume that the Spirit is fully incarnate in each living creature – and how far and to what extent can the work of the Spirit really be identified with evolutionary processes?[32] Edwards seems to hint at this in his understanding of the Spirit as 'animating Breath' and 'immanent divine principle'. Edwards is also more traditional than

Wallace in acknowledging the work of creation to be that of both Word and Spirit.[33]

He also is able to complement the view of the Spirit as a vitalising principle with the idea of the Creator Spirit being present to each creature in love.[34] This is a very important idea, for it allows there to be a sense of interrelationship with each creature, thus distinguishing this view from the pantheism espoused by Wallace. It also allows some questioning of the suffering in evolution.[35] Moreover, while Edwards does speak at times as if he thinks of the Spirit as the energising principle of creation, he wants to distance himself from vitalism, the view that this principle could be discovered by science, so 'The Spirit is not to be understood as a physical force. The Spirit is a personal divine presence, closer to individual creatures than they are to themselves ... She is not a power accessible to science.'[36] The idea of personal presence is also important, for it allows us to think of the Spirit as not just an amorphous other, or even as a bond of love, for example, but as personal communion in a way that is entirely appropriate to each and every living creature, expressed eventually in human beings as one who is both grace-filled and self-conscious.

In order to fill out his understanding of the work of the Spirit in the processes of creation which allow the new to emerge, Edwards needs to turn to more contemporary theologians, for the early Church fathers had little understanding of evolutionary processes and emergence in creation. He draws on Karl Rahner to put forward the view that the new in creation is the work of God as 'active self-transcendence'.[37] The language that Rahner uses here is the language of God, expressed also in the person of Jesus who is both the self-transcendence of the universe, and the self-communication of God to that universe. Edwards' particular contribution here is to expand the work of Rahner so the language is more specifically related to the work of the Spirit, understood in a Trinitarian way.

Finally, Edwards suggests that we understand the work of the Spirit as one that overflows from the Divine communion of persons in ecstatic (*ek-stasis*) love. He follows Moltmann and other more traditional theologians such as Yves Congar in perceiving the Spirit as one who 'goes out' from the Trinitarian communion of love, and so can be understood as the principle through which God communicates with creation, expressing the dynamism and abundance of Trinitarian communion. An understanding of what this love means helps to solve the puzzle of how the work of the Spirit can be both empowering in creation, but also in some way linked with the processes of evolution mentioned above. For Edwards (and Moltmann) the power of the ongoing Creator Spirit is necessarily one that is self-limiting – that is, one that expresses the power of love in self-limiting ways. In this sense Edwards can suggest that 'The Creator Spirit relates with creatures in a compassionate, self-limiting love that respects each creature's proper nature and autonomy. The spirit works with kenotic power in every creature ...'[38] The concept of kenosis succeeds in allowing a notion of the Spirit in creation, while giving creatures and biological processes an appropriate autonomy. Of course, we are still left with the limits of language: how can the Spirit be thought of as really 'enabling' and 'animating' the processes of creation, while being profoundly 'self-limiting' in its love?

Creation set free

Jürgen Moltmann, among others, has appropriated the theme of liberation to the work of the Spirit, and this liberation includes the whole of creation. He suggests that the creation cries out for liberation from the 'destructibility of nature itself' and the 'progressive destruction of nature by human beings'.[39] The prayer for the coming of the Holy Spirit expressed in Romans 8:26 informed the work of the seventh assembly of the World Council of Churches, which met in Canberra in 1991 and also linked the coming of the Holy Spirit with the renewal of creation. Within the earliest period of Christian reflection on the Spirit, the Cappodician theologian Gregory of Nazianzus has also been appropriated in order to expand notions of the Spirit to include the whole community of creation. Sigurd Bergmann's *Creation Set Free: The Spirit as Liberator of Nature* reviews the work of Gregory of Naziansus, who was also a contemporary of Basil of Caesarea.[40] Bergmann suggests that such dialogue with ancient pre-modern writers can be useful for a number of reasons. Firstly, some of the philosophical issues that occupied pre-modern thought were eventually translated into modernity, so there is some historical continuity. Secondly, the way in which Gregory sought to transform the thinking in his world can provide both contrasts with and inspiration for present theological reflection.[41]

Gregory is similar to Basil in wanting to put emphasis on the social nature of God, and incorporate this into his understanding of the relationship between God and the world.[42] He also views the liberation of creation as being related to the development of sociality. Bergmann interprets Gregory as putting most emphasis on the work of the Son in creation and the work of the Spirit in its role as perfector and completer of creation, so that the Spirit is more particularly related to deification and redemption, even though both the Son and the Spirit work together.[43] For Gregory the beginning of creation is an expansion of the divine community, even though such expansion cannot be thought of as 'necessary' to the Godhead. There are some parallels, however, in that the unity of the Godhead is a unity of different persons, so the intention of God to allow the world to participate in the sociality of God also expresses a unity analogous to that existing in God.[44] The combination of unity through difference is important in his understanding of creation, but 'God is always the subject that connects and fits together opposing elements within creation, without himself being connected by nature with the creature, and without representing any sort of connecting link.'[45] This idea provides an important contrast with that of Wallace, who views the Spirit in purely *natural* terms. For

Gregory the unity of the created and uncreated natures is found only in the person of Christ.[46]

The difference between the movement of creation and that of the Spirit is related to the finiteness of creatures. Movement of creatures is relational, while that of the Spirit is completely free, or self-movement. For according to Gregory the movement of the Spirit is perpetual, eternal, without beginning or end, and independent of time and space.[47] The boundary existing between the created and the Creator is only applicable to creation, for the Creator is always 'efficaciously present in creation in free movement within the Spirit'.[48] Gregory also insists that the Spirit is much more than simply 'energy', for it also includes this capacity for self-movement. In this sense the Spirit can be described as one who 'fulfils, guides, sanctifies, deifies, consummates, creates, brings about, bestows life', but in such a way that created movement is not identified with the self-movement of the Spirit. In this view Gregory is insisting on maintaining both intense involvement of the Spirit in creation, without tying the work of the Spirit into the processes of the created world.[49] Yet at the same time, he also insists that God is the ground and initiator of all movement in the created world, so the movements of the created and uncreated are not unrelated, and all the movements in creation are dependent on their Creator. He also suggests that creatures that have movement and spirit can direct their movements either towards or away from God.

For Gregory, the Spirit creates life in the beginning, is constant in bestowal of life, and is orientated towards the future, so that the work of the Spirit is best thought of more as one that is constantly moving, and in this way is connected more with soteriology, rather than ontology. The Spirit is, further, the very presupposition of the world's beauty.[50] The material world is, in other words, in the first place fully permeated by the Spirit and preserves its life and being. A second stage of the Spirit's activity is *incarnational* in the community of believers. A third stage of the Spirit's activity is *liberating*, thus binding up the liberation of both humanity and the world.

Bergmann suggests that the ancient idea of movement can be translated into ecological concepts that describe both the patterns of relationships and the processes of exchange and change in ecological terms. He also retains a distinction between the forms of movement in God, and that in the world, so that God can be understood as coming from the future, from recollection of the past, and also from the present through cooperation. Like Wallace, he links his interpretation of God to specific practices, suggesting that the human theological task has three stages. The first one is to discern where movement is counter to the liberating movement of God. The second stage is to find practical ways through such discernment. The third stage is to imitate the liberating movement of God so that movements working towards evil become instead movements for the good.[51] Bergmann also sounds a note of caution: namely, that we cannot simply identify the spirit of evolution or ecology with the Holy Spirit – that is, we need to be fully aware of the apophatic principle of the self-limitation of reason, both with respect to the natural world and to God.[52] The Spirit is to be thought of not so much as a mediator between God and the world, but as the Triune God who acts in order to liberate creation.

Bergmann has helpfully pointed to the significant resonance between Gregory's work and ecological theology in the present context. The question that needs to be addressed is whether the liberating theme that he correctly highlights does sufficient justice to the work of the Spirit in creation – in other words, does he formulate theological reflection in such a way that the Spirit is understood as one that fosters a positive encounter with creation, as well as pointing to the work of the Spirit in redemption? By concentrating on the liberative aspects of the work of the Spirit, the latter seems to dominate the former.

The Spirit of wisdom

Many theologians have hesitated to identify the Spirit with wisdom, perhaps because the Holy Spirit is more often than not associated with the prophetic tradition, while wisdom is more often than not aligned with everyday reasoning or even secular traditions.[53] Wisdom, traditionally understood, could be thought of as a habit of mind, while the Spirit is associated with spontaneity. Yet there are biblical precedents for linking the Spirit and wisdom, just as there are biblical precedents for linking the Spirit with creation. In Exodus 28:3, the Spirit is associated with everyday activities; those making priests' garments, for example, are given the Spirit of wisdom. In Genesis 1:2 the Spirit of God hovers over creation, but this is parallel to the way wisdom is spoken about in creation in Proverbs 8:30. In wisdom 7:25–27, Wisdom is described as the 'breath of the power of God, pure emanation of the Glory of the Almighty'. In Wisdom 1:6–7 wisdom is linked directly with the Spirit, so that 'Wisdom is a spirit … The Spirit of the Lord fills the whole earth.'

Based on the earlier discussion, I suggest that Irenaeus' seeming priority of the Word in establishing creation and the Spirit in its perfection, reflected somewhat analogously in Bergmann's interpretation of Gregory's idea of the Spirit as liberator, places the Spirit in a secondary place chronologically in the creation account compared with the Word, so that the Word has priority over the Spirit. Instead, I suggest that we need to find ways to express the activity of the Spirit from the beginning as the creative source of life – as Edwards has suggested, the breath of life. How can we understand this breath? Of course, identifying the breath of the Spirit with love has some advantages in the sense that the movement towards creation in the beginning is a movement of over-flowing love. I am not suggesting, by drawing attention to the integration of the Spirit and wisdom, that love is not also present in the work of the Spirit. Rather, just as love is the defining characteristic of all persons of the Trinity, so too, wisdom is there in Trinitarian fashion, enabling each of the persons to act in appropriate ways.

Wisdom is associated not only with the Spirit, but also with the other two persons of the Trinity. In Irenaeus, the Father is the ultimate source of all created being, which is established through the Word, but the Spirit is there as the one who perfects creation through Wisdom.[54] Augustine also named Wisdom as being associated with all three persons of the Trinity.[55] By suggesting Wisdom as important to all persons of the Trinity, I am also alluding to the importance of perceiving Wisdom as the *feminine face of God*. This prevents femininity in God being confined to the work of the Holy Spirit as in traditional dogmatics, thereby marginalising its importance through association with feminine categories. Bulgakov's understanding of the Spirit as feminine conforms to this stereotype, describing the Spirit as the 'female Comforter', based on a Syriac translation of John 14:26.[56] Such an understanding can also incorporate the idea of mutual indwelling of all persons of the Trinity in *perichoresis*.[57]

Elisabeth Johnson's *She Who Is* argues for femininity in all three persons of the Trinity. She is unhesitant in her attribution of Spirit-Sophia as evident in all life forms, so that 'life itself with all its complexities, abundance, threat, misery, and joy becomes a primary mediation of the dialectic of presence and absence of divine mystery'.[58] Hildegard of Bingen reminds us of a rich plethora of images that can be used to describe the work of the Spirit in creation, from the life of life itself, to connectedness, to a burning fire, a guide in the fog, a healing balm, a shining serenity, an overflowing fountain and so on.[59] Johnson describes the work of the Spirit in creation as 'like a great mother bird over her egg', but one who is also continually energising the world, holding all the world together (Wisd. 1:7).[60] Like other authors, Johnson points to the renewing power of the Spirit's work in creation, but it is a power expressed through Sophia, Wisdom, so that 'Spirit-Sophia is the source of transforming energy among all creatures. She initiates novelty, instigates change, transforms what is dead into new stretches of life. Fertility is intimately related to her creative power, as is the attractiveness of sex. It is she who is ultimately playful, fascinating, pure and wise, luring human beings into the depths of love.'[61] But how are these natural, biological activities to be understood as specifically the work of the Holy Spirit and in what manner do they express the divine?

Bulgakov's distinction between creaturely and divine Wisdom may be helpful here, for it allows us to speak of the spirit of creaturely wisdom in relation to the Holy Spirit of Divine Wisdom when dealing with the difficult task of relating our human knowledge of the natural sciences and ecology to that of theology. The use of language reaches its limits here, for how on the one hand can we reasonably suggest that God's Spirit is actively present in all creatures, while on the other hand arguing that all creatures have their own integrity and autonomy according to evolutionary and ecological processes found in the natural world? If we argue for kenosis, often understood as the spatial withdrawal of God to make room for the other, does this really appropriate sufficiently well the idea of God sustaining the world?[62] Such an idea might give the impression that creation is no longer dependent on God, and in this sense I find spatial conceptions of kenosis unconvincing. How can we argue that the Spirit is the presence that leads to vibrant life in the world, while acknowledging that this life is also more often than not at the expense of other life, and ultimately death and suffering, leading to victims of predation, violence and evolutionary extinction through, for example, loss of habitat? If Divine Wisdom is the movement of God that Gregory of Nazianzus speaks about, then we reach an antimony that needs to be faced and acknowledged: God is both present as Wisdom in the natural world, and suffers with its suffering victims, but is not subject to transitory changes and contingency in the manner of finite creatures. Creaturely wisdom, on the other hand, is subject to such changes, and in as much as it echoes Divine Wisdom it fulfils its vocation to demonstrate the vestiges of God in the natural world as in a mirror of the Divine.

Bulgakov, however, shows that there is also one sense in which it may be possible to use the language of kenosis, but this is in relation to the fact that God has chosen to reveal himself in creaturely Sophia as both Word and Spirit. Bulgakov claims that:

> In the creation of the world this kenosis is expressed in the fact that the Holy Spirit, who is the fullness and depth of Divinity, diminished Himself to *becoming* in His revelation in the creaturely Sophia. In the Divine life, the Holy Spirit realizes the fullness adequate to this life and plumbs the depths of God by a unique eternal act. In creaturely being, the Holy Spirit is the force of being and giver of life, but, according to the very concept of creation, this being and this life exist only as becoming, that is, not in fullness but only in the striving towards fullness.[63]

This distinction between creaturely Sophia and Divine Sophia and their relationship to the Holy Spirit is very important, for it allows us to attest that the Holy Spirit is working in the natural creativity of the world, without identifying those processes with the Divine. In this sense Bulgakov can also suggest that 'The immeasurableness of Fullness is included in the measure proper to unfullness, which is inevitable for creation with its "evolution" and growth.'[64] The form that the kenosis takes is also the creative 'let there be' in creation, and Bulgakov names this 'natural grace'. Such natural grace accompanies creation from the beginning through to the final transfiguration of the earth. Moreover, by naming the natural grace of creation as natural, this work of the Spirit is to be found in the matter of the world, its material being. It becomes, he suggests, the precondition for sanctification of that matter, the reception of God's grace. He suggests that in as much as matter bears the imprint of creaturely Sophia, it is capable of receiving divine Sophia. Such reception is not, therefore, an 'intervention' of God, but a uniting of creaturely Sophia with divine Sophia, a deification of creation.

Conclusions

The role of the Holy Spirit in the processes of the natural world – specifically, how it is related to creaturely being and becoming – is an area that lends itself to careful theological reflection. Traditional theology has confined the work of the Holy Spirit to the experiences of grace in the human community. I have only touched briefly on this aspect in this chapter. Such consideration is an important aspect of theological anthropology, but falls short in that, on its own, it can serve to devalue the theological significance of creation as a whole. Furthermore, contra Moltmann, I suggest that there is room for consideration of how the Spirit might influence the human community as a *second* movement of thought – that is, once there is a deeper appreciation of the work of the Spirit in creation as such. These considerations are also relevant to human practices that seek to alleviate some of the damage inflicted on the environment.

There are various ways in which it is possible to reinstate the importance of the Spirit in a cosmic sense, as inclusive of both the human and non-human communities. Drawing on biblical and traditional texts, we can argue for the presence of God in creation through the Spirit, understood as the breath of God, one who gives life to the world. Once we see the work of God in a Trinitarian way, then it becomes possible to view creation as the work of the Trinity, including the Spirit. Moltmann argues that we need to find analogies between the work of the Holy Spirit in the human community and that in creation, though keeping the work of the Spirit within such boundaries is unconvincing for authors such as Mark Wallace, who argue strongly for a vital presence of God the Spirit in creation as the starting point of discussion. Wallace also believes that it is necessary to view the Spirit in pantheistic ways, as a wild bird, identified with natural, material being, if we are to respond adequately to environmental collapse. Ecocide becomes, in his scheme, deicide. However, if we tie God too closely into the life and suffering of the material world, what hope might we have for its renewal?

Denis Edwards is more traditional in this respect, arguing for the Spirit as the breath of God, but one who is committed, in love, to allowing the creation to be itself. Drawing on Basil of Caesarea, he argues for a Trinitarian view of the Spirit as the life-giving and renewing breath of Life, ever present in the universe as one who brings communion. Bergmann, similarly, argues for a recovery of the thought of Gregory of Nazianzus, finding his view of the Spirit as liberator of creation informative for contemporary discussion of both theology and ethical praxis. I have suggested that, drawing on Bulgakov, viewing the Spirit as Wisdom, Sophia, is also relevant, for it allows us to perceive the work of the Spirit through the dialectic of creaturely Sophia and Divine

Sophia. The kenosis experienced in this respect is not so much a spatial with-drawal, as a determination to allow creaturely Sophia to exist, to shape the world as informed by the Holy Spirit. The Sophianic interpretation of the Spirit's work is also thoroughly Trinitarian, for Sophia is common to all three persons of the Trinity. In addition, given that Sophia is a feminine term, it reminds us to interpret the work of the Spirit in feminine categories – Sophia becomes the feminine face of God. But how might we extend this discussion to include eco-feminist theology? The chapter that follows seeks to outline some of the issues relevant in this respect.

Further reading

Bergmann, S., *Creation Set Free: The Spirit as Liberator of Nature* (Grand Rapids, Eerdmans, 2005)

Bulgakov, S., *The Comforter*, trans. from Russian by Boris Jokim (Grand Rapids, Eerdmans, 2004)

Deane-Drummond, C., *Creation through Wisdom* (Edinburgh, T. & T. Clark, 2000)

Edwards, D., *Breath of Life: A Theology of the Creator Spirit* (Maryknoll, Orbis Books, 2004)

Johnson, E., *She Who Is* (New York, Crossroad, 1992)

Moltmann, J., *History and the Triune God* (London, SCM Press, 1991)

Moltmann, J., *God in Creation* (London, SCM Press, 1985)

Wallace, M., *Finding God in the Singing River* (Minneapolis, Fortress Press, 2005)

Wallace, M., *Fragments of the Spirit: Nature, Violence and the Renewal of Creation* (Harrisburg, Trinity Press International, 2002)

Chapter 11

Eco-feminist theology

FEMINISTS HAVE TAKEN WHAT MIGHT BE CALLED a leading role in active concern for environmental questions and issues. This is spurred on by the twin beliefs that not only are women historically associated with nature, but also cultural oppressions that have served to inhibit women through dualisms inherent in patriarchy, have also had a negative impact on humanity's treatment of the natural world. Some feminists are so convinced of the vitality of this connection that they have described eco-feminism as the 'third wave' of feminism. In a manner similar to liberation theology, feminist thinking puts most emphasis on *praxis* – that is, the active concern for the way more theoretical concepts feed into practices and vice versa. Yet political positions within eco-feminism vary considerably, from more conservative ones that speak of environmental concern through to more radical re-visioning of politics. This chapter will highlight not just the variety, but also debates within eco-feminist theology. It will also focus on Christian theology, rather than religion more generally or other religious traditions, even though this will inevitably narrow the limits of the discourse. Heather Eaton compares eco-feminism with an intersection of different roadways, a meeting place of activists, environmentalists and feminists, along with local and national groups.[1] The huge variety within eco-feminist thinking means that this chapter will also necessarily be illustrative rather than exhaustive in scope, and will focus particularly on the spiritual and theological aspects of the debates emerging out of historical and cultural critiques of social structures. Given the contextual nature of feminist thinking, there is also a conscious effort to think within the context of both environmental issues themselves, especially as related to women, and particular practices – in other words, ethics.

Eco-feminist spiritualities

Not all eco-feminists consider religion as fundamental to their concerns, but within eco-feminist theology there are debates about how God might be re-conceived. In particular, many seek to find an alternative way of expressing spirituality that, for traditional thinkers at least, is at the borders of what has been defined as acceptable from a Christian theological position. Given the number of examples of the way women are portrayed negatively in the biblical record and demeaned in the Christian tradition, it is, perhaps, not surprising that some eco-feminists have given up seeking inspiration in Scripture.[2] Some accounts of spirituality have reverberated in the writings of many other authors, even if there are differences in opinion in terms of content. Susan Griffin, for example, offers a poetic interpretation of the intense closeness between humanity and nature in her book *Woman and Nature: The Roaring Inside Her*.[3] Griffin traces the dualisms between soul–flesh, mind–feelings and culture–nature as the outcome of men being confronted with the terror of mortality. Instead of facing such mortality, she suggests that men oppress women and nature. Hence, for her, the solution is to identify with the earth in its mortality. The voice of nature that is joined with those of women becomes embodied and impassioned. Carol Christ welcomes ideas such as the Goddess, Earth and Life as symbolic of the whole of which we are part, so that the 'divinity which shapes our ends is life, death and change, understood both literally and as a metaphor for our daily lives'.[4] What is important to Christ is recognition that we are part of the cyclical process of life and death.

Such ideas have served to influence the way eco-feminist theologians have sought to develop a spirituality that engages with more explicit Christian theologies. Such writers are more often than not suspicious of the notion of the goddess, on the basis that this serves to reinforce the identification between women and the earth that is inherent in the patriarchy that is opposed. However, in general eco-feminist theologies have a different methodological starting point compared with traditional theology in that more often than not they begin with an earth-centred approach that then offers an analysis of tradition, rather than focusing first on tradition as such.[5] Rosemary Radford Ruether, for example, rejects those aspects of a goddess theology that promote religious practices without taking into account economic and social structures that have led to particular patterns of oppression. She is drawn to the new creation story of Thomas Berry, but weaves it into her version of a way of thinking about the earth as an interacting organism. In her book *Gaia and God* she seeks to stress the Judaeo-Christian covenantal theme expressed in an ethic of caretaking.[6] For her, Gaia represents the sacramental tradition – in particular, the cosmological presence of the divine in the natural world. Yet like writers such as Griffin, she is anxious to identify with the mortal processes of the earth, so that for her resurrection becomes interpreted in terms of the continuation of our bodily matter in future life forms on earth, leading to what she terms a 'spirituality of recyling' that is only possible once humanity has experienced a 'deep conversion of consciousness'.[7]

Mary Grey turns less to the covenantal and sacramental spirituality that is at the background of Ruether's analysis, but more to biblical prophetic themes so that they become sources of inspiration in what she calls 'an outrageous pursuit of hope'.[8] Like Ruether, she situates her discussion in cultural analysis, highlighting the culture of consumerism as of critical importance in fostering a culture where wants become needs, indirectly leading to exploitative attitudes towards the environment. Instead, she argues for a prophetic vision taken from Isaiah as a vision of flourishing, one that is inclusive of both people and planet, and one that does not split ecology from social justice.[9] She also suggests that Isaiah fosters an ecological wisdom, embedded in a liturgical context so that it becomes the source of change and renewal:

> The emphasis is on *Leitourgia*, the authentic work of the gathered community: a people who grieve, lament, give thanks, and at the same time work to free the land from the poison of pesticide, the long death of nuclear radiation and nuclear winter, and the injustice of being wrenched away from the ownership of indigenous peoples, with all the conflict and complexity that this means.[10]

For Grey, eco-feminist spirituality arises from the margins and out of the concrete concerns linking the devastation of the earth and the suffering of vulnerable people. This comes through even more clearly in her later book, *Sacred Longings*.[11] Here she argues not just for an alternative spirituality that is sensitive to the needs of the earth, but also for one that takes particular cognisance of the threats posed to human societies through globalisation. In particular, she argues that globalisation poses as an effective spirituality, a misplaced desire of the heart, that needs to be tackled through providing an alternative, one that re-educates desire. She uses alternative ways of communicating that appeal to the person as a whole – that is, reasoning combined with story-telling, along with parables and myths that are deliberately interlaced so as to appeal to the imagination and emotions. In this book she is more self-conscious in her tracing of particular sacramental traditions. Grey is also actively involved in a non-government organisation (NGO) that builds wells in India, and this practical experience filters through into the way she writes with both passion and conviction about the experience of Indian women in the lowest castes and their struggle for human dignity. In particular, she challenges her readers, who are likely mostly to be Western, to embrace a way of renunciation, simplicity and sacrifice. In offering an alternative spirituality this book succeeds in the possibility of appealing to those from a variety of religious perspectives. Like many other eco-feminist writings, it is more concerned with engaging with practical contexts and the challenges they pose, than with more specific theological analysis that tends to be more theoretical.

Of course, close identification between women and the earth is problematic for many writers, who believe that such views amount to an essentialist connection between women and nature that cannot be defended. It has set up a sharp debate within eco-feminist discourse as to whether women should be identified with nature or not. Stacy Alaimo has been strongly critical of such identification, for she suggests that while it sings of unity with nature, it un-wittingly widens still further the divide between nature and culture. To some extent I share her reservations. Alaimo writes: 'speaking for nature can be yet another form of silencing, as nature is *blanketed in the human voice*. Even a feminist voice is nonetheless human: representing cows as ruminating over the beauty of the mother–child bond no doubt says more about cultural feminism than it does about cows.'[12]

Other concerns about eco-feminist spirituality centre on the extent to which it is relevant only to Western middle-class women and out of touch with the real needs of those in the poorer communities of the world. Eco-feminists have sought to correct this tendency by concentrating on listening to the voices of those in the Third World.[13] Mary Grey's *Sacred Longings*, discussed above, has also taken into account this critique by consciously incorporating religious elements from religious traditions outside Christianity in the work of Mahatma Gandhi. Mary Ress has also described an emerging shift towards eco-feminism among Latin American activists who are committed to the poor and to the Christian faith. Some of these women are reluctant to give the label 'eco-feminism' to the shift in their understanding of the human and divine, since they 'long for a more adequate metaphor, a more poetic, authentic term that would also reflect the region's earlier cosmologies'.[14] There are other examples where an eco-feminist approach is explicitly unhelpful in some social contexts, and this issue needs to be faced. Although environmental problems affect women in a disproportionate way in most parts of the world, eco-feminism needs to be connected with specific practices. In particular, some societies show that women are not inevitably more nature friendly than men – as, for example, in the case of the farming people of the Mijikenda in Kenya, or women in highland Chiapas in Mexico.[15]

There is also a growing body of literature that begins from a discussion of social, political and economic issues. For example, in a special issue of the journal *Ecotheology* (2006) edited by Heather Eaton, the majority of the articles drew on fieldwork and social analysis of particular contexts where women were actively engaged in practical projects.[16] The contexts varied geo-graphically and culturally, from the poorest communities in Vietnam and China, to Pentecostalism in Mexico, through to student groups in the University of the Western Cape in South Africa. Although such studies were indebted to methodologies more naturally associated with religious studies, the contributions are important in broadening out the possible scope of meanings for the term 'eco-theology' as such, so that it is no longer strictly concerned with systematic questions, but encompasses issues from other disciplinary perspectives, such as social anthropology, development studies, gender studies and so on.[17] The grounding of such articles is perhaps illustrated by Sarah McFarland Taylor's commentary on the eating habits, rituals and lifestyles of the Roman Catholic religious (the 'green sisters') in North America.[18]

Another assumption in virtually all writing on eco-feminist theology and spirituality is that patriarchy is essentially linked to dualism, and that this dualism is a destructive way of thinking of relationships between men and women, along with God and humanity and the earth.[19] However, Gillian McCulloch argues that patriarchal patterns of relationships are not inevitably and essentially linked with all forms of dualism.[20] She argues for a more sophisticated critique of dualism that allows for distinction in unity in a way that is actually more in tune with other more recent strands in feminist thinking that speak of difference.[21] In other words, a socio-cultural critique of patriarchy need not necessarily go hand in hand with a primary critique of theological dualism and secondary associated pantheistic notions of God.

Models of God: the earth as God's body

Grace Jantzen's book *God's World: God's Body* and Sallie McFague's *The Body of God* have been influential not just as eco-feminist theologies, but also within debates in systematic theology.[22] Jantzen suggests that just as humans are embodied, rather than existing as detached souls and bodies, so God too is embodied in the world, and God's transcendence is analogous to that of human beings. Such an approach is radically different from interpreting God as Other as in much classical theology. She also believes that more intermediate positions (such as found in a panentheistic understanding of God in which God somehow bears the world in a way analogous to a mother bearing a child) put too great a distance between God and the world. For her, it is the universe as such that is expressive of the intentions and will of God. God as embodiment is costly to God in that God's power is self-limited by the desire to love. While notions such as the self-limitation of God's power are not unique to eco-feminism, Jantzen takes this up in a new way by incorporating the idea of God as feminine divine, especially in *Becoming Divine*.[23] Like many other feminist writers, she is strongly critical of dualistic tendencies that she finds in Western culture, believing that under such dualism is a desire to control, leading to controlling attitudes not just towards women and nature, but also towards sexuality, feelings and other races. She believes that the fear that underlies this dualism is fear of the body, which has some resemblance to Griffin's belief that such fear stems from mortality. She is explicit in her celebration of pantheism, so that 'instead of mastery over the earth which is rapidly bringing about its destruction, there would be reverence and sensitivity; instead of seeing domination as godlike we would recognize it as utterly contradictory to divinity'.[24] However, would such a change in attitude necessarily follow in the way she suggests? For her transcendence is related to the idea of becoming, expressed in the feminine divine. She believes that those who reject such a view express a fear of being swallowed up in the maternal womb, associated with a loss of boundaries. But are not some boundaries helpful in maintaining distinctions, as indicated above?

McFague, like Jantzen, argues for an embodied model of God that has implications for the way we think about the earth. Instead of viewing the earth through an arrogant eye, as if it were a machine that we then seek to control, she suggests that we need to pay attention to the earth, come in tune with that earth and become conscious of its vibrant subjectivity. Although she is conscious of the earth sciences and evolutionary theory, by giving the earth subjectivity this clearly moves outside this brief. For her, sin becomes a refusal to accept our place on the earth. The planet is a reflection of 'God's back' and the idea of the earth as God's body is deliberately metaphorical, so that we are 'invited to see the creator in the creation, the source of all existence in and through what is bodied forth from that source'.[25] God is spirit expressed as agent in a way that expresses deep connectivity. Hence her view allows for some distinction between God and the world, and thus parts company with Jantzen's more explicitly pantheistic approach. Yet we need to question how helpful the image of the body might be for an understanding of God in feminist terms. Bodies today become subjects that can be manipulated and altered through medical practices and technology; consumerism pressurises women to conceive of idealistic images of the body; cyberspace replaces the image of the body with a virtual world that is no longer subject to earthly constraints. All such cultural trends give bodiliness as such an ambiguity that then can overshadow any more positive advantages of such identification.

It is significant, perhaps, that McFague's later book, *Life Abundant*, focuses much greater attention on social and cultural issues of economics.[26] Like Grey, she is concerned above all with the culture of consumerism that dominates the Western world and its economy. However, she still holds to her earlier position of combining the agential and organic models through the panentheistic metaphor of the world as God's body.[27] Here she develops the idea of God's love as creator, liberator and sustainer in a way that is concerned with creaturely flourishing as such. For her, the glory of God expressed in the gift of life is concerned about the well-being of all creatures, including the way relationships are worked out in an economy. Hence, understanding the doctrine of creation is 'about God's total graciousness in the gift of life and total commitment to the life so created'.[28]

McFague also understands God as liberator in Jesus Christ as a continuation of that which finds expression in understanding God as creator. McFague turns her attention to Christology, believing that in its classical form it encourages individualism and 'spiritualism', by which she means a detachment from economic, political and cosmic concerns, which she believes is ironic in view of the deeper meaning of the incarnation as physical embodiment. Like Mary Grey, McFague argues for a prophetic and sacramental theology, but unlike Grey, McFague revisits Christology in such a way as to draw out these dimensions. Drawing out the notion of 'God with us', she suggests that an ecologically sensitive Christology centres on God as present with human beings as well as all other life forms. She believes, in particular, that the significance of Jesus is not so much in understanding who Jesus is in what she terms 'Jesusolatry' as in showing us what God is like. She suggests that it is the liberative and prophetic ministry of Jesus towards those who are oppressed that needs to be extended to all creatures, including the natural world. She seems to accept the idea that all of reality has a 'cruciform shape', so that 'Jesus did not invent the idea that from death comes new life'.[29] For her the sacramental dimension of Christology is both inclusive and embodied; the entire creation is *imago Dei*, rather than just human beings. She also believes, correctly in my view, that sacramental Christology also adds a vital ingredient for contemporary discussion, namely that of hope. Yet for her the resurrection is interpreted as symbolic of the triumph of life over death; Christ's resurrection is 'emblematic of the power of God on the side of life and its fulfillment'.[30] The question in this case is whether such hope, that seems to be interpreted as akin to natural re-growth, is sufficient to sustain us in the face of the terrible tragedies facing creaturely worlds. Yet she is also prepared to state that life for Christians is about a following after Jesus as incarnate; the resurrection expresses God's Yes to all that is for life abundant in spite of suffering and pain. This is a different model of salvation compared with the traditional atonement images of substitution and sacrifice. For her sin is not just individual misdeeds, as in much traditional theology; rather, it is the movement away from such flourishing, whether it be at individual or institutional levels. She is also critical of theodicies which she believes fret about how God could have caused or permitted evil, when in fact we have not faced adequately the extent to which human beings are involved in evils. She aptly suggests that:

> Whether we consider poverty and starvation, genocide, ethnic hatred and warfare, racial and sexual discrimination, greed and hoarding, species decline, deforestation, air and water pollution, land degradation, global warming and even floods, droughts and tornadoes, human beings are now responsible, directly or indirectly, to a lesser or greater degree – and some more than others – for all the above.[31]

Yet while acknowledging the full extent and breadth of human sin, extending beyond the human community, which is a view I share, how far does her christological model deal adequately with that sin? If Christ's resurrection is wedded to natural cycles of re-birth, in what sense is reconciliation achieved for the human or wider cosmic community, other than a solidarity in suffering and rising again? In her resistance to stark images of God as one who punishes the Son, as in some penal or substitutionary versions of Christ's atonement, she has moved away altogether from recognising the importance of atonement as such; Christology is reduced to incarnation, where, like Ruether, even the resurrection is resumed under the cycles of nature. We need, in other words, to find a way of expressing Christ's reconciling work on the cross that includes ecological and structural sin, without resorting to images of a brutal or un-loving God. This also need not include 'satisfaction' theories of the atonement, which implies that God somehow has to be placated or can undergo a change of mind – such a view represents anthropocentrism writ large. Yet in resisting penal or satisfaction theories, the theme of reconciliation should not be lost, but it is reconciliation sought in love and holiness, rather than anger. For with-out any reconciliation there can be little hope of redemption, unless that redemption is simply reduced to a natural process in the manner she suggests. Human history suggests that a natural recovery is rarely sufficient; instead, what is needed is God's grace working in creatures in order to restore relation-ships, and that grace is expressed in the Christian tradition through the wisdom of the cross.

Models of God: the promise of Gaia

An alternative way of identifying human beings with the earth without resorting to notions of the body as such is through exploring alternative systems that represent the earth in holistic ways. Anne Primavesi is an eco-feminist theologian who has drawn on the imagery of Gaia, but in a way that is distinctive compared with Ruether, for it draws explicitly on the scientific theory of James Lovelock that envisages the earth as a homeostatic self-regulating organic system.[32] Eco-feminists are generally suspicious about the merits of Western science – in particular, the oppression of women implicit in its practices in the Western world and through its colonisation of other cul-tures.[33] Yet this does not mean that scientific considerations are redundant, and Primavesi is among those eco-feminist theologians who wish to take science seriously. Primavesi's theology is also in tune with the wider contemporary shift in understanding the natural world as sacred. For Lovelock, Gaia is not simply a shift in thinking away from reductionism, though it is certainly this; it also reflects the idea of emergence, in which a whole behaves differently from the sum of its parts.[34] For Primavesi the language of Gaia is useful in as far as it allows theology to become translated into a scientific language in a way that she believes will make theology accessible to a much wider audi-ence.[35] I am in full agreement with her premise that constructive dialogue between science and theology can and must take place, with science providing insights into complex relationships with our environment and theology prob-ing into the reasons why our lives are validated by our religious beliefs. While she attributes to Gaia theory the role of increasing awareness of dependence on other species, much the same could be said of ecology in general. Like the philosopher Mary Midgley, Primavesi sees in Gaia a means of shifting Western consciousness away from individual competition towards co-operation, though she identifies particularly with the non-violent connected-ness normally associated with Buddhism. Yet she suggests that this particular interpretation of Gaia is not just significant ethically, for theology takes on the characteristics of Gaia and becomes 'another earth science'.[36] In particular it is an *embedded theology*, for

> Whatever we may say about our environment, or about God, will relate God, ultimately, to every process and organism seen within the evolution of life on earth. Seeing myself embedded there will affect how I speak about God.[37]

Primavesi, like McFague, finds much traditional theology too individualistic. She highlights the traditional Augustinian theological focus on the story of one individual, Adam, whose sin polluted the human race until the arrival of the one man, Jesus Christ. In other words, she suggests that the story of the human race has been limited to the story of fall and redemption, focused on the death and resurrection of Christ.[38] It seems to me that Primavesi is correct to challenge Christian dogma that claims either that human beings were created in a state of perfection, or did not evolve in the same way as other species.[39] However, does Christianity necessarily posit Jesus Christ as 'outside the flow of evolution' in the way she suggests? For her, Christ is no more unique than any other human life and in this sense he manifests the sacredness of all life. Yet the fact that theological tradition affirms the uniqueness of Christ's incarnation does not necessarily mean that it is *unable* to affirm the worth of all creatures in the manner that she quite correctly believes is necessary. McFague has, it seems to me, succeeded in doing just that by paying attention to Eastern religious traditions in her interpretation of Christology.

Primavesi intends to set up a contrast between what she believes is a damaging interpretation of Christianity and her own view that draws heavily on the idea of Gaia understood as connectedness. The language that she uses to describe our embeddedness is instructive. The particular boundaries around ourselves – that is, our body in relation to place, or our individual experience of coupling – are known as the *SelfScape*.[40] It represents personal subjectivity. Next we have *SocialScape*. As the name implies, this is suggestive of social interactions ranging from 'food to Internet access ... and includes language, ritual, sex, education, play, culture and religion', that affirm the scope of SelfScape in some respects, but curtail it in others.[41] Our *EarthScape* reflects a more general interaction with our environment, but different objects may have a different purpose for those with a different EarthScape. For example, a stone may be used by a crab for shelter, but by a thrush to crack open a snail, or by humans as a missile.[42]

However, Primavesi includes another dimension as well that echoes the intention of Mary Grey and other eco-feminists, and this is the *PoieticScape* – that is, the 'linguistic, poetic, intellectual, creative, imaginative and expressive dimension of our co-evolutionary environment: the place where we "make" and remake our images of ourselves and of our relationships and express them through various media.'[43] It is significant that she describes this as a fourth dimension that goes beyond the Self-, Social- and EarthScapes, for it links up with the idea of autopoiesis, which literally means 'self-making', that refers to a dynamic movement of self-renewal normally found within living organisms.[44] For Lovelock Gaia is an autopoietic system expressing a structural integrity between living organisms and their environment. For Primavesi theology understood in terms of the PoieticScape corresponds to the link between belief and practice.[45] More important, perhaps, she suggests that the PoieticScape serves as a reminder of the partial theological perspectives that we all bring to a discussion.

While it is clear that Primavesi's particular definition of PoieticScape allows for diversity, it is only very loosely connected with the autopoiesis of Gaia through the ideas of both co-evolution and emergence, in the sense that we have somehow missed giving full recognition to this particular 'field' or fourth dimension emerging from our other embedded relationships. Primavesi argues that a Gaian perspective moves us away from anthropocentrism to a more holistic understanding of our place from a co-evolutionary perspective.[46] However, for Primavesi autopoietic description is more than just cooperation, for she sees it as bringing together paradoxical ideas such as the fact that there is both connection, but also distinction between organisms and their environment. Importantly, she suggests that autopoietic language can serve to emphasise the paradoxical nature of relationality in terms of its competition/cooperation, as well as its autonomy/bonding, distinction/obliteration, dependence/separation and so on. This may be one reason why Primavesi can claim that PoieticScape allows for diversity, while at the same time suggesting that it draws on Gaian imagery. Yet in spite of such qualifications, it is the monistic tendency in Gaia understood as a single organism that may win through unless the metaphor is very carefully handled. In other words, we return to a question that has plagued environmental ethics. Does holistic valuing lead to an over-emphasis on the whole at the expense of individuals?[47] How far we can really cross between linguistic codes in a way that is in excess of the original meaning of the terms in the manner that Primavesi suggests is a moot point.[48]

Primavesi suggests that the appropriate theological response to a greater awareness of our embeddedness in the natural world is acceptance of life as a gift event, one that is sensitively aware of our creaturely dependence on all other life for our own existence, so that 'other species have not evaded or ignored the demands I make on them'.[49] The appropriate response becomes one of gratitude and sin is now violence against the earth community.[50] Primavesi also makes a distinctive contribution in the way her eco-theology points to ethical outcomes, so ecological justice and interpersonal justice are grounded in a particular view of the earth as sacred through the notion of Gaia. She insists that the unitary view of the earth as sacred counters the damaging theological apartheid that affirms the superiority of the human that she believes has contributed to environmental degradation.[51] Instead we see God as integral to the earth systems that she describes. Yet in a way that is not entirely clear, God is distinct from the earth as well. Hence, God is the 'God of the whole earth system: enchanting and terrible, giver of life and death, not separate from and not confused with the world and its sacred gift events.'[52] Yet how can God, especially God that draws on Gaian imagery, be 'not confused' or distinct from the world? Moreover, God as 'terrible', while being 'sacred', seems not only to deny the possibility of intimacy with God, but also the goodness of God, so that the future outcome of the God–human relationship is not secure. While I welcome her suggestion that humanity needs to be more aware of its biological and evolutionary origins, her conflation of God's being with the world seems to undermine her assertions about the real possibility for change. While process theologians can look to the promise of nature by exploring the cosmological context of evolution, such a dimension seems to be missing in Primavesi's version of sacred Gaia. Her implication seems to be that God is a Gaian Goddess, though for some reason she resists making an explicit identification of one with the other in the same way as other eco-feminist writers such as Rosemary Radford Ruether.

Osborn has suggested that one of the reasons why Gaia provokes such a strong reaction, either in its favour or against, is because it represents a particular archetype. According to Jungian psychology, archetypes 'tend to have irrational (or, perhaps more accurately, pre-rational) emotions associated with them – they tend to become objects of devotion (or vilification).'[53] Ruether identifies religious narratives of apocalypse, as well as classical narratives of sin and evil as taking hold of Western cultural heritage. Her alternative is to promote a sacramental and covenantal healing tradition, with Gaia *incorporated* into that vision. For her, as for Primavesi and other eco-feminists such as Carolyn Merchant, the archetype of the earth as a machine needs to be replaced with the archetype of the world as an organism. However, it is only some eco-feminist appropriations of Gaia that reflect the *maternal* archetype in the manner Osborn suggests.[54] Anne Primavesi also integrates her understanding of Gaia with her view of God, though she resists using the language of the goddess, or even suggesting that this is a 'female' voice of God. Primavesi is certainly aware of the patriarchal oppression of women identified by other eco-feminists.[55] However, her view of Gaia differs significantly from Ruether's in that it takes far more cognisance of the scientific understanding of the Gaia hypothesis and seeks to ground her understanding of theology in such science. Yet, as I indicated above, she feels free not to remain restricted to the language of science in reformulating theological models.

Lawrence Osborn suggests that the next step after attributing consciousness to Gaia is for eco-feminists to attribute to her a religious identity.[56] There are certainly examples of eco-feminists using the language of Gaia to describe the earth as a goddess. Charlene Spretnak, for example, rejects the idea that transcendence is the 'sky God' of patriarchy; rather she suggests that transcendence is the 'sacred whole' or the 'infinite complexity of the universe'.[57] The answer to the loneliness of fragmentation characteristic of modernity is to discover one's inner connectedness with all that exists, embracing both life and death, celebrating the erotic and sensual. While she seems to recognise that there are some difficulties in close identification between the earth and femaleness as such, she insists that the most important idea to retain is an understanding of the planet as a body, an organism. Yet this admission seems to contradict her call for a reinstatement of goddess spirituality.

Primavesi's view of theology as embeddedness in Gaia also has ethical implications. While she roots her ideas about theology in an understanding of Gaia as autopoeisis, it is the notion of connectedness that dominates. She also believes that Gaia supports non-violence and freedom from competition. While Ruether suggests that our attitude towards nature needs to be kindness, Primavesi argues that it should be gratuitousness – an awareness of our lives as a gift-event, reflected in a sense of deep dependence on the natural processes of the earth.[58] For Primavesi the ultimate basis for ethics is through consideration of the system as a whole, rather than distinguishing ourselves from other species in order to sanction violence against them. Hence a Gaian ethic for Primavesi is also an ethic of non-violence.

Yet I suggest that positive characteristics such as cooperation do not automatically flow from understanding the earth system as interconnected. Moreover, once we put the system as a whole as an adjudicator of other interrelationships, a different problem emerges, one that is associated with other forms of Deep Ecology as well. This is the tendency for holism to take on negative ethical dimensions, especially in terms of different individual species. If a particular life form does not contribute to the stabilising of environmental/climatic conditions, what reasons could there be for conserving it? The loss of such a species, including humans, might not seem particularly problematic.[59] For all the rhetoric of interconnectedness, the preservation of a particular kind of biodiversity is all that seems to be required.

It is even possible to use Gaia in such a way as to support negative environmental action.[60] The robustness of the system is such that negative environmental consequences of industrial waste are a relatively minor player in the overall scheme of the earth's history as a whole. This could encourage an irresponsible attitude to human activity, rather than its opposite. Rather than an ethic of Gaia, I suggest that a true sensitivity to all life forms comes through reflecting more closely on a *local* as well as a global level, and recognising fragility and capacity for change as part of the picture as much as the overall stabilising effects. How far these stabilising effects are coordinated at a planetary level is impossible to prove, given the current status of scientific knowledge. It seems doubtful that any kind of conscious or unconscious organism can be read into these stabilising effects, though I grant that such systems do include the biota as well as inorganic processes. Hence, the only real ethical lesson to be learnt from Gaia is the importance of trying to understand the whole, rather than just focusing on the individual components. Another difficulty with Gaian imagery that is also implicit in earlier models such as the world as God's body, discussed above, is that by putting most emphasis on the system as a whole, new versions of marginalisation can emerge.

Although not specifically focused on spirituality as such, Susan Hawthorne's book *Wild Politics* is particularly interesting as it counters such a turn to holism by a focus on local knowledge and local politics.[61] In other words, it lays stress on the importance of diversity at a local level – diversity that would be eclipsed by a Gaian model that would seek to preserve only those systems that were needed for the functioning of the whole. She also draws on the work of Vandana Shiva in her critical analysis of Western biotechnologies. For Hawthorne, the particular 'seeds' of Western culture that need to be challenged are universalism and separation. The diversity of equals that the latter engenders implies that context is no longer relevant. Instead, she argues that the 'wild' has to become the generating seed so that biodiversity rather than universalism becomes the inspiration for a culture. Although Primavesi's embeddedness stresses connection in a way that is not apparent in the Western models she is seeking to replace, the universalistic overtones in this and other accounts, such as the currently popular 'new creation story', or even forms of New Age spirituality that extract elements of the 'wild', could far too easily diminish the importance of the local, contextual elements. For Hawthorne wild politics is not the cultural voyeurism that picks and chooses elements from other cultures, but rather is a strategy for resistance in different local contexts. The wild also portrays the world as neither entirely knowable nor controllable. She is critical of concepts of God as being too universalist, along with science and Western culture in general. She is attracted to Hegelian thinking in as much as she sees the antithesis of resistance from diversity in response to the thesis of globalisation as leading to a synthesis of wild politics.[62] How such a wild politics might incorporate globalisation is not entirely clear. Like other feminists, she argues for *associative thinking* that engages with images, symbols and patterns of thinking as well as disassociative thinking that detaches from feeling. She believes that the problem that humanity faces is that cultures are under pressure to conform to the most powerful norm. An economy that took account of such issues would promote participation and acknowledge complexity so that 'place matters'.[63] Her vision that we should adopt the Aboriginal position in taking account of the future in the long term, understood as the next 40,000 years, seems somewhat unrealistic. Yet her critique of the privatisation of public spaces and practical suggestions about the specific issues connected with the patenting of life forms are well placed.

Models of God: the promise of wisdom

An alternative to Gaian imagery, but one that still allows for the use of imagination in constructing the way we see ourselves in relation to the natural world, is that of wisdom.[64] While in earlier work Primavesi identified Gaia and wisdom in the Hebrew Bible, this line of thought has not been developed in her later works on Gaia.[65] She argues that the concept of wisdom as that which is mediated through knowledge of the relationship between God and creation qualifies what human wisdom means. She argues that this is a mediating role of Gaia. But why call this Gaia? It seems to me that it is Wisdom/Sophia that has this mediating role – Sophia understood as expressed in the creaturely world as a whole, leading to a similar conclusion to Primavesi, namely, a challenge to all forms of human arrogance. Contrary, perhaps, to expectations, wisdom drawn from the classical tradition in theology can point to a more poetic way of perceiving the world, but is also one that encourages the habit of paying attention to the relational aspects of existence. Wisdom *per se* can serve to fill the gap that Primavesi identifies in our relationship with the natural world, by becoming more conscious of the wisdom of God as the feminine face of God manifested in the intricate community of all creatures and our kinship with them. However, unlike PoieticScape, wisdom is not simply an emergent property *within* nature, but rather is also given as gift from God, reflecting the Trinitarian community of persons, expressive of ultimate Wisdom. Instead of seeing the earth as divine in a pantheistic way like Jantzen, for example, the perspective of wisdom encourages those with faith to find in creation the marks of Trinitarian love. Wisdom, in addition, is not a romantic idealism that ignores the suffering of creation, for wisdom includes the wisdom of the cross.[66] Aquinas, too, believed that creation is an expression of God's wisdom, for 'Just as the universe is governed by divine wisdom, so everything was made by God's wisdom, according to the Psalmist, *Thou has made all things in wisdom.*'[67] His own view of a hierarchical universe created through a chain of being obviously needs some adjustment in the light of evolutionary biology. However, his notion that all life is both expressive of divine Wisdom, but at the same time that 'divine wisdom is the cause of variety in things' serves to emphasise the embeddedness of the action of wisdom in the creative processes of the world.[68] He also believed that all creation expressed the divine goodness; indeed, it was the *diversity* of creaturely existence that allowed the single goodness of God to be 'in creatures multiple and scattered'. Given such affirmation of creaturely goodness, any violation of creatures would be sinful. The place of humans is one of qualified responsibility due to particular powers given to humanity, rather than superiority.

Mary Grey has pointed to the fruitfulness for wisdom in generating an adequate spirituality. She suggests that our failure to perceive our own entanglement in consumerism is a failure of wisdom. Embodied wisdom is deep connectedness to the earth that, according to Grey, echoes the thought of

Susan Griffin.[69] Mary Grey is right to include within practical wisdom the idea that it is inseparable from the wisdom of ordinary experience, embodied in the lives of the poor and uneducated. Knowing becomes a subversive form of knowing, celebrated in the Eucharist, which she names as the feast of wisdom.[70] A perspective of wisdom would also be one that highlights the value of the local community and its wisdom, for wisdom is learned in the context of community and family life, while having a political dimension as well through political prudence. It therefore combines the local and the universal streams of thought and, in a manner akin to the wild in Susan Hawthorne's position, encourages lateral thinking 'outside the box'.

I have argued that Sophia (Wisdom) is a metaphor for eco-theology in that it is fruitful for thinking through how God may be perceived in an ecological context.[71] In the first place wisdom, like Gaian imagery, provides an important link between the secular and the sacred. The difference with Gaia is that wisdom is embedded in the Hebrew Bible and the New Testament – that is, it has roots deep into the particular Judaeo-Christian religious tradition. Wisdom would also include the possibility of Gaian science, but it is science *kept in its place as science*, rather than allowed to grow into a mythology beyond its original intention.[72] Wisdom is also identified with secular longing for knowledge, but it is a form of knowing that critiques claims for superior knowledge from one perspective, including reductionism in science, but also exaggerated forms of holism. In other words, wisdom acknowledges that the world offers insights into the nature of reality, yet looks beyond this to the divine ideal that criticises all wisdoms that are against the commandments of God. This juridicial role is not found in those eco-feminist theologies that simply affirm nature as such. It therefore resists forms of naturalism that suggest that we can automatically derive a good from what is, while being thoroughly grounded in the daily practical lives and tasks of ordinary people, men and women included. I am also critical of those eco-feminist writers who have used Sophia as a basis for Isis Goddess theology, for it seems to me that this detracts from the power of the symbol in Christian thought.[73] Such theologies are not helpful in that they identify too strongly with the earth in a manner analogous to other goddess imageries critiqued by Rosemary Radford Ruether and others.

Wisdom provides a means for reaffirming the feminine in the Trinity so that all three persons are considered the feminine divine, rather than femininity being exclusively confined to the Holy Spirit, as in much classical thought. With Elizabeth Johnson we can claim Sophia as *She who Is*, who shakes off previous stereotypes of femininity and patriarchy.[74] It provides a Christian image of God that is a corrective to those male images of God that have existed in the past, while drawing explicitly on biblical thought. I prefer to see the role of Sophia as transforming the way we think about who God is so that a feminine dimension is included in all three persons of the Trinity. Such a feminine dimension celebrates the complementary difference between masculine and feminine as well as common ground between them, and resists stereo-typing the female image to that which automatically is closer to nature, earth-bound and, by implication, irrational. Wisdom, understood in the manner I have indicated, also allows for a panentheistic concept of God, one that is Sophiological and is just as concerned with practical immanent expressions of wisdom as transcendent images of God as Holy Sophia. The Wisdom of God understood in a transcendent sense is, therefore, more than simply the sum total of those immanent wisdoms found in the world, in a manner analogous to reflection on the world as the body of God, especially in Jantzen's interpre-tation. Yet reflection on Divine Wisdom is also set in the context of our own experience of frailty and limited understanding, for the Wisdom of God is also the Wisdom of the Cross.[75]

In this sense Divine and creaturely wisdom allows for a clear distinction between God and creation that is resisted by some feminist scholars in the name of *all* forms of anti-dualism. In this sense it is important to distinguish between those distinctions that are helpful, and those that are harmful in terms of their impact on women. I suggest that the blurring of the difference between God and creation is unnecessary in the first place because there is no direct link between oppressive forms of patriarchy and retaining distinctions between God and creation. In the second place, just because God is distinct from creation does not mean that God is not involved with creation, as classic notions of immanence of God testify. There is no need to dispense with trans-cendence in the name of immanence in the manner that authors such as Primavesi suggest. In the third place, it is the failure of humankind to acknowl-edge its difference from God and its dependency both on God and on God as incarnate Wisdom and humble self-emptying servant that paves the way for other abuses of human power and authority. Those feminist scholars that have resisted christological images of humble service, claiming that they have been used to put women in their place, have failed to appreciate properly that the servanthood image applies to the human race as a whole, not just women. Such a servanthood image is also the appropriate attitude that humanity needs to take in relation to the wider creation at large. In the fourth place, set loose from any pattern of higher authority, humankind sets itself up as master and controller of nature, and controller of other groups, including women and mar-ginalised communities. Hence, what needs to be rejected in this case is not so much *all* distinctions, but the use of distinctions in order to oppress women, or stereotype the roles of men and women in particular ways, thus associating women with nature, and men with reason and so on. This is one reason why I argue for a retrieval of elements of the work of the Orthodox theologian Sergii Bulgakov, for although the explicitly sexist elements of his work need to be dealt with, including his priority of the work of the Father, for example, his sophianic vision of God offers a way of bringing the idea of the feminine into a transcendent vision of God, rather than reducing God to human visions of an idealistic de-patriarchal society.

Conclusions

The development of eco-feminist spirituality and theology has highlighted the tensions within eco-feminism as such. Some have been more inclined to stress the social, political or environmental elements in the plight of women, viewing the development of spirituality suspiciously as too theoretical to be useful. Others argue for a robust theology that also takes into account particular social and political aspects of thought, and in some cases, as in Mary Grey's work, emerges from within the context of activism on behalf of poor and marginalised communities. Attention to the way we perceive God and re-descriptions that take into account feminist and ecological concerns have become broadened to include economic and social agendas, as in the work of Sallie McFague. Some feminists believe that we should take our cue from science, since science has dominated the cultural agenda for so long in the Western world. An alternative way of practising science in Gaia that lends itself to ecological and holistic ways of thinking becomes for Primavesi a way of thinking theologically as well. It sets up powerful imagery that is strong enough to have influence not just within feminist circles, but outside these too. Although there are many merits to this model, there are drawbacks as well, given the implicit universalism that Gaia represents. An alternative approach that avoids the theoretical and political limitations of Isis theology is Wisdom, for Sophia can also be fruitfully grounded in the Judaeo-Christian tradition in a way that is helpful for thinking not only about God, but also about particular practices and ecological decision-making. Sophia also takes up the eco-feminist concern of seeking to provide alternative ways of thinking about the feminine and the divine in a way that, on the one hand, is closely connected to nature, but on the other hand, fully acknowledges differences. Yet eco-feminist thinking more often than not resists consideration of eco-eschatology, for it is grounded firmly in earthly practices. But arguably, eschatology is vitally important in furnishing Christian hope, not just for humans, but for the earth as well.

Further reading

Deane-Drummond, C., 'Sophia: The Feminine Face of God as a Metaphor for an Ecotheology', *Feminist Theology*, 16 (1997), pp. 11–31

Eaton, H., *Introducing Ecofeminist Theologies* (London, Continuum, 2005)

Eaton, H. and Lorenzen, L., *Ecofeminism and Globalisation: Exploring Culture, Context and Religion* (Lanham, Rowman and Littlefield, 2003)

Grey, M., *Sacred Longings: Ecofeminist Theology and Globalization* (London, SCM Press, 2003)

Jantzen, G., *Becoming Divine: Towards a Feminist Philosophy of Religion* (Manchester, Manchester University Press, 1998)

Jantzen, G., *God's World: God's Body* (London, DLT, 1984)

McFague, S., *Life Abundant: Rethinking Theology and Economy for a Planet in Peril* (Minneapolis, Fortress Press, 2001)

McFague, S., *The Body of God: An Ecological Theology* (London, SCM Press, 1993)

Mies, M. and Shiva, Vandana, *Ecofeminism* (London, Zed Books, 1993)

Plaskow, J. and Christ, C. (eds.), *Weaving the Visions: New Patterns in Feminist Spirituality* (San Francisco, Harper and Row, 1989)

Primavesi, A., *Sacred Gaia: Holistic Theology and Earth System Science* (London, Routledge, 2000)

Ruether, R. Radford, *Gaia and God: An Ecofeminist Theology of Earth Healing* (London, SCM Press, 1993)

Ruether, R. Radford, *Women Healing Earth: Third World Women on Ecology, Feminism and Religion* (London, SCM Press, 1996)

Ress, M. J., *Ecofeminism in Latin America: Women from the Margins* (Maryknoll, Orbis Books, 2006)

Chapter 12

Eco-eschatology

ESCHATOLOGY HAS TRADITIONALLY BEEN CONCERNED ABOUT 'last things' – what will happen at the last judgement, what kind of eternal future might be expected for believers and unbelievers, and so on. Contemporary theologians have pointed to the limitations of such a view, pointing out that hints of a new kingdom may be experienced now, in a 'realised' eschatology, through the activity of God's Spirit in the world. Jürgen Moltmann has even suggested that all theology should be in an *eschatological key*, the hope of the resurrection life pivotal in shaping expectations that are present both now and in the future.[1] An adequate eschatology is also particularly important in the light of the limitations of theodicy discussed in Chapter 9. But where should we begin? I suggest that given the awesome nature of the calamity that we are now facing in terms of potential threats and real threat to the environment, a starting point for theological reflection on eschatology needs to be that of the apocalyptic. Some care is needed here, however, for apocalyptic is not just a branch of eschatology, for the eschatological expectations embedded in apocalyptic traditions are diverse. Starting with apocalyptic traditions has the advantage of helping to situate eschatological discussions in the light of the signs of the times that we find in contemporary debate on the environment. In particular we will ask, in what sense might the suffering of the natural world be thought of as being redeemed through Christ? We can then move to a discussion of how the future of creation is expected in other scriptural traditions in a way that serves to paint a portrait of the future hope for creation. How far are we justified in naming the future hope for creation in the light of a cosmic Christology and reflection on the significance of the resurrection?

Apocalypse now: the ecological 'crisis'

Stories of gloom and potential disaster may immediately call to mind the apocalyptic strand in the Christian tradition, a strand that has habitually flourished in situations where the future seemed hopeless. Most notable among these is James Lovelock's recent book *The Revenge of Gaia*.[2] His personification of the earth is unabashed, for he believes that we need such metaphors in order to appreciate the significance of what human beings are doing to the planet. Here, instead of apocalyptic disaster happening in some far-flung future, he anticipates climate change triggering a quite literal hell on earth, 'so hot, so deadly, that only a handful of the teeming billions now alive will survive'.[3] While a popular understanding of biblical apocalypses is that they point to a future that is outside history, in actual fact 'their authors expected a vindication of their righteousness within the world of men, not in some intangible existence beyond the sphere of history'.[4] This is crucially important, for if the lessons of apocalyptic are interpreted as beyond this world, then it has negative ethical implications with respect to humanity's treatment of the earth. On the other hand, if the apocalyptic is seen as symbolic language that is relevant for the present, then its lessons may have some bearing on how to view the difficulties faced on earth aright and how to put such insights into practice.[5] One of the most significant constituents of apocalyptic literature is wisdom. This might seem surprising for us. A common understanding of the sage is one who expresses confidence in the order, harmony and balance of God's creation; while the seer seems to despair of order. How then is wisdom found in apocalyptic, and why might this be significant? According to the apocalyptic book of Enoch, the Fall amounts to a misuse of power and abuse of wisdom, manifesting on earth as abuse of women and corruption of creation.[6] This strand of apocalyptic literature also associates knowledge of the workings of creation with a vision of God, contrasting with the book of Job where such knowledge was inaccessible. The Fall, on the other hand, in this tradition, is associated with pride in such a way that knowledge itself becomes corrupting. Even in the apocalyptic literature of the Hebrew Bible, the contrast set up was to encourage a transformation in the present, rather than a dualistic separation of heaven and earth.[7]

It strikes me that an echo of this truth still reverberates in our present context of ecological calamity. On the one hand scientific knowledge of the way different ecosystems work and are interconnected can lead to a profound sense of awe, wonder and beauty reflected in natural wisdom. One might suggest it leads to the threshold of a vision of God, reflecting God, as it were, in the mirror of God's works. On the other hand our lack of appropriate use of science and technology through the project of modernity itself with its drive towards progress and consumption has led to an arrogant disregard for the natural world and its workings, putting us on the brink of ecological collapse. Human knowledge has itself become corrupting, as it has disregarded the wisdom that is implicit in the natural world.

What about the New Testament apocalypse? Perhaps one of the best-known examples of this appears in the book of Revelation. In this case wisdom is revelation. The secrets of the end time are revealed, but for a purpose, so that action can take place now. In Revelation 5:12 and 7:12 hymns are sung to the throne of wisdom, but only God and the Lamb are worthy to receive wisdom. Sophia is personified as Mother of the Messiah, the Son of Man and the Spirit. But just as the book of Genesis finds its distortion in more literal interpretations such as found in creationism, so the book of Revelation should not be interpreted literally. Rather, the sea monster and earth monster are not supernatural powers, but political powers that will ultimately be overthrown. The vision of the Woman in the Sun may be interpreted as the Church, or, more commonly in Orthodox or Roman Catholic theology, as the Virgin Mary. The final goal of creation is one that is redeemed through Christ, and Mary, the Mother of God, anticipates the Wisdom possible in all of creation, but Mary also becomes the icon of the glory of the wisdom of all creation.

Revelation 21—22 clarifies still further the importance of Christ as one who inaugurates 'a new heaven and a new earth'. Should we take this to mean a literal disappearance of the present earth so that 'there is no longer any sea' (21:1)? This is extremely unlikely, given the symbolic language of the book of Revelation. There are also hints at a connection with the first creation. Here, just as Adam and Eve represent the dawn of human existence, rather than being literal figures, so the disappearance of the sea described in Revelation is symbolic language for powerful and chaotically disruptive forces at work, overall the new coming out of the old, God removing sin and chaos. In addition, the description of the tree of life hints once more at the language of Genesis and thus seeks to instil the idea of a paradise regained, but it is also a paradise that is *transformed*. The river is symbolic of the continuing presence of the grace of God, and the tree of life is for the healing of the nations. The tree is inaugural of the blessing for all, rather than a curse, as in the Genesis account. Christ as Alpha and Omega implies that what he has begun in the creation of the world will be brought to completion. The encounter with God in Christ face to face also serves to remove all doubt about the future. His name on their foreheads implies that there are none who are unknown or unloved; all have an accepted dignity and identity in the new heaven and earth. The word used for 'new' here is *kainos*, meaning 'new' in terms of quality, rather than *neos*, 'totally new'.[8] Perhaps 'renewed' is the more appropriate term in this context.

Margaret Barker is one of the few biblical scholars who argues that the newness described here *is* a radical departure from the old after the end of time, believing that the prophetic tradition that speaks of total annihilation is also present in other passages in both the Hebrew Bible (e.g. Jer. 4:23–26; Ps. 102:25–27) and the New Testament (e.g. Mark 13:31; 2 Pet. 3:10).[9] Clearly, the way we interpret such passages will be crucial to an understanding of the continuation or otherwise of the created, material world. It is important to face the possibility that the book of Revelation might imply a total destruction of the earth, rather than project our own concerns onto the passage at hand. Yet, it strikes me that Stephen Smalley is on safer ground when he suggests that the whole of Johannine theology *associates* heaven and earth, rather than trying to split them apart. The closest analogy here is with the resurrection event itself, so that there are lines of continuity and discontinuity.[10] In addition there are some parallels with the idea of a new creation in Christ described in 2 Corinthians 5:17. There is no sense of a completely new body; rather, the newness is related to the spiritual life of the believer which, understood holistically, may, of course, also have bodily impacts, but it is the same body that is renewed. Also, if the creation was annihilated, this would seem to suggest that God's creation had somehow failed, even though Christ is the 'first born' of all creation and the purpose of creation is fulfilled in the Son.[11] Other passages in the New Testament which speak of a 'burning up' of the earth, such as 2 Peter 3:3–13, also make most sense when compared with the story of the Genesis Flood account. In this the elements that are destroyed, such as the sea, are those principles that work against the will of God. God is portrayed as one who cleanses evil, laying bare the earth, with a connotation of rediscovery, rather than replacement. Moreover, the sea did not disappear because it was in itself evil, but because in Hebrew thought it represented the deceptive nature of evildoers, so that its removal symbolised the unity of humankind and its security in a transformed creation.

Expectant reality: the groaning of creation

In order to ground the vision of redemption described in the book of Revelation in the reality of this worldly suffering, we need to consider once more the meaning of the suffering of Christ and Christ's atonement. This is not so much a theodicy – that is, seeking to explain in rational terms why the world suffers the way it does even though God is also declared good; rather, it is a way of reshaping theological thinking so that it is inclusive, rather than exclusive. I am also interpreting atonement to mean more than just the reconciliation that is possible in spite of human, moral sin. Of course, perhaps it is as well to be reminded of this, given the human propensity to greed and over-consumption that underlies much of the strain in the carrying capacity of the planet. Rather, atonement means 'at-one-ment', a right ordering of relationships that is achieved paradoxically through Christ's own descent into suffering, death and hell. This last element is not always appreciated, or it is diffused through a re-description in existential language in order to express the horror of Christ's sense of abandonment by the Father.

However, perhaps a contemporary understanding of hell could include the abyss that lies beyond extinction – what philosophers have sometimes described as 'horrendous evils'.[12] Hans Urs von Balthasar has written graphically of Christ's entry into hell on Holy Saturday. He suggests that the purpose of theology that reflects on this moment is the 'realisation of all the godlessness of all the sins of the world, now experienced as agony and a sinking down into the "second death" and "second chaos", outside of the world ordained from the beginning by God'.[13] Christ's solidarity in this sense goes deeper than simply mortality; for it enters into that space that humanity fears most. Although von Balthasar did not extend his theology beyond the human community, a fear beyond that of simple mortality for non-human species would be that of extinction. Moreover, it is in that descent that Christ is most able to 'become the ascent of all from the same depths'.[14] The logic of such a movement is one that expresses the deep love of God for all creation, and it is consonant with the sentiment of Colossians 1. Yet, I think that von Balthasar is correct to resist the idea that the passage from death to life that Christ shows in his own death and resurrection is just one example of that renewing principle found on earth. Rosemary Radford Ruether suggests as much in her interpretation of the resurrection as a kind of 'recycling'.[15] Rather, the scandal of the cross remains, for it is a unique event, more than simply symbolic of what happens on earth. In this we can say with von Balthasar that

> The redeeming act consists of a wholly unique bearing of the total sin of the world by the Father's wholly unique Son, whose Godmanhood (which is more than the 'highest cast' of a transcendental anthropology) is alone capable of such an office.[16]

Although von Balthasar may not have had ecological issues in mind, his concept of 'total sin' also, in the light of earlier discussion, needs to include anthropogenic sin as well as the breakdown in relationship with God that is the root of the breakdown of all relationships. The weight of natural evil, even though it is perhaps improperly called 'sin', is also borne by Christ, and it is in this sense that Christ is 'victim', along with other 'victims' of evolution in the manner that Moltmann suggests.[17]. Yet Christ is not just victim, for Christ reconciles as well as bears the sins of the world. In this way, the redeeming and reconciling act encompasses evil beyond the human community.

But what is the relationship between redeemed humanity and redeemed creation? For this we need to turn to Romans 8:19–23, which speaks of the 'groaning of all of creation'. It is worth repeating it in full here:

> For the creation waits with eager longing for the revealing of the children of God; for the creation was subjected to futility, not of its own will but by the will of the one who subjected it, in hope that the creation itself will be set free from the bondage to decay and will obtain the freedom of the glory of the children of God. We know that the whole of creation has been groaning in labour pains until now; and not only the creation, but we ourselves, who have the first fruits of the Spirit, groan inwardly while we wait for adoption, the redemption of our bodies.

Although early commentators sometimes restricted the meaning of such verses narrowly in terms of the human community, this is less likely in contemporary scholarship. Cranfield comments that 'Paul sees the whole splendid theatre of the universe, together with all sub-human life within it eagerly awaiting the time when the sons of God will be made manifest in their true glory.'[18] He suggests that the freedom that is proper to the created order will only be experienced when the children of God are glorified; while humanity is still in disgrace, the whole of creation suffers accordingly. The allusion is to the Genesis text where the earth becomes cursed through Adam and is subject to decay because of human activities. The frustration is present 'not of its own choice'; in other words, it is not a latent aspect of creaturely being as such, but inflicted because of human activities. Just as the ground is cursed through human activity, so also is the possibility of sharing humanity's liberation. The eager expectation is, according to James Dunn, rather like an audience eager to see the way humans play their part on a world stage.[19] This passage is particularly relevant in terms of the anthropogenic effects on the natural order that have been variously described in terms of an ecological crisis, even if Paul did not have such a compass in view at the time of writing. Of course, mortality as such came long before human beings entered the world, but it is the additional frustration caused by human activity that is noted here. It also implies that where human beings turn towards their future glorification, then the healing of human–non-human relationships becomes possible. Human futility is that lack of realisation of dependence on God. Disappointingly, Dunn suggests that the purpose of the restoration of creation is that humanity can have a 'fitting environment';[20] though there is nothing to suggest that such a goal is narrowed to anthropocentric gains in this way. Sustainability is often talked about in such language – namely, for the benefit of future generations – in a way that truncates the needs and interests of creatures as such. Interestingly, the background to this passage is likely to be apocalyptic – that is, it is shaped in the context of belief in an ordered, but precarious creation. It seems to me that Romans 8 is supportive of a cosmic understanding of the Holy Spirit, rather than a cosmic Christology. It is through the Spirit that the suffering of all creation comes to be identified with Christ's death and through the Spirit that creation finds hope in Christ's resurrection. The difference between Jewish apocalyptic and Christian hope is worth reciting again here. The expected 'turn of the age' does not just take place at the end of history, but as Moltmann notes, already begins in the midst of this world.[21] But what might this mean in theological terms?

Moltmann's vision of hope: the redemption of nature

In theological terms Jürgen Moltmann has urged us to distinguish between what he terms *futurans* and *adventus*.[22] In the former, *futurans*, the future just emerges out of the present. There is a continuous line with the present, and our projections into the future are based on what has happened in the past. This is the method of science: we predict based on what we know and have experienced. On the other hand *futurans* is about a breaking into the present from the future – the idea that the present anticipates in some way the future that is to follow, for it is a foretaste of a transformed reality. But what form does the breaking into the present take and how might we understand it? The scope of the Christology in Colossians 1:15–20 speaks of all of creation as being caught up in the redemption wrought in Christ. Instead of seeing the catastrophic end of the world as bringing in the second coming of Christ, rather, Christ's coming inaugurates a new beginning, even in the midst of chaos. The fear of disaster is the reverse side of hope for the future, so there is, according to Moltmann, 'no hope without fear'. By this he means that even in hope we are aware of the opposite expressed in calamity. By comparison, the reverse side of fear is not hope, in other words, hope includes fear, but fear does not necessarily include hope. Apocalyptic thus keeps hope real in the sense of reminding it of what is being hoped against. He suggests that with the advent of modern science, it was hardly surprising that theologians withdrew consideration of redemption from the natural world and restricted it to human history. Yet without cosmology, eschatology becomes a 'gnostic myth of redemption', separating humanity from its material ground in creation that is paradoxically also attested to by modern science.[23]

Moltmann also suggests that creation should be understood in the light of redemption, not the other way round. This is because if creation takes priority, then redemption would just amount to a restoration to a pristine state. On the other hand, if creation takes its place in the context of the creation of a history of God's will which is only consummated when God will be all in all, then redemption arches beyond simply restoration to earlier origins. The second position also makes more sense in the light of evolutionary theory. For if redemption is simply restoration of prior perfection, then we might expect to find that perfection in history. There is no evidence whatsoever that this is the case even prior to the emergence of humans. Hence, the idea of a future new heaven and earth is one that reaches out beyond present or past.[24]

Moltmann suggests, further, that the sabbath itself points to this future consummation, so that the beginning is always more about what it might become, rather than what it presently is. In other words, future hope is about the renewal of all things, rather than their restoration. Moltmann works out how this happens through his idea of the Shekinah, the presence of God. For him,

> sabbath and Shekinah are related as promise and fulfilment, beginning and completion … In the eschatological Shekinah the new creation takes the whole of the first creation into itself, as its own harbinger and prelude, and completes it. Creation begins in time and is completed in space.[25]

He also relates the sabbath and Shekinah through the rest found in God in the sabbath of creation. It is here that we find the 'eternal bliss and eternal peace of God himself'. The Church, it seems, acts as an anticipated place for this expectation, for in the forgiveness of sins comes the hope for a new creation where God will dwell universally. For him, the future hope is one that is implied in Orthodox theology, namely that the whole earth will take up the divine image and become the *imago Dei*.[26]

Above all, Moltmann sees a close correspondence between this world and the next, so that

> This earth with its world of the living, is the real and sensorily experienceable promise of the new earth, as truly as this early, mortal life here is the experienceable promise of the life that is eternal, immortal … Love for Christ and hope for him embrace love and hope for the earth.[27]

Yet at the same time this new earth will no longer suffer under the contingencies of time and space. For,

> The temporal creation will then become the eternal creation, because all of created beings will participate in God's eternity. The spatial creation will then become an omnipresent creation, because all created beings will participate in God's omnipresence.[28]

Such a transition means the end of mortality as such, but all times will be caught up into the time of eternity, taken up into the aeon of the new creation. He envisages here a 'final moment' which echoes the first 'primordial moment' in the beginning. It is a time that is the very opposite of where creation has come from; it is the transformation of 'deathlike silence' to 'eternal livingness'.[29] In this sense the cosmic *perichoresis* that he envisages takes up both eternity and time so that they exist in mutual relation, for this God has to *restrict* his eternity so that it is possible to speak of a 'time of eternity', and *restrict* his omnipresence so that room is made for creation through divine withdrawal. Moltmann has already laid out the case for divine withdrawal in order for God to be the Creator of all that is.[30] Now this same kenotic theology is taken into the end times, the culmination of eschatological hope. While in some respects this way of speaking about God offers a systematic solution to the problem of relating God and creation, its speculative nature begins to cast doubt over its likelihood. More promising, it seems to me, is Moltmann's insistence that the future will be one that is marked by both holiness and glory.[31] Yet how holiness might be understood to be 'politically, economically and morally' in the time of eternity is particularly hard to envisage, for that would suggest not just a measure of material continuity as in resurrection faith, but a continuity in the structures of society as well. He goes on further to suggest that:

[the] glory lies in the unfolding of the divine splendour and its in-exhaustible beauty ... The light that shines through everything is a visible sign of the all-interpenetrating presence of God, and of the perichoresis which does not destroy created beings but full-fills them. The countless and multifariously bright reflections of the divine light show the richness and the eternal participation of created beings in the present glory of God. The holiness and glory of the eternal indwelling of God is the eschatological goal of creation as a whole and of all individual created beings. This gives cosmic eschatology a theological dimension and an aesthetic one.[32]

Although Moltmann has sometimes been accused of being influenced by Hegel's philosophy, he is keen to distance himself from Hegel's ideas when it comes to reflecting on the final future in God. For Hegel, there can be 'nothing new', for even a reconciled world is not a new world.[33] This is important, for if we think that reconciliation is already possible in this world in its entirety, then this can give rise to forms of justification of suffering on the basis of expected reconciliation. A parallel exists in some interpretations of evolutionary suffering, as discussed above, for if that suffering is seen as somehow necessary for the process, it implicitly endorses that suffering as justified and thereby acceptable. Instead, Moltmann urges a Trinitarian understanding of the future in the light of the resurrection. Here death is overcome and life is imperishable, eternal life. Moltmann draws particularly on an Eastern Orthodox approach to resurrection here: *charis* is that life drawn from the fullness of God, not simply the reconciliation of sinners. Such transformation is also the beginning of the transformation of the cosmos, so that 'the risen Christ ... draws all things into his future, so that they may become new and participate in the feast of God's eternal joy'. Further, it is expressed through the 'cosmic liturgy', a 'universal Easter laughter' that includes the rejoicing of all created being.[34]

Given that the future that Moltmann envisages is a thoroughgoing deification of the cosmos, what might this mean for individual creatures? How does it work out in practical terms in relation to the countless victims of evolutionary extinction and those extinctions resulting from human activities? Moltmann's theology does not deal with this question thoroughly, but there are in places hints at what he envisages. For example, in *The Way of Jesus Christ* he suggests that:

If Christ has died not merely for the reconciliation of human beings, but the reconciliation of all other creatures too, then every created being enjoys infinite value in God's sight and has its own right to live; this is not true of human beings alone.[35]

This passage, however, seems to refer to the reconciliation of creatures here on earth now, rather than in the new aeon that he calls the 'time' of eternity. It is also not clear how this reconciliation experienced now through the cosmic scope of Christ's redemptive power will actually impinge on non-human creatures here and now. Does he really mean that all of the natural world in some way finds redemption on earth? It is hard to envisage for non-human creatures his view of the Christian community, who, through the work of the Holy Spirit, lose any sense of the power of death over them, and so experience a foretaste of redemption. He seems, rather, to express this as a 'right to live' as being of worth in God's sight. But do we really need a theology of *redemption* in order to express this? Would not the incarnation suffice?

Yet Moltmann also speaks of Christ's resurrection as the 'embodied promise for the whole creation' that is then spelt out more explicitly to include all evolved creatures; this is the 'divine tempest of the new creation, which sweeps out of God's future over history's fields of the dead, waking and gathering every last created being'.[36] Moreover, it is a future for nature where, as for humanity, 'death will be no more', so that 'with vulnerable human nature the non-human nature of the earth is transformed as well', leading to its 'eternal healing'.[37] Moltmann also believes that in the new earth humans will still depend on the earth for food, air, climate and so on, arguing that if this were not so, then this would be a 'gnostic' interpretation and an 'end to the earthly community of creation in which human beings live bodily and practically'.[38] But is this suggestion, along with the suggestion of the literal resurrection of all creatures that ever lived on earth, coherent? In the first place, if the earth has any resemblance to our experience in the present, there would not be room for such a literal resurrection of all creatures that ever lived – the community of creation could not be sustained on this basis. In addition, if, as he suggests, death is no more in the context of redeemed nature, then how can there possibly exist bodily dependencies which rely on death, such as that which informs an ecological food chain? Furthermore, it all depends on how one might envisage the new earth as to the extent to which the redeemed life is 'gnostic'. I suggest that it is a transformed earth and one that is cosmic in scope, but how far and to what extent the same conditions prevail as in our present experience is quite simply outside the boundary of human knowing.

How might we envisage the ultimate future of nature?

The question that needs to be addressed is, in what sense might we envisage the future of the earth, in as much as we are justified to speculate on the redemption of nature? While I agree with Moltmann that nature – that is, the natural world as inclusive of humans and non-human creatures – will in some sense be redeemed together, what might be entailed in that redemption requires further reflection. Understanding biblical hope as a peaceful restoration of creation in covenant relationship in the manner of Gerhard Liedke does not help matters in this respect, for it still does not express lines of continuity and discontinuity, except in as much as the community envisaged at the end changes from one of conflict, to one of reconciliation and peace.[39] Ernst Conradie, for example, suggests that the natural world finds its ultimate future through focusing on continuity in the creative love of God, 'in the faithfulness of God to the beloved creation'.[40] He approves of Moltmann's emphasis on the Holy Spirit as a way of linking Christology and eschatology. But how might we symbolise what happens in the redemption of nature? Conradie draws on the process theology of Whitehead, who introduced the concept of 'objective immortality'.[41] By this he means that all events, embracing all cosmic and creaturely events, are 'inscribed' into history in a way that will make a difference to the future, including the long-term future. Everything, including what has happened in the cosmos, becomes 'inscribed' into the 'mind' of God.[42] This inscription takes place in the consequent nature of God and for this reason has 'objective immortality'. Other theologians have taken up this idea of the cosmic memory and described it in terms of an active organic process – reorganising, perhaps even through love changing the way something is remembered. John Haught, in particular, suggests that creation in its suffering also becomes taken up into divine existence, and thereby experiences salvation.[43] Conradie suggests that one of the difficulties with objective immortality is that it no longer gives creation independence. I suggest that independence is not as important as the fact that identity seems evacuated by such remembering; would I really *want* to become just a memory in the mind of God? Authors like Ian Barbour have tried to overcome this by suggesting that there is also a form of *subjective* immortality,[44] but in what sense is this subjectivity real if it seemingly exists in God's memory? This problem is not really overcome by Conradie's similar belief that panentheism avoids some of the difficulties associated with this view. He suggests that we exist now 'only' in the mind of God, for this is what participation in the life of God means, and as such, this participation continues after death for both humanity and the earth through God's loving memory.

He also draws on the idea of cosmic pilgrimage, a sense of the whole journey of the cosmos being caught up into the future with God. But how might this take place? For this he develops the idea of inscription, which seems to be a modified version of the 'objective immortality' of Whitehead. He suggests that 'The history of the cosmos, this cosmic pilgrimage, is *inscribed* in the eschaton.'[45] He imagines that the inscription that takes place during our life history is like the writing on two sides of a cube; only in the eschaton will this take on additional dimensions, and thus gain 'depth'. He suggests that such inscriptions are permanent, so that

> Once this inscription has taken place, it can never be obliterated, not even by an omnipotent God. Eternity does not imply the annihilation of time. Nothing that is past can pass away ... This inscription will be completed when the history of the cosmos finally comes to an end (*finis*).[46]

This view has many advantages in ecological terms. In the first place, it is a reminder that what happens here on earth will have consequences in the future, so that earth's journey is one that is vital not just for now, but also for the future that is to come. It implies an ethic of responsibility, so that, 'Through caring for the earth now, the building materials for the new earth are now being gathered.'[47] He is also aware that this view does not deal with the Christian hope of forgiveness adequately, so for this reason, he suggests that what happens in time will be judged in the light of God's loving, healing and indwelling presence. This includes the hope for the earth, so, according to our own consciousness, is sanctified in the presence of a holy God, and remain in the eschaton through an unlimited capacity for healing and forgiveness. Clearly there are dangers in this move as well, for such unlimited capacity for forgiveness in the future life seemingly after death might encourage a lack of responsible action now, even though this is not what he intends. Furthermore, while he has hinted that human life will be *conscious* life, which therefore implies some sort of bodily resurrection, this is not normally how the notion of inscription is understood; in other words, the latter seems more impersonal rather than personal. In addition, if it is the conscious personal self that is raised, how will this also take place for myriads of species that have no experience of consciousness? This model of inscription seems to work best for non-human species, for there is a sense in which, as long as the new earth includes a memory of their existence, the individual raising of each and every creature that ever existed no longer seems to be of such vital importance. In Jürgen Moltmann's most recent book on the practical experiences of hope in the resurrection, there is, perhaps not surprisingly, relatively scant attention paid to the redemption of the cosmos. However, it is significant that he does also seem to endorse the notion of inscription, for he claims that

> the history of creation is etched into his memory and preserved for its consummation in the eternal kingdom of his glory. In the restoration of all things, everything that happened in sequence in the progress of time will be present in the eternal moment. It is only then that what God promises in Rev. 21:5 can come to fulfilment; behold I make *all things new*.[48]

In this respect he seems to hold onto his earlier suggestion that all things will be restored, but now includes the idea of inscription as a temporary aspect of the process; in other words, the inscription is not equivalent to consummation. While Conradie does allow for some change in terms of healing and so on, this is a less luxuriant vision compared with Moltmann's.

Denis Edwards discusses the various alternatives possible in envisaging a new earth.[49] He suggests that Moltmann's emphasis on the new creation detracts from affirming the present creation, while the idea of objective immortality is too minimalist. Of course, the idea of eschatology coming 'from ahead' that Moltmann anticipates might seem at first sight to denigrate present existence. However, it strikes me that Moltmann overcomes this difficulty by insisting not just on a 'new earth', but also on the reconciliation of the present earth through a cosmic Christology that gathers up both creative and redemptive movements. I do have other problems with his portrayal of the future of creation in terms of its coherence, as discussed above, but I doubt that his theology is 'gnostic'; rather, it is simply over-luxuriant in its anticipation of the future of the earth. Edwards has a number of helpful suggestions as to how to approach the difficult question of the redemption of nature:[50]

- 'The future of creation remains obscure and surrounded in mystery.' I agree with this and also with his insistence that what we do have is a promise, based on the hope of the resurrection, but this does not give us a clear view of the future.
- 'Individual creatures are inscribed in the eternal divine life through the Holy Spirit.' Edwards suggests, correctly in my view, that the Spirit of God gives life to all creatures in their bodiliness, and that this is expressed in terms of resurrection through inscription into the divine life. This seems to include both non-humans and humans, so that all are 'inscribed eternally into the life of the Trinity'.
- 'Individual creatures find healing and fulfilment in Christ.' Such a healing is one that is inclusive of all creatures in their suffering on earth.
- 'Redemption in Christ will be specific to each kind of creature.' For this to be authentic, redemption needs to be specific to the creature involved, so 'God relates to each creature on its own terms.' The fulfilment of a creature will be appropriate to that creature; for human beings this is personal, but for mosquitoes it will be non-personal. I think that Edwards is sensible to suggest a differential expression of Christ's redemption, and to argue for a richer interpretation of human experience than that envisaged by inscription. It also allows for the possibility of redemption of creatures that have a degree of self-consciousness, though he does not specifically address this aspect.
- 'Some individual creatures may find redemption in the living memory and the eternal life of the Trinity and the Communion of the Saints.' Edwards seems to understand the treasuring of memory to be in the divine life of the Trinity, but then this is also included in the way the Saints share in this communion through celebration. He believes, correctly in my view, that bodily resurrection may be inappropriate for 'bacteria or a dinosaur'.

Yet there are also some difficulties with Edwards' inclusive belief 'that we can proclaim that the dynamic shared life of God will involve the holding and treasuring of every creature of every time in the living present of the Trinity'. How might, for example, we celebrate those creaturely lives that depend entirely on the destruction of other life forms, such as viruses or cancers? If a cancer is a distorted form of life that already exists, one might envisage such transcription taking the form of a memory that is celebrated because it no longer exists or takes hold. Yet if redemption of such a creature is envisaged, as in the fourth suggestion above, then we face an identity problem: the creature no longer has the same identity in heaven as it did on earth, for it has been radically transformed. The dark side of natural, creaturely existence does not seem to be adequately addressed here, even while I would agree with the general principle that creatures might find permanence in the memory of God. For this we need to be reminded of characteristics of the eschaton that Moltmann has highlighted – namely, holiness and glory. A holy God will not tolerate aspects of creation that are 'evil' or work against divine purposes. Some aspects of creation, therefore, may be discarded. This is not a Gnostic rejection of the material world, but an acknowledgement of the idea of God's holy judgement alongside God's love.

Conclusions

I have suggested in this chapter that the way we approach eco-eschatology needs to be done with a certain amount of caution, partly because there is very little said on this subject in the scriptural and traditional canons. However, in the light of our own understanding of evolutionary science and ecology, we can make some tentative suggestions as to what this might entail. There exists a number of paradoxical tensions in approaching this subject. In the first place, the secular attraction to speaking of current environmental problems through a secular appropriation of apocalyptic needs to be faced. Realism about the present state of the planet is important, but not exaggeration of imminent collapse. Yet even these stories make most sense when compared with biblical accounts of apocalyptic, for such apocalyptic literature always surfaced when the threat of annihilation loomed near. The challenge for the apocalyptic writers was to encourage responsible action now, rather than offer hope through utopias that could never find realisation in the present. Such literature shows that humanity has gone astray through its lack of wisdom and exploitation of the earth. Moreover, the future of the earth is one that includes the possibility of the redemption of all natural existence. Yet it would be premature to consider what this might entail without first considering the way suffering in nature can be understood theologically. I have argued that consideration of what lies beyond death through von Balthasar's notion of Christ's descent into hell on Holy Saturday can be expanded to encompass that hell which includes the extinction of species. The shock of that loss must not be allowed to lose its force, even though its sting is taken away through subsequent reflection on the redemption of nature. Such redemption, in Moltmann's terms, takes a form that is rich in its inclusiveness of every creature that ever existed. However, it is hard to reconcile this with his suggestion that the new life will be built on this earth, for such an earth would be impossible if all life forms that have ever existed were to be raised. A more realistic alternative, therefore, is to envisage some form of inscription in the memory of God for creaturely being, but a rather more robust interpretation of resurrection for conscious beings. The shape of resurrection and how this will be expressed in detail is a matter for speculative theology, and the wisest course in this case may be silence, for there are some things that we cannot know, since they are hidden in the heart of God. What we do know, however, is that since God is a God of love, the new life we experience will be one that is inclusive of creatures in some way, and that this life will be rich in its experiences, taking up the historical memory of different phases of our own history and biography, as well as wider in terms of the cosmos as a whole. The question now becomes, in the light of this future, how are we to express such a hope through our own actions and behaviour? While ethics is not a specifically theological task, it is towards the consideration of practices that much eco-theology points; and indeed, this could be regarded the beginning and end of eco-theological reflection. It is the beginning in that it is more often than not the motivation for such intense reflection. It is the end in as much as it lays out a theological rationale for specific earth-keeping practices that are particularly prominent in different Church statements advocating a position on how Christians need to act.

Further reading

Conradie, Ernst, *Hope for the Earth* (Bellville, University of the Western Cape, 2000)

Edwards, Denis, 'Every Sparrow that Falls to the Ground: The Cost of Evolution and the Christ Event', *Ecotheology*, 11.1 (2006), pp. 103–23

Moltmann, J., *In the End: The Beginning* (London, SCM Press, 2004)

Moltmann, J., *The Coming of God* (London, SCM Press, 1996)

Moltmann, J., *The Way of Jesus Christ* (London, SCM Press, 1990)

von Balthasar, Hans Urs, *Mysterium Paschale*, trans. with an Introduction by Aidan Nichols (Edinburgh, T. & T. Clark, 1990), pp. 51–2.

Towards theological eco-praxis

THE INTENTION OF THIS POSTSCRIPT IS to point the way for further development of theological ethics and practice in the light of the earlier theological discussion. I am fully aware that there is so much more literature here that could be discussed – indeed a full expansive textbook on theological eco-ethics is called for! I am also conscious that many other religious organisations and groups are fully engaged in what might be termed eco-sensitive practice, and that these groups offer practical help and encouragement to practise living lightly on the earth.[1] However, it is important to highlight reasons why ecological practices are so important for eco-theology, for they serve to inform that theology and in some senses are also an expression of it. I will suggest here that ecology needs to inform the way of being a church community – not just practical encouragement towards recycling or cutting down car use and so on. This book has argued for an interweaving of ecological themes into different aspects of Christian teaching from a variety of diverse starting points, including different doctrinal bases as well as different geographical and social locations. This implies that ecology is a *universal vocation* for all Christians, even if the interpretation of what this means will differ, depending on the cultural context and the particular Christian traditions of the individuals and communities concerned. Ecological concern serves to join seemingly disparate groups, from Eastern Orthodox to Radical Feminist, and even beyond this to other religious traditions as well. In other words, ecology needs to become integrated into the heart of Christian faith and practice. The question is, how might this be achieved?

One of the first places that is important in this respect is how to perceive the mission of the Church. The proclamation of the good news cannot be detached from concern about the natural world in which people are placed: people and planet form an interwoven community that needs to be considered together, rather than separately. Of course, there are different styles of evangelisation, but it seems to me that ecology is relevant, whatever the particular starting point for Christian mission, or the model of that mission. Those committed to an evangelical view of the Church need to recognise that given the cosmic scope of key doctrines in the Church, from Christology through to doctrines of creation and redemption, then the Gospel message would be impoverished if this aspect was somehow omitted. In other words, the Gospel needs to include the idea of an *ecological conversion*,[2] integrated into a conversion towards Christ and the message of the Gospel. Perhaps this is one reason why the fifth mark of mission is 'to strive to safeguard the integrity of creation and sustain and renew the earth'.[3] Indeed, I would argue, like others, that the experience of grace through the Holy Spirit active in the human community includes the determination to protect and care for the earth, ever groaning under the weight of what I would term anthropogenic evils.[4] Some groups have even made it their vocation as Christians to express the mission to the world through active ecological conservation projects throughout the world.[5] Such projects have obvious benefits for the creatures under threat, but they are not detached from beneficial impacts on human communities as well, many of whom have come together in new ways in order to cooperate with the projects, or subsequently gain benefit following transformation of landscapes. Some Christian-based projects in India have even begun with the environmental action first, for both human and ecological communities were being eroded through the destruction of mangrove forests. The Christian Coastal Development Project achieved remarkable success in a relatively short time. Over a hundred hectares are now regenerated, but this was motivated by a careful concern for both people and land.[6]

In addition, once we appreciate the differential impact on the poorest communities, action for the earth also becomes a matter of environmental and ecological justice. While authors sensitive to eco-theology have been writing about this for some time, Deiter Hessel and Larry Ramussen being good examples, filtering these insights to ecclesial practices on the ground is perhaps more patchy.[7] The importance of this has been recognised by Christian development agencies in the United Kingdom, including, for example, CAFOD in their *Live Simply* project launched in January 2007. This project reflects Roman Catholic social teaching on ecology, inspired by the work of Pope John Paul II, who was bold enough to suggest the need for *ecological conversion*. He suggests that:

> What is required is an act of repentance on our part and a renewed attempt to view ourselves, one another, and the world around us within the perspective of the divine design for creation. The problem is not simply economic and technological; it is moral and spiritual. A solution at the economic and technological level can be found only if we undergo, in the most radical way, an *inner change of heart*, which can lead to a change in lifestyle and of unsustainable patterns of consumption and production. A genuine conversion in Christ will enable us to change the way we think and act.[8]

This statement from the Pontiff of the largest Christian community in the world is highly significant, for he implies that if we really desire to follow Christ, then we will act responsibly towards the environment. In other words, ecology is not just a mark of mission, it is also a mark of discipleship. He also similarly suggests that:

> Above all in our time man has devastated wooded plains and valleys, polluted the waters, deformed the earth's habitat ... humiliating – to use an image of Dante Alighieri (*Paradiso*, Xxii, 151), the earth, that flower bed that is our dwelling. It is necessary therefore, to stimulate and sustain the 'ecological conversion', which over these last decades has made humanity more sensitive when facing the catastrophe towards which it is moving ... Therefore, not only is a 'physical' ecology at stake, attentive to safeguarding the habitat of different living beings, but also a 'human' ecology that will render the life of creatures more dignified, protecting the radical good of life in all its manifestations and preparing an environment for future generations that is closer to the plan of the Creator.[9]

He seems here to be translating the need for ecological interrelationships into an understanding of what it means to function adequately as a human society – what he terms a *human ecology*. Of course, some might argue that this approach is still too anthropocentric, implying, as he does, that the environment for future generations is in need of protection, rather than more radical claims about the protection of nature in and of itself. In other words, he opts for a stewardship approach to ethics that is still focused on human needs, especially the needs of the poor.

Yet, in spite of this reservation, we can welcome this as a start towards reminding those in the Church of the need for care-giving in relation to the planet and its creatures. Denis Edwards follows through these themes in suggesting in his *Ecology at the Heart of Faith* that once we perceive Christian faith in ecological terms, then it becomes necessary to practise a new way of living on the earth that is more responsible and sensitive to the needs of all creatures.[10] He includes in this practical ways of expressing this faith in terms of the worship and liturgy of the Christian community. This seems to me to be vitally important if ecological ideas are to become embedded into Christian consciousness. A change of heart is best affected if we are reminded of such change through worship and celebration. The Eucharist is a celebration of the death and resurrection of Christ, but through it we also lift up all of creation, and through the cosmic Christ, we remember the victims of ecocide. Moreover, through this remembering the possibility of a change of ethos in the human community becomes realised.

I suggest that prior to such a transformation, we also need to foster the notion of *keeping the Sabbath*, transformed in Christian terms as respect for the Lord's Day.[11] The Old Testement scholar, Claus Westerman, argues that P, the author of the passage in Genesis 2.1, takes over the ancient tradition of a rest for the Creator and joins it with history, creating an original synthesis by describing this rest in the language of the Sabbath. However, its purpose is not to reinforce Sabbath institutional observance; the seventh day is sanctified by God regardless of human practice – in other words, it is a way of making holy time universal in character.[12] It gives the holy 'a special place in the stream of events'.[13] The blessing of the seventh day is also similar to the blessing of fertility; it bestows a 'power that makes it fruitful for human experience', for the human community as a whole. This is significant, for it points to the importance of keeping a cycle of time that includes a day of rest, beyond whether there is conformity to institutional observance. In other words, its significance goes beyond Sabbath (or Sunday) observances. Yet where there are such observances, then these also need to reflect the creation Sabbath.

Keeping the Sabbath day holy was a reminder of the analogous relationship with the work of God in the creation of the world on the seventh day, as described in Genesis. It is also a reminder to 'let creation be', to change from practices that seek to exploit and harm creation, to those that approach creation with due respect and humility. It is also important to note that the Hebrew word 'rest' means 'to cease from'; it is not passive, but a ceasing from the *specific* work of creating. It amounts to a balance, in time, of work and being-with, a holding out against evil, arising out of an affirmation of the good. Why is this significant for an ecological theology? I suggest it is important because it emphasises letting creation be in a way that is more difficult for models such as God as gardener or humanity as steward of creation, or even more recent debates about sustainability.[14]

Christian scholars have sought to translate some of the ideals of the Jewish Sabbath to the Lord's Day in the Christian tradition. While legalistic adherence to institutional practices is not what is being recommended here, there are some advantages in making this analogy in order to support the ecological basis for becoming in tune with rhythms of rest and vitality that is built into an understanding of the seventh day. While the seventh day *begins* with creation, the Lord's Day *begins* with a transfigured creation.[15] Hence living from the Sabbath/seventh day is not simply a general theology of creation, but goes much deeper than this in providing a starting point for ecological Christology and soteriology through consideration of the Lord's Day, and an ecological pneumatology through its opening up of the themes of eschatology and new creation.[16]

Living from the Sabbath in a Christian context can, then, be inclusive of living from the Lord's Day. Both are reminders of *covenant*, a setting aside of time to reflect on God, a renewal of relationships with God and creation, and a making space for being with both God and the natural world. Hence, the Sabbath is primarily about re-connection with God and with all creatures in order to allow the flourishing and plenitude that is spoken about in the Genesis account. The connection with the Lord's Day is a reminder of the forgiveness and healing possible in Christ, giving Christology and its associated redemptive themes an ecological dimension that is also reflected in passages such as the great christological hymn in Colossians 1.

I suggest that living *from* the Sabbath leads to *transformation*, a transformation of encounter, of renewal of covenant, which we can rightly name as a *cosmic covenant* of the kind that we might associate with the early experience of the first Israelite wanderers in the desert.[17] Living from the Sabbath implies going beyond what simply happens on the Lord's Day, but every day of the week becomes influenced by its transforming power. Such a transformation includes a deep sensitivity to the created world in a way that weaves together some of the threads discussed in this book, so that we:

- Give time and space to reaffirming a sense of covenant between God, humanity and creation.
- Acknowledge the dependence of all creation on God and God's authority over evil and chaos.
- Acknowledge the contribution of human sinfulness to the destruction and devastation of creation, including loss of biodiversity and the need for conversion or *metanoia*.
- Move away from those cycles of behaviour that urge more and more economic growth, in favour of a deeper balancing of human activity and rest as integral to that in the natural world.
- Celebrate the presence of Christ in the midst of creation and acknowledge Christ's redeeming power for all the brokenness in creation, including sinful humanity.
- Learn to appreciate the value of all of creation in and of itself, as God's creation, rather than just a resource for human benefit.
- Develop a sense of *wonder*, which includes a deep joy in creation as it is now, in all its richness and diversity, as well as what it might become in glory.
- Acknowledge an ignorance of the complexity of the natural world and through this develop the virtue of *humility*, or realistic appreciation of who we are in relationship to creation.
- Enter into an understanding of creation as manifesting the wisdom of God, and seek to practise *wisdom* and *prudence* in our dealings with creation.
- Learn to *love* creation as gift, as it is in itself, and as expressive of the love of God.
- Find ways to recognise how to balance competing demands and promote ecological justice.

Fired up by such reflection, we can learn to live from the Sabbath in such a way so as to express these virtues for the benefit of the human community and the community of creation.

In this, an understanding of what to do through practical wisdom, or prudence, becomes translated into forms of ecological justice, for the common good. What shape might this prudence take?[18] Certainly, it is informed by the appreciation of wisdom that has surfaced in the theological discussion of much of this book. This is not to say that other virtues are unimportant or relevant, as authors like Steven Boumer-Prediger shows clearly,[19] but rather that wisdom, expressed as prudence, helps us to decide how to express these virtues, including eco-justice and environmental justice, so, from this perspective, it needs to take priority. Yet, if wisdom is primarily about our human relationship with God, our theology, practical wisdom is about how to translate such belief into given practices, or praxis – practices informed by theory and vice versa. Practical wisdom is needed, therefore, in dealing with the earth, for it involves more than mere logical reasoning in trying to decide what to do when faced with complex issues such as climate change.

Prudence includes deliberation, judgement and action. The basis for deliberation includes consideration of past, present and future. We need a clear appreciation of the actual history of human relationships with the natural world, including its history of abuse and appreciation. It is from here that we learn more about helpful models of human being and living, whether it be by tuning into the Celtic traditions in the context of Europe, or Aboriginal or African traditions elsewhere. Such traditions can be a reminder to modern readers of what it means to live in tune with the natural world, while being realistic about the possibility for human sin and abuse, whatever particular tradition is evoked. Christian believers will want to recover aspects of the Christian tradition that have served them well in the past. In other words, while it is important to appreciate the scope and variety of different religious traditions and their relationship with creation, I do not think it is necessary to blend these beliefs with Christian ones in order to inform good practice. Such memory also lends itself to a degree of caution that is also characteristic of prudence, expressed in secular terms as the precautionary principle.

In relation to the present we need to be conscious of the insights from scientific and social scientific analysis, and philosophical reflection, as well as the work of contemporary theologians. This consciousness presupposes a degree of teachableness, or *docilitas* in classical terminology, but it is teachableness that has an eye to what is *reasonable*. In other words, the task is necessarily a multidisciplinary one. Even though we need to acknowledge that our own particular standpoint will influence the way we perceive particular issues, some appreciation of alternatives is possible through empathetic reasoning. I suggest that given the global scale of environmental issues and their impacts, a similar global approach to theology and other traditions is needed.

In addition, some perception of what might happen in the future, or foresight, is a necessary ingredient. Prudence thinks not just about present gains, but has its eye on future scenarios, including the fate of the earth. Of course, all this might become unmanageable were it not for the need within prudence to arrive at a judgement where there are issues of conflict to solve. How do we adjudicate between the demands of an impoverished human community and the possibility of species extinction? Such local judgements require the virtue of prudence. How do we decide what political measures to put in place in order to effect the greatest positive impact on the climate? Again, such political decisions require prudence. What does deliberative justice mean in relation to the human and non-human communities of which we are a part? Such decisions require political prudence.

In naming prudence as active for the earth in this way, I am not suggesting that we neglect the needs of human beings. Rather, in the light of a consideration of the community of creation, our actions need to be informed by our prudential judgements, rather than just conscience-salving exercises that make us feel better about ourselves. There is a balance to be struck here as well. Deciding not to recycle our waste because we think it would not reasonably make any difference to global climate effects also shows a lack of vision, for it absolves us from any responsibility to act at all. Rather, it is through cooperation in such ventures that differences can become visible and practical. In this sense, the Church has an even greater responsibility to encourage its members to act in ways that reflect ecological responsibility, for as a collective group it does have the power to effect such changes. There are signs that this is beginning to take place in a variety of church groups.[20]

I have urged a recovery of prudence as flowing out of a deep respect for the earth that can be fostered by reminding ourselves of the importance of balance of time in the cycle of nature and human life. Such ecological practices will be demanding on our energy and therefore we need to recover once again the importance of simply spending time in the natural world, or reflect on aspects of that world if the former is impossible for us. Such paying attention to life itself is something that comes naturally for most biologists, who generally have a passion for life, for it has informed their way of being in the world. Yet openness and appreciation of life in all its richness is also open to the non-specialist, and can lead to a profound sense of wonder in believers and non-believers alike.[21] Such experiences of wonder give us pause for thought, for through faith they can take us into the presence of the Divine, understood as the Wisdom of God. It is here that eco-praxis reaches its climax, for by seeking to conserve the natural world in all its richness, we are given insights from the Maker of all that is, and enter into the Presence of God in mystical communion with the natural world. It is in this spirit of contemplation that we find courage to start again, in spite of human frailties and weaknesses. Nature becomes our teacher and healer, through the natural grace of creation, and we learn once again that human being and becoming is not the measure of all things. The glory of God is the cosmos fully alive.

Questions for Discussion

Individuals may use these questions in order to reinforce their comprehension of a particular chapter, or they can be used by discussion groups, taking each chapter in turn as a basis for reflection and discussion.

Chapter 1: Trends in Ecology and Environment

1. What are the impacts of climate change on (a) human and (b) non-human species? How are the two related?
2. What are the benefits of biodiversity? Which one is likely to be the most important in encouraging change in practice?
3. What values are the most significant in addressing the problems of global ecology? Why?

Chapter 2: Economics and Environmental Justice

1. What practical steps might be taken to render globalisation more environmentally responsible?
2. What do you understand by 'sustainability'? How might this be achieved?
3. Discuss the arguments for genetically modified crops in commercial agriculture. Are they convincing?
4. What are the key features of environmental justice? How does this impact on future generations?

Chapter 3: Eco-theology from the North

1. Do you find Deep Ecology convincing?
2. To what extent can Teilhard's mystical approach be appropriated for eco-theology? Is Thomas Berry more successful in this respect?
3. Compare Teilhard with Matthew Fox. What distinctive elements do you find?

Chapter 4: Eco-theology from the South

1. Why is it impossible to separate concerns about development from environmental issues? Can you give any examples?
2. According to Boff, how is eco-theology related to liberation theology?

3. What distinctive issues for eco-theology are raised by indigenous communities?

Chapter 5: Eco-theology from the East
1. What are the essential features of a doctrine of creation according to Eastern Orthodox traditions? Do you find this approach convincing?
2. What advantages and disadvantages for eco-theology follow from the strong emphasis on theology as informed by liturgical practices in Eastern Orthodox traditions?
3. Is the idea of humanity as priests of creation compatible with eco-theology?
4. What contribution to eco-theology emerges from Bulgakov's discussion of divine and creaturely Wisdom (Sophia)?

Chapter 6: Eco-theology from the West
1. In what ways are Bookchin's ideas relevant for eco-theology?
2. What implicit theology emerges from socio-political analysis of GMOs? In what ways might this be useful for eco-theology?
3. What are the different disciplinary dialogue partners emerging in Western traditions? What are the advantages and disadvantages of such diversity?

Chapter 7: Biblical Eco-theology
1. Do you find the arguments for a biblical basis for creation care convincing?
2. What are the advantages and disadvantages of biblically based ethical models, such as stewardship? How far is this an appropriate reading for ecological ethics?
3. What are the different eco-justice principles? Do you find this a valid way of appropriating biblical texts?

Chapter 8: Ecology and Christology
1. How would you convince a sceptic of the ecological importance of cosmic Christology?
2. What are the key features emerging in the Gospel accounts that relate Jesus to the land? Why is this particularly important in an ecological context?
3. How do you think one might begin to understand different aspects of Christology, such as incarnation and atonement, in ecological terms?
4. Why is understanding Jesus as the Wisdom of God important for eco-theology?

Chapter 9: Ecology and Theodicy
1. Which aspects of the suffering present in the natural world raise issues for

theodicy and why?

2. What are the five different possible approaches to thoedicy? Which one(s) do you find convincing in relation to large-scale ecological suffering?
3. How helpful do you find speaking of evil as 'shadow sophia' as a theological approach to creaturely suffering?

Chapter 10: Ecology and Spirit

1. In what ways is it possible to envisage the Spirit as involved in the creation? How helpful is the image of the Spirit as a wild bird? Are you convinced by arguments for pantheism?
2. In what sense is thinking of the Spirit in Trinitarian terms important for eco-theology? Are there problems with this view?
3. What does the idea of the Spirit as Divine Wisdom contribute to discussion on the Spirit in an ecological context?

Chapter 11: Eco-feminist Theology

1. What are the distinctive marks and varieties of eco-feminist thinking?
2. Compare McFague's understanding of the earth as a model of God with Primavesi's Gaian approach. What are the strengths and limitations of each?
3. What are the special characteristics of Wisdom that emerge in the context of eco-feminist thought?

Chapter 12: Eco-eschatology

1. What theological argument might be brought to bear in considering future redemption as inclusive of the earth and its creatures?
2. How does Moltmann envisage the future of creation? Are you convinced by his approach?
3. What are the merits of Conradies' interpretation of eschatological inscription in ecological terms?
4. What are Edwards' five principles for the redemption of nature? What are the advantages and drawbacks of each of these?

Select Bibliography

Altner, G., *Natutvergessenheit: Grundlagen einer umfassenden Bioethic* (Darmstadt, Wissenschafliche Buchgesellschaft, 1991)

Altner, G. (ed)., *Ökologische Theologies: Perspektiven zur Orientierung* (Stuttgart, Radius Verlag, 1989)

Barker, M., *The Lost Prophet: The Book of Enoch and its Influence on Christianity* (London, SPCK, 1988)

Barker, M., *The Older Testament: The Survival of Themes from the Ancient Royal Cult in Sectarian Judaism and Early Christianity* (London, SPCK, 1987)

Barker, M., *The Revelation of Jesus Christ* (Edinburgh, T. & T. Clark, 2000)

Barth, Marcus and Blanke, Helmut, *Colossians: A New Translation with Introduction and Commentary* (The Anchor Bible), trans. Ashid B. Beck (New York, Doubleday, 1994)

Bauckham, Richard, 'Joining Creation's Praise of God', *Ecotheology*, 7.1 (2002), pp. 45–59

Beck, Ulrich, *What is Globalisation?*, trans. Patrick Camiller (Cambridge, Polity Press, 2000)

Bergmann, S., *Creation Set Free: The Spirit as Liberator of Nature* (Grand Rapids, Eerdmans, 2005)

Bernstein, Ellen, *The Splendour of Creation: A Biblical Ecology* (Cleveland, The Pilgrim Press, 2005)

Berry, R. J. (ed.), *The Care of Creation: Fostering Concern and Action* (Leicester, Inter-Varsity Press, 2000)

Berry, R. J. (ed.), *When Enough is Enough; A Christian Framework for Environmental Sustainability* (Nottingham, Apollos/Inter-Varsity Press, 2007)

Berry, R. J., *God's Book of Works* (London, T. & T. Clark/Continuum, 2003)

Berry, R. J. (ed.), *Environmental Stewardship* (London, Continuum, 2006)

Boff, Leonardo, *Cry of the Earth: Cry of the Poor* (Maryknoll, Orbis Books, 1997)

Boff, Leonardo, *Ecology and Liberation: A New Paradigm* (Maryknoll, Orbis Books, 1995)

Bookchin, M., *The Philosophy of Social Ecology: Essays on Dialectical Naturalism* (2nd edn, London, Black Rose Books, 1996)

Boumer-Prediger, S., *For the Beauty of the Earth: A Christian Vision for Creation Care* (Grand Rapids, Baker Academic, 2001)

Bouma-Prediger, S. and Bakken, P. (eds.), *Evocations of Grace: Joseph Sittler's Writings on Ecology, Theology and Ethics* (Grand Rapids, Eerdmans, 2000)

Brown, W. S. (ed), *Understanding Wisdom* (Philadelphia, Templeton Foundation Press, 2000)

Bruce, D. and Bruce, A. (eds.), *Engineering Genesis: The Ethics of Genetic Engineering in Non-Human Species* (London, Earthscan, 1998)

Bulgakov, S., *The Bride of the Lamb*, trans. B. Jakim (Grand Rapids, Eerdmans, 2002)

Bulgakov, S., *The Comforter*, trans. B. Jakim (Grand Rapids, Eerdmans, 2004)

Bulgakov, S., *Sophia: The Wisdom of God: An Outline of Sophiology* (Hudson, NY, Lindisfarne Press, 1993)

Caird, G. B., *Paul's Letters from Prison* (Oxford, Oxford University Press, 1984)

Carson, R., *Silent Spring* (Boston, Houghton Miflin, 1961)

Carson, R., *A Sense of Wonder* (New York, Harper and Row, 1965)

Ceccarelli, L., *Shaping Science with Rhetoric* (Chicago and London, University of Chicago Press, 2001)

Clayton, P. and Peacocke, A. (eds.), *In Whom we Live and Move and Have Our Being: Panentheistic Reflections on God's Presence in a Scientific World* (Grand Rapids/Cambridge, Eerdmans, 2004)

Conradie, Ernst, *Hope for the Earth* (Bellville, University of the Western Cape, 2000)

Conradie, Ernst, *An Ecological Christian Anthropology: At Home on Earth?* (Aldershot, Ashgate, 2005)

Conradie, Ernst, 'Towards an Agenda for Ecological Theology: An Intercontinental Dialogue', *Ecotheology*, 10.3 (2005), pp. 281–43

Conradie, Ernst, *Christianity and Ecological Theology: Resources for Further Research, Study Guides in Religion and Theology 11* (Stellenbosch, Sun Press/University of the Western Cape, 2005)

Cranfield, C. E. B., *The Epistle to the Romans*, Vol. 1, 1–VIII (Edinburgh, T. & T. Clark, 1975)

De Lobel, J. (ed.), *Logia – Les Paroles de Jesus (The Sayings of Jesus)* (Leuven, Leuven University Press, 1982)

Deane-Drummond, C., *A Handbook in Theology and Ecology* (London, SCM Press, 1996)

Deane-Drummond, C. (ed.), *Teilhard de Chardin on People and Planet* (London, Equinox, 2006)

Deane-Drummond, C., 'Environmental Justice and the Economy: A Christian Theologian's View', *Ecotheology*, 11.3 (2006), pp. 294–310

Deane-Drummond, C., *Creation through Wisdom: Theology and the New Biology* (Edinburgh, T. & T. Clark, 2000)

Deane-Drummond, C., *The Ethics of Nature* (Oxford, Blackwell, 2004)

Deane-Drummond, C., *Wonder and Wisdom: Conversations in Science, Spirituality and Theology* (London, Darton, Longman and Todd, 2006)

Deane-Drummond, C., 'Where Streams Meet: Ecology, Wisdom and Beauty in Bulgakov, von Balthasar and Aquinas', in H. Meisinger, W. B. Drees and Z. Liana (eds.), *Wisdom or Knowledge? Science, Theology and Cultural Dynamics* (London, T. & T. Clark, 2006), pp. 108–26

Deane-Drummond, C., 'Sophia: The Feminine Face of God as a Metaphor for an Ecotheology', *Feminist Theology*, 16 (1997), pp. 11–31.

Deane-Drummond, C. and Szerszynski, B., *Re-Ordering Nature: Theology, Society and Genetics* (London, Continuum, 2003)

Devall, Bill and Sessions, George, *Deep Ecology* (Salt Lake City, Peregrine Smith Books, 1985)

Dobson, A., *Justice and the Environment: Conceptions of Environmental Sustainability and Dimensions of Social Justice* (Oxford, Oxford University Press, 1998)

Duchrow, Ulrich and Liedke, Gerhard, *Shalom: Biblical Perspectives on Creation, Justice and Peace* (Geneva, WCC, 1989)

Dunn, J., *Christology in the Making* (London, SCM Press, 1989)

Dunn, James, *Word Biblical Commentary, Romans 1—8* (Dallas, Word Books, 1988)

Eaton, H. and Lorenzen, L., *Ecofeminism and Globalisation: Exploring Culture, Context and Religion* (Lanham, Rowman and Littlefield, 2003)

Eaton, H., *Introducing Ecofeminist Theologies* (London, Continuum, 2005)

Echlin, E., *Earth Spirituality: Jesus at the Centre* (London, John Hunt, 1999)

Edwards, D. (ed.), *Earth Revealing, Earth Healing* (Collegeville, The Liturgical Press, 2001)

Edwards, D., 'Every Sparrow that Falls to the Ground: The Cost of Evolution and the Christ Event', *Ecotheology*, 11.1 (2006), pp. 103–23

Edwards, D., *Jesus, the Wisdom of God: An Ecological Theology* (Homebush, St Pauls, 1995)

Edwards, D., *Breath of Life: A Theology of the Creator Spirit* (Maryknoll, Orbis Books, 2004)

Edwards, D. and Worthing, M. (eds.), *Biodiversity and Ecology* (Adelaide, ATF Press, 2004)

Flader, Susan and Callicott, J. Baird (eds.), *The River of the Mother of God and Other Essays* (Madison, University of Wisconsin Press, 1991)

Fox, M., *The Coming of the Cosmic Christ: The Healing of Mother Earth and the Birth of Global Resistance* (San Francisco, Harper and Row, 1988)

Fox, Matthew, *Original Blessing* (Santa Fe, Bear and Co., 1983)

Gaston, K. J. and Spicer, J. I., *Biodiversity* (2nd edn, Oxford, Blackwell, 2004)

Gottlieb, Roger S. (ed.), *Liberating Faith: Religious Voices for Justice, Peace and Ecological Wisdom* (Lanham, Rowman and Littlefield, 2003)

Gregorios, P. mar, *The Human Presence: An Orthodox View of Nature* (Geneva, WCC, 1978)

Grey, M., *Sacred Longings: Ecofeminist Theology and Globalization* (London, SCM Press, 2003)

Grey, M., *The Outrageous Pursuit of Hope: Prophetic Dreams for the Twenty-first Century* (London, Darton, Longman and Todd, 2000)

Griffin, S., *Women and Nature: The Roaring Inside Her* (London, The Women's Press, 1984)

Habel, Norman C. (ed.), *Readings from the Perspective of Earth, The Earth Bible 1*, (Sheffield, Sheffield Academic Press, 2000)

Habel, Norman and Wurst, Shirley (eds.), *The Earth Story in Genesis, The Earth Bible 2* (Sheffield, Sheffield Academic Press, 2000)

Habel, Norman and Wurst, Shirley (eds.), *The Earth Story in Wisdom Traditions, The Earth Bible 3* (Sheffield, Sheffield Academic Press, 2001)

Hall, J., *The Steward: A Biblical Symbol Come of Age* (2nd edn, Grand Rapids, Eerdmans, 1990)

Hall, John, *Imaging God: Dominion as Stewardship* (Grand Rapids, Eerdmans, 1986)

Hallman, D. (ed.), *Ecotheology: Voices from South and North* (Geneva, WCC, 1994)

Haught, John, *God after Darwin* (Boulder, Westview Press, 2000)

Hefner, Philip, *Technology and Human Becoming* (Minneapolis, Fortress Press, 2003)

Hessel, Dieter T. and Ruether, Rosemary Radford (eds.), *Christianity and Ecology: Seeking the Well Being of Earth and Humans* (Cambridge, Harvard University Press, 2000)

Hessel, D. and Ramussen, L. (eds.), *Earth Habitat: EcoJustices and the Churches' Response* (Minneapolis, Fortress Press, 2001)

Houghton, J., *Global Warming: The Complete Briefing* (3rd edn, Cambridge, Cambridge University Press, 2004)

Hughes, P. E., *The Book of Revelation: A Commentary* (Grand Rapids, Eerdmans, 1990)

IPCC, *Climate Change 2001: Synthesis Report of the Third Assessment of the Intergovernmental Panel on Climate Change* (Cambridge, Cambridge University Press, 2001)

IPCC, *Climate Change 2007: Mitigation of Climate Change Working Group 111 Contribution to the Fourth Assessment Report* (Cambridge, Cambridge University Press, 2007)

IPCC, *Climate Change 2007: Physical Science Basis, Working Group 1 Contribution to the Fourth Assessment Report* (Cambridge, Cambridge University Press, 2007)

Jantzen, G., *Becoming Divine: Towards a Feminist Philosophy of Religion* (Manchester, Manchester University Press, 1998)

Jantzen, G., *God's World: God's Body* (London, DLT, 1984)

Jenkins, Willis, *Ecologies of Grace: Environmental Ethics and Christian Theology* (New York, Oxford University Press, 2008)

Johnson, E., *She Who Is* (New York, Crossroad, 1992)

Jones, J., *Jesus and the Earth* (London, SPCK, 2003)

Kearns, Laurel and Keller, Catherine, *EcoSpirit: Religions and Philosophies for the Earth* (New York, Fordham University Press, 2007)

Kent, Homer, Vaughan, Curtis and Rupprecht, Arthur, *The Expositors Bible Commentary with the New International Version, Colossians* (Grand Rapids, Zondervan Publishing, 1996)

Keselopoulos, A. G., *Man and the Environment: A Study of St Symeon* (Crestwood, St Vladimir's Seminary Press, 2001)

Lash, N., *Holiness, Speech and Silence* (Aldershot, Ashgate, 2004)

Liedke, G., *Im Bauch des Fisches: Ökologische Theologie* (4th edn, Stuttgart, Kreuz-Verlag 1984)

Light, A. (ed.), *Social Ecology after Bookchin* (London, The Guildford Press, 1998)

Light, Andrew and Rolson III, Holmes (eds.), *Environmental Ethics: An Anthology* (Oxford, Blackwell, 2003)

Link, C., *Schöpfung: Schöpfungstheologie angesichts der Herausforderungen des 20. Jahrhunderts*, Handbuch Systematischer Theologie 7/2 (Gütersloh, Gütersloher Verlagshaus, 1991)

Locker, T. and Bruchac, J., *Rachel Carson: Preserving a Sense of Wonder* (Golden, Fulchrum Publishing, 2004)

Lovelock, J., *Gaia: A New Look at Life on Earth* (2nd edn, Oxford, Oxford University

Press, 1987)

Lovelock, J., *The Revenge of Gaia* (London, Penguin, 2006)

Médaille, J. C., *The Vocation of Business: Social Justice in the Market Place* (London, T. & T. Clark International/Continuum, 2007)

McDonagh, S., *To Care for the Earth: A Call to a New Theology* (London, Geoffrey Chapman, 1986)

McDonagh, S., *Climate Change: The Challenge to All of Us* (Blackrock, The Columba Press, 2006)

McDonagh, S., *The Greening of the Church* (London, Geoffrey Chapman, 1990)

McDonagh, Sean, *Patenting Life: Stop* (Dublin, Columba Press, 2004)

McFague, S., *Life Abundant*: *Rethinking Theology and Economy for a Planet in Peril* (Minneapolis, Fortress Press, 2001)

McFague, S., *The Body of God: An Ecological Theology* (London, SCM Press, 1993)

Midgley, M., *Gaia* (London, Demos, 2001)

Mies, M. and Shiva, Vandana, *Ecofeminism* (London, Zed Books, 1993)

Moltmann, J., *The Coming of God* (London, SCM Press, 1996)

Moltmann, J., *God in Creation* (London, SCM Press, 1985)

Moltmann, J., *In the End: The Beginning* (London, SCM Press, 2004)

Moltmann, J., *The Crucified God* (London, SCM Press, 1974)

Moltmann, J., *The Experiment Hope* (London, SCM Press, 1975)

Moltmann, J., *The Future of Creation* (London, SCM Press, 1979)

Moltmann, J., *The Way of Jesus Christ* (London, SCM Press, 1990)

Moltmann, J., *Theology of Hope: On the Grounds and Implications of a Christian Eschatology* (London, SCM Press, 1967)

Moltmann, J., *History and the Triune God* (London, SCM Press, 1991)

Murray, Robert, *The Cosmic Covenant* (London, Sheed and Ward, 1992)

Newton, David E., *From Global Warming to Dolly the Sheep: An Encylopedia of Social Issues in Science and Technology* (Santa Barbara/Oxford, ABC-CLIO, 1990)

Northcott, M., *The Environment and Christian Ethics* (Cambridge, Cambridge University Press, 1996)

Northcott, M., *A Moral Climate: The Ethics of Global Warming* (London, DLT, 2007)

Peters, T. (ed.), *Playing God: Genetic Determinism and Human Freedom* (London, Routledge, 1997)

Peters, T., Russell, R. J. and Welker, M. (eds.), *Resurrection: Theological and Scientific Assessments* (Grand Rapids, Eerdmans, 2002)

Peters, Ted, Bennett, Gaymon, Hewlett, Martinez and Russell, Robert John, *The Evolution of Evil* (Dordrecht, Vandenhoek and Ruprecht, 2008)

Pickett, S. T. A, Kolasa, J. and Jones, C. G., *Ecological Understanding*: *The Nature of Theory and the Theory of Nature* (London, Academic Press, 1994)

Plaskow, J. and Christ, C. (eds.), *Weaving the Visions: New Patterns in Feminist Spirituality* (San Francisco, Harper and Row, 1989)

Polkinghorne, J. (ed.), *The Work of Love: Creation as Kenosis* (Grand Rapids, Eerdmans, 2001)

Primavesi, A., *Gaia's Gift* (London, Routledge, 2003)

Primavesi, A., *Sacred Gaia: Holistic Theology and Earth System Science* (London, Routledge, 2000)

Ramussen, L., *Earth Community, Earth Ethics* (Maryknoll, Orbis Books, 1996)

Ress, M. J., *Ecofeminism in Latin America: Women from the Margins* (Maryknoll, Orbis Books, 2006)

Rossi, V., 'Christian Ecology is Cosmic Christology', *Epiphany*, 8 (1987), pp. 52–62

Rowland, C., *The Open Heaven* (London, SPCK, 1982)

Ruether, R. Radford, *Gaia and God: An Ecofeminist Theology of Earth Healing* (London, SCM Press, 1993)

Ruether, R. Radford, *Women Healing Earth: Third World Women on Ecology, Feminism and Religion* (London, SCM Press, 1996)

Santmire, H. Paul, *Nature Reborn: The Ecological and Cosmic Promise of Christian Theology* (Minneapolis, Fortress Press, 2000)

Santmire, P., *The Travail of Nature: The Ambiguous Promise of Christian Theology* (Philadelphia, Fortress Press, 1985)

Schememann, A., *For the Life of the World* (Crestwood, St Vladimir's Seminary Press, 1973)

Schumacher, E. F., *Small is Beautiful: Economics as if People Mattered* (London, Blond and Briggs, 1973)

Scott, Peter, *A Political Theology of Nature* (Cambridge, Cambridge University Press, 2003)

Sen, A., *Inequality Re-examined* (Oxford, Sage, 1992)

Sen, A., *Development as Freedom* (New York, Alfred Knopf, 1999)

Sherrard, Philip, *Human Image: World Image* (Ipswich, Golgonoosa Press, 1992)

Smalley, S., *The Revelation to John: Commentary on the Greek Text of the Apocalypse* (London, SPCK, 2005)

Southgate, C. B. (ed.), *God, Humanity and the Cosmos: A Companion to the Science and Religion Debate* (2nd edn, London, Continuum, 2005)

Swimme, Brian and Berry, Thomas, *The Universe Story* (San Francisco, HarperCollins, 1992)

Teilhard de Chardin, P., *Christianity and Evolution*, trans. R. Hague (New York, Harcourt Brace Jovanovich, 1971)

Teilhard de Chardin, P., *Towards the Future*, trans. R. Hague (New York, Harcourt Brace Jovanovich, 1975)

Teilhard de Chardin, P., *L'activation de l'énergie* (Paris, Seuil, 1965)

Teilhard de Chardin, P., *The Human Phenomenon*, trans. Sarah Appleton Weber (Brighton, Sussex Academic Press, 1999)

Teilhard de Chardin, P., *Writings in Time of War*, trans. R. Hague (New York, Harper and Row, 1968)

Theokritoff, E., 'Creation and Priesthood in Modern Orthodox Thinking', *Ecotheology*, 10.3 (2005), pp. 344–63

Theokritoff, E., 'Creation and Salvation in Orthodox Worship', *Ecotheology*, 10 (2001), pp. 97–108

UNEP, *Global Environmental Outlook 4 Report* (London, Earthscan, 2007)

von Balthasar, Hans Urs, *Mysterium Paschale*, trans. with an Introduction by Aidan Nichols (Edinburgh, T. & T. Clark, 1990)

Walker, A. and Carras, C. (eds.), *Living Orthodoxy in the Modern World* (London, SPCK, 1996)

Wallace, M., *Finding God in the Singing River* (Minneapolis, Fortress Press, 2005)

Wallace, M., *Fragments of the Spirit: Nature, Violence and the Renewal of Creation*

(Harrisburg, Trinity Press International, 2002)

Wenham, D., 'Kingdom and Creation from Jesus to Paul: Does the New Testament Give us an Ecological Mandate?', *Theology in Green*, 3 (July 1992), pp. 27–38

Westermann, C., *Genesis 1—11, A Commentary*, trans. John J. Scullion (London, SPCK, 1984)

White, Lynn, 'The Historical Roots of Our Ecologic Crisis', *Science*, 155 (10 March 1967), pp. 1203–7

White, Sarah and Tiongco, Romy, *Doing Theology and Development: Meeting the Challenge of Poverty* (Edinburgh, St Andrew's Press, 1997)

Whitehead, A. N., *Process and Reality: An Essay in Immortality* (1st edn 1929, 2nd edn New York, Harper and Row, 1957)

Wilson, E. O., *Consilience* (London, Abacus, 1999)

Wilson, E. O., *Biophilia* (Cambridge, Mass., Harvard University Press, 1984)

Wilson, E. O., *In Search of Nature* (Washington, Island Press/Shearwater Books, 1996)

World Watch Institute, *Vital Signs 2006–7* (W. N. Norton, 2006)

Worster, D., *Nature's Economy* (New York, Cambridge University Press, 1977)

Zizioulas, J. , 'Symbolism and Realism in Orthodox Worship', *Sourozh*, 79 (February 2000), pp. 3–17

Zizioulas, J., 'Preserving God's Creation' (Part 3), *Sourozh*, 40 (May 1990), pp. 31–40

Notes

Preface: The Turn to Ecology

1. Roger Gottlieb, *A Greener Faith: Religious Environmentalism and Our Planet's Future* (Oxford, Oxford University Press, 2006).
2. My book, *A Handbook in Theology and Ecology* (London, SCM Press, 1996), is written in an even more accessible way, and could be read first where this topic is completely new. Those students with a basic knowledge of theology would find the present volume accessible. For example, I assume that readers are familiar with basic theological terms such as Christology, theodicy and so on.
3. I am on the steering committee of an international global project entitled *Christian Faith and the Earth*, directed by Professor Ernst Conradie from the University of the Western Cape, South Africa. Students and others can hope for a number of resources for their research emerging out of this project. See also his *Christianity and Ecological Theology: Resources for Further Research, Study Guides in Religion and Theology 11* (Stellenbosch, Sun Press/University of the Western Cape, 2006).
4. I have also mostly cited those works available in English or available as English translations, based on my knowledge of the average linguistic skills of students in English-speaking nations. This is not intended to demean the work of my European or international colleagues writing in other languages, but to be realistic about the audience that this work is intending to reach. The German scholar, Christian Link, for example, discusses two rather different methodological approaches to ecological theology: either an ecological dogmatics, or by starting with ecology and examining the problems in a theological context. C. Link, *Schöpfung: Schöpfungstheologie angesichts der Herausforderungen des 20. Jahrhunderts*, Handbuch Systematischer Theologie 7/2 (Gütersloh, Gütersloher Verlagshaus, 1991). To some extent, the present text is intended to embrace both approaches to ecological theology.
5. I am aware that another such text is needed, but it seems to me that there are rather more accessible works written in this vein compared with eco-theology as such.
6. See, for example, the book series from the Harvard University Centre for the Study of World Religions. It is significant, perhaps, that the text on *Christianity and Ecology*, edited by D. T. Hessel and R. Radford Ruether (Cambridge, Harvard University Press, 2000), focused primarily on ecological practices, rather than more systematic concerns. A further anthology that includes other religious traditions and practices has just been published: L. Kearns and C. Keller (eds.), *Eco-Spirit: Religions and Philosophies for the Earth* (New York, Fortress Press, 2007).
7. There are, of course, important historical antecedents as in, for example, the works and traditions of St Francis of Assisi or St Bonaventure or St Benedict, but none

of these writers or their later interpreters were self-consciously aware of environmental concerns in the manner of eco-theology today. Even modern Eastern Orthodox theology claims its relevance to the present context.

8. A good example of this can be found in, for example, Mary H. MacKinnon and Moni McIntyre, *Readings in Ecology and Feminist Theology* (Kansas City, Sheed and Ward, 1995), where a whole section is devoted to 'Postmodern Horizons'. It is clear, however, that this is what I would term 'soft' postmodernism that still accepts that the demands of ecology are real, rather than illusory. What might be termed 'harder' forms of deconstruction would doubt the concrete basis on which eco-theology and environmental ethics rely – that is, that there is an environmental problem in the first place. While there may be much discussion and debate about, for example, the extent of climate change, and the values embedded in the project of modernity on which the natural sciences depend, few would doubt that climate change exists or that it is simply illusory in the human mind.

9. Laurel Kearns and Catherine Keller (eds.), *EcoSpirit: Religions and Philosophies for the Earth* (New York, Fordham University Press, 2007).

10. Ibid., Preface, p. xii.

11. This is a point made by a number of authors, and particularly forcefully by Ernst Conradie in his *An Ecological Christian Anthropology: At Home on Earth?* (Aldershot, Ashgate, 2005), p. 1.

12. Ibid., p. 13.

13. Conradie throws down the gauntlet in his challenging and thought-provoking article, 'Towards an Agenda for Ecological Theology: An Intercontinental Dialogue', *Ecotheology*, 10.3 (2005), pp. 281–343.

14. Ibid., p. 283.

15. C. Deane-Drummond, *Creation through Wisdom: Theology and the New Biology* (Edinburgh, T. & T. Clark, 2000); *Wonder and Wisdom: Conversations in Science, Spirituality and Theology* (London, DLT, 2006).

Chapter 1: Trends in Ecology and Environment

1. R. J. Berry, *God's Book of Works* (London, Continuum, 2003), p. 131.

2. David E. Newton, 'Population', in *From Global Warming to Dolly the Sheep: An Encyclopedia of Social Issues in Science and Technology* (Santa Barbara/Oxford, ABC-CLIO, 1990), pp. 216–20.

3. http://www.worldwatch.org/node/4298, accessed 5 July 2007.

4. World Watch Institute, *Vital Signs: 2006–7* (New York, W. B. Norton, 2006), pp. 22–3.

5. UNEP, *Global Environmental Outlook 3 Report* (London, Earthscan, 2002), esp. pp. 34–6. The most recent Global Outlook Report 4 is now available in late 2007 as this book goes to press, and individual facts can also be retrieved on line.

6. http://www.worldwatch.org/node/4322, accessed 5 July 2007.

7. http://www.unep.org/geo/geo4/media/fact_sheets/Fact_Sheet_6_Water.pdf, accessed 5 March 2008.

8. http://www.worldwatch.org/node/4314, accessed 5 July 2007.

9. http://www.worldwatch.org/node/4226, accessed 5 July 2007; World Watch Institute, *Vital Signs: 2006–7*, op. cit., pp. 24–5.

10. http://www.worldwatch.org/node/4238, accessed 5 July 2007.

11. http://www.worldwatch.org/node/4243, accessed 5 July 2007.

12. World Watch Institute, *Vital Signs: 2006–7*, op. cit., pp. 38–9.

13. This overview is limited in scope. The IPCC has issued four major reports; the fourth was released in 2007. This latest report seeks to validate its earlier estimates of global warming due to climate change, using climate models. Between 1990 and 2005 models predicted a change between 0.15 and 0.29 °C, though the actual increase of 0.33 °C shows that the models predict, if anything, slightly low estimates. See http://www. ipcc.ch/activity/ar.htm.

14. For an excellent overview see J. Houghton, *Global Warming: The Complete Briefing* (3rd edn, Cambridge, Cambridge University Press, 2004).

15. World Watch Institute, *Vital Signs: 2006–7*, op. cit., pp. 42–3. See also http://www. worldwatch.org/node/4400, accessed 5 July 2007.

16. Scientists still debate as to whether 2005 or 1998 saw the highest global temperatures on record overall, due to statistical variation in measurement of the results. See http://data. giss.nasa.gov/gistemp/2005/, accessed 11 July 2007. As this book goes to press, the results suggest that 2007 was in the same category as 1998, see http://www.sciencedaily.com/releases/2008/01/080116114150.htm, accessed 3 March 2008.

17. The carbon cycle refers to those natural processes of the respiratory release of carbon dioxide by living things, which lead to an overall increase in carbon dioxide levels, followed by carbon fixation – that is, the conversion of free carbon dioxide to sugars and other carbohydrates, primarily through photosynthesis.

18. D. A. Stainforth, T. Aina *et al.*, 'Uncertainty in Predictions of the Climate Response to Rising Levels of Greenhouse Gases', *Nature*, 405 (January 2005), pp. 403–6.

19. Anthropogenic effects are those effects directly related to human activities, such as burning fossil fuels.

20. The 'biosphere' is the change in atmospheric conditions caused by the activities of the biota – that is, the sum total of living things on the planet.

21. The hydrological cycle is, as the name suggests, the cycling of water from rivers, to sea, then evaporation into clouds and eventually back into rivers.

22. World Watch Institute, *Vital Signs: 2006–7*, op. cit., pp. 44–5.

23. The Kyoto agreement of 1997 was an international agreement aimed to encourage all nations to reduce carbon dioxide emissions.

24. Discussion of the economics of climate change can be found in *The Stern Review: The Economics of Climate Change* (Cambridge, Cambridge University Press, 2007).

25. http://www.hm-treasury.gov.uk/media/4/7/WorldEconomics2.pdf and http://www. hm-treasury.gov.uk/media/E/8/World_Economics1.pdf, also published in *World Economics*, 8 (1), accessed 5 July 2007.

26. http://www.defra.gov.uk/environment/statistics/globatmos/gagccukem.htm, accessed 5 July 2007.

27. We will return to this in the next chapter on giving economic value to environmental goods. For a more detailed review of climate change by Christian scholars, see S. McDonagh, *Climate Change: The Challenge to All of Us* (Blackrock, The Columba Press, 2006) and M. Northcott, *A Moral Climate: The Ethics of Global Warming* (London, DLT, 2007)

28. Northcott, *A Moral Climate*, op. cit., ch. 5.
29. http://www.worldwatch.org/node/4253, accessed 5 July 2007. There is also talk of how the human ecological footprint draws down the 'ecological capital', i.e. it is spoken of as an economic commodity.
30. See K. J. Gaston and J. I. Spicer, *Biodiversity* (2nd edn, Oxford, Blackwell, 2004), p. 110.
31. http://www.worldwatch.org/node/4258, accessed 5 July 2007; also in *Vital Signs: 2006–7*, op. cit., pp. 98–9.
32. Figures are from *Birdlife International*. By 2100 scientists predict that 6–14% will be extinct and 7–25% functionally extinct – that is, only a few remain, who are not able to reproduce. See *Vital Signs: 2006–7*, op. cit., pp. 96–7.
33. http://www.worldwatch.org/node/4267, accessed 5 July 2007.
34. http://www.worldwatch.org/node/4260, accessed 5 July 2007; also in *Vital Signs: 2006–7*, op. cit., pp. 102–3.
35. http://www.worldwatch.org/node/4259, accessed 5 July 2007; also in *Vital Signs: 2006–7*, op. cit., pp. 100–1.
36. http://www.worldwatch.org/node/4265, accessed 5 July 2007.
37. http://www.worldwatch.org/node/4255, accessed 5 July 2007; also in *Vital Signs: 2006–7*, op. cit., pp. 94–5.
38. C. M. Roberts, C. J. McClean, J. E. N. Veron, J. P. Hawkins, G. R. Allen, D. E. McAllister, C. G. Mittermeir, F. W. Schueler, M. Spalding, F. Wells, C. Vynne and T. B. Werner, 'Marine biodiversity hotspots and conservation priorities for tropical reefs', *Science*, 295 (2002), pp. 1280–84.
39. Gaston and Spicer, *Biodiversity*, op. cit., pp. 100–3.
40. Anne Platt McGinn, 'Harmful Algae Blooming Worldwide', in *Vital Signs, 1999-2000*, ed. Lester R. Brown, Michael Renner and Brian Halweil (World London, Earthscan/Watch Institute, 1999), pp. 126–7. See also http://www.arlington institute.org/wbp/species-extinction/443#, accessed 3 March 2008.
41. World Watch Institute, *Vital Signs: 1999–2000* (London, Earthscan, 1999), pp. 122–3; *Vital Signs: 2002–3* (London, Earthscan, 2001), pp. 102–3.
42. M. Midgley, *Gaia* (London, Demos, 2001); A. Primavesi, *Gaia's Gift* (London, Routledge, 2003).
43. J. Lovelock, *Gaia: A New Look at Life on Earth* (2nd edn, Oxford, Oxford University Press, 1987).
44. D. Worster, *Nature's Economy* (New York, Cambridge University Press, 1977).
45. M. Northcott, *Christianity and Environmental Ethics* (Cambridge, Cambridge University Press, 1996).
46. For further discussion see C. Deane-Drummond, *The Ethics of Nature* (Oxford, Blackwell, 2004), pp. 36–7.
47. For further discussion see C. Deane-Drummond, *Wonder and Wisdom: Conversations in Science, Spirituality and Theology* (London, DLT, 2006).
48. J. Schloss, 'Wisdom Traditions as Mechanisms for Organismal Integration', in W. S. Brown (ed.), *Understanding Wisdom* (Philadelphia, Templeton Foundation Press, 2000), p. 156.
49. E. O. Wilson, *Biophilia* (Cambridge, Mass., Harvard University Press, 1984).
50. E. O. Wilson, *In Search of Nature* (Washington, DC, Island Press/Shearwater Books, 1996).

51. E. O. Wilson, *Consilience* (London, Abacus, 1999).

52. L. Ceccarelli, *Shaping Science with Rhetoric* (Chicago and London, University of Chicago Press, 2001), p. 138.

53. R. Carson, *A Sense of Wonder* (New York, Harper and Row, 1965).

54. R. Carson, *Silent Spring* (Boston, Houghton Miflin, 1961).

55. Cited in T. Locker and J. Bruchac, *Rachel Carson*: *Preserving a Sense of Wonder* (Golden, Fulchrum Publishing, 2004), p. 32.

56. Hans Urs von Balthasar has argued for a recovery of a beauty, but it is one marked by the presence of the cross. For more discussion of the importance of a recovery of beauty and wisdom in the context of climate change, see C. Deane-Drummond, 'Where Streams Meet; Ecology, Wisdom and Beauty in Bulgakov, von Balthasar and Aquinas', in H. Meisinger, W. B. Drees and Z. Liana (eds.), *Wisdom or Knowledge? Science, Theology and Cultural Dynamics* (London, T. & T. Clark, 2006), pp. 108–26.

57. Northcott, *A Moral Climate*, op. cit., Introduction, p. 16.

Chapter 2: Economics and Environmental Justice

1. See John O'Neill, 'King Darius and the Environmental Economist', in Tim Haywood and John O'Neill (eds.), *Justice, Property and the Environment* (Aldershot, Ashgate, 1997), pp. 114–30.

2. G. Smith, *Deliberative Democracy and the Environment* (London, Routledge, 2003), pp. 29–49.

3. H. Cox, 'Mammon and the Culture of the Market: A Socio-Theological Critique', in Roger S. Gottlieb (ed.), *Liberating Faith: Religious Voices for Justice, Peace and Ecological Wisdom* (Lanham, Rowman and Littlefield, 2003), p. 277.

4. Ulrich Beck, *What is Globalisation?*, trans. Patrick Camiller (Cambridge, Polity Press, 2000), p. 4.

5. Ibid., pp. 9–13.

6. Benefit sharing is the distribution of some profits for the common good through recognition of responsibility that comes with attainment of power in the economy.

7. M. Stenmark, *Environmental Ethics and Policy Making* (Basingstoke, Ashgate, 2002).

8. Joseph R. des Jardins, *Environmental Ethics: An Introduction to Environmental Philosophy* (Belmont, Wadsworth, 2001), pp. 60–2.

9. M. Northcott, *A Moral Climate: The Ethics of Global Warming* (London, DLT, 2007), ch. 4, 'Climate Economics', pp. 120–56.

10. John C. Médaille has argued from a Roman Catholic perspective for social justice in the market-place. This is certainly a step in the right direction. I would urge further that environmental and ecological justice are required as well. See J. C. Médaille, *The Vocation of Business: Social Justice in the Market Place* (London, T. & T. Clark International/Continuum, 2007). I am grateful to Catherine Cowley for pointing me to this reference.

11. John B. Cobb, 'Towards a Just and Sustainable Economic Order', in Andrew Light and Holmes Rolson III (eds.), *Environmental Ethics: An Anthology* (Oxford, Blackwell, 2003), pp. 359–70.

12. E. F. Schumacher, *Small is Beautiful: Economics as if People Mattered* (London, Blond and Briggs, 1973).

13. C. Deane-Drummond and B. Szerszynski (eds.), *Re-Ordering Nature: Theology, Society and the New Genetics* (Edinburgh, T. & T. Clark, 2003).

14. C. Deane-Drummond, 'Chapter 11: Biotechnology', in C. Southgate (ed.), *God, Humanity and the Cosmos* (2nd edn, London, Continuum, 2006), pp. 361–92.

15. See report of WCC consultation on genetics in December 2007; 'Aide Memoire from the Global Consultation on Genetics and New Biotechnologies and the Ministry of the Church' http://www.oikoumene.org/en/news/news-management/eng/a/article/1722/genetic-advances-and-new.html, accessed 3 March 2007.

16. For these and other examples see Donald and Ann Bruce, *Engineering Genesis* (London, Earthscan, 1999).

17. See C. Deane-Drummond, 'Genetic Interventions in Nature: Perspectives from a Christian Ethic of Wisdom' in Denis Edwards and Mark Worthing (eds.), *Biodiversity and Ecology: An Interdisciplinary Challenge* (Adelaide, ATF Press, 2004), pp. 30–44.

18. For a fuller discussion of patenting and genetics see C. Deane-Drummond, *Genetics and Christian Ethics* (Cambridge, Cambridge University Press, 2006), pp. 160–90.

19. Citation in Mark Sagoff, paper for American Association for the Advancement in Science Dialogue Group on Genetic Patenting (1996), p. 13; also quoted in A. Chapman, *Unprecedented Choices: Religious Ethics at the Frontiers of Genetic Science* (Minneapolis, Fortress Press, 1999), p. 132.

20. A fuller discussion can be found in C. Deane-Drummond, 'Environmental Justice and the Economy: A Christian Theologian's View', *Ecotheology* 11.3 (2006), pp. 294–330.

21. C. Stephens, S. Bullock and A. Scott, *Environmental Justice: Rights and Means to a Healthy Environment for All, ESRC Briefing Paper No. 7* (London, Economic and Social Science Research Council, 2001).

22. J. Rawls, *A Theory of Justice* (Cambridge, Harvard University Press, 1971).

23. D. Bell, 'Environmental Justice and Rawls' Difference Principle', *Environmental Ethics*, 26.3 (Fall 2004), pp. 297–306.

24. T. Gorringe, *A Theology of the Built Environment: Justice, Empowerment, Redemption* (Cambridge, Cambridge University Press, 2002).

25. M. Grey, *Sacred Longings* (London, SCM Press, 2003); S. McFague, *Life Abundant: Rethinking Theology and Economy for a Planet in Peril* (Minneapolis, Fortress Press, 2001).

26. Amartya Sen, *Inequality Re-examined* (Oxford, Sage, 1992). Also developed in A. Sen, *Development as Freedom* (New York, Alfred Knopf, 1999).

27. This strikes me as a more realistic approach to the economy compared with Michael Northcott, whose somewhat strident attack shows up the clear environmental and social limitations of global politics and the economy, without really offering an alternative that is realisable in practical terms. See M. Northcott, *A Moral Climate*, op. cit. His comparison of the use of cedars in the ancient biblical world with the fuel economy in the present world (pp. 101–7, 116) also seems a little strained. The common ground in both may be underlying greed and abuse of power, but how does this really help us in ethical terms, other than pointing to the flaws in the systems common in the history of humanity? For a review of Northcott's book see C. Deane-Drummond, *Expository Times*, 2008, in press.

28. Arguably, the gathering pace and likely extent of climate change has also forced this issue for present as well as future generations.
29. R. Muers, 'Pushing the Limit: Theology and the Responsibility to Future Generations', *Studies in Christian Ethics*, 16.2 (2004), pp. 36–45, citation, p. 41.
30. W. Beckerman and J. Pasek, *Justice, Posterity and the Environment* (Oxford, Oxford University Press, 2001).
31. P. M. Wood, 'Intergenerational Justice and Curtailments on the Discretionary Powers of Governments', *Environmental Ethics*, Vol. 26.4 (Winter 2004), pp. 411–28.

Chapter 3: Eco-theology from the North

1. Aldo Leopold, *A Sand County Almanac – and Sketches Here and There* (1949; New York, Ballantine, 1970). See also extracts in Mark J. Smith (ed.), *Thinking through the Environment: A Reader* (London, The Open University/Routledge, 1999), pp. 189–96. For other essays see Susan Flader and J. Baird Callicott, *The River of the Mother of God and Other Essays* (Madison, University of Wisconsin Press, 1991).
2. A. Leopold, 'The Land Ethic', in *A Sand County Almanac*, op. cit., p. 262.
3. J. Lovelock, *Gaia: A New Look at Life on Earth* (2nd edn, Oxford, Oxford University Press, 1987).
4. For a good summary of these issues see Joseph R. des Jardins, *Environmental Ethics: An Introduction to Environmental Philosophy* (3rd edn, London, Wadsworth, 2001), pp. 192–206.
5. J. Baird Callicott, 'The Land Ethic in a Time of Change', in Richard L. Knight and Suzanne Riedel (eds.), *Aldo Leopold and the Ecological Conscience* (Oxford, Oxford University Press, 2002), p. 104.
6. Peter S. Wenz, *Environmental Ethics Today* (Oxford, Oxford University Press, 2001), p. 158.
7. For discussion, see S. Conway Morris (ed.), *The Deep Structure of Biology: Is Convergence Sufficiently Ubiquitous to Give a Directional Signal?* (Philadelphia, Templeton Foundation Press, forthcoming 2008).
8. See S. Conway Morris, *Life's Solution: Inevitable Humans in a Lonely Universe* (Cambridge, Cambridge University Press, 2002).
9. Steven Bouma-Prediger, *For the Beauty of the Earth* (Grand Rapids, Baker Academic, 2001), p. 133.
10. Arne Naess, 'The Shallow and the Deep, Long Range Ecology Movement', *Inquiry*, 16 (1973), pp. 95–100.
11. For a summary see Bill Devall and George Sessions, *Deep Ecology* (Salt Lake City, Peregrine Smith Books, 1985), pp. 69–70.
12. See des Jardins, *Environmental Ethics*, op. cit., pp. 210–13.
13. Scientific reductionism as a methodology is the view that science understands wholes only in relation to its separate elements. As a theory of knowledge or epistemology, it goes further than this and argues for the reduction of other explanations to scientific ones.
14. For helpful analysis from an Indian perspective see Guha Ramachandra, 'Radical American Environmentalism and Wilderness Preservation: A Third World Critique', *Environmental Ethics*, 11 (Spring 1989), pp. 71–84.

15. See, for example, Pierre Teilhard de Chardin, *The Human Phenomenon*, trans. Susan Appleton-Weber (Brighton, Sussex Academic Press, 1999); Pierre Teilhard de Chardin, *The Divine Milieu*, trans. Sion Cowell (Brighton, Sussex Academic Press, 2003).

16. C. Deane-Drummond (ed.), *Teilhard de Chardin on People and Planet* (London, Equinox, 2006), esp. J. Skehan, 'Exploring Teilhard's "New Mysticism": "Building the Cosmos"', pp. 13–36.

17. See, in particular, the essay by John Grim and Mary Tucker, 'An Overview of Teilhard's Commitment to "Seeing" as Expressed in His Phenomenology, Metaphysics, and Mysticism' in Deane-Drummond, *Teilhard de Chardin*, op. cit., pp. 55–73.

18. U. King, 'One Planet, One Spirit: Searching for an Ecologically Balanced Spirituality', in Deane-Drummond, *Teilhard de Chardin*, op. cit., pp. 74–95. Diarmuid Ó Murchú similarly argues in the same collection that there are resources embedded in Teilhard's work that can meet the need of contemporary spiritualities that seek to identify more fully with the earth. See D. Ó Murchú, 'Teilhard: A Mystical Survivor!', in Deane-Drummond, *Teilhard de Chardin*, op. cit., pp. 96–104.

19. See C. Deane-Drummond, 'Sophia, Mary and the Eternal Feminine in Pierre Teilhard de Chardin and Sergei Bulgakov', in Deane-Drummond, *Teilhard de Chardin*, op. cit., pp. 209–25.

20. See S. Cowell, 'Newman and Teilhard: The Challenge of the East', in Deane-Drummond, *Teilhard de Chardin*, op. cit., pp. 193–208.

21. See Robert Faricy, 'The Exploitation of Nature and Teilhard's Ecotheology Of Love', in Deane-Drummond, *Teilhard de Chardin*, op. cit., pp. 123–37.

22. See Richard Kropf, 'Our Environmental Responsibilities in the Light of Contemporary Cosmology: A Teilhardian Retrospect', in Deane-Drummond, *Teilhard de Chardin*, op. cit., pp. 141–59.

23. See Ludovico Galleni and Francesco Scalfari, 'Teilhard de Chardin's Engagement with the Relationship between Science and Theology in the Light of Discussions about Environmental Ethics', in Deane-Drummond, *Teilhard de Chardin*, op. cit., pp. 160–78.

24. See Mary Grey, 'Cosmic Communion: A Contemporary Reflection on the Eucharistic Vision of Teilhard de Chardin', in Deane-Drummond, *Teilhard de Chardin*, op. cit., pp. 107–22.

25. Deane-Drummond, 'Sophia, Mary and the Eternal Feminine', op. cit.

26. Thomas King, 'Teilhard and the Environment', in Deane-Drummond, *Teilhard de Chardin*, op. cit., pp. 179–92.

27. For a helpful critical review of Fox's work, see David Keen, 'Creation Spirituality and the Environment Debate', *Ecotheology*, 7.1 (2002), pp. 10–29.

28. For example, Matthew Fox, *Original Blessing* (Santa Fe, Bear and Co., 1983); *A Spirituality Named Compassion for the Healing of the Global Village, Humpty Dumpty and Us* (2nd edn, New York, Harper, 1990); *Creation Spirituality-Liberating Gifts for the Peoples of the Earth* (San Francisco, HarperCollins, 1991).

29. Pantheism in this case means identification of the divine with the world as such.

30. Thomas Berry, *The Dream of the Earth* (San Francisco, Sierra Club Books, 1988),

p. 22.
31. See, for example, Elisabeth Sahourtis, *Gaia: The Human Journey from Chaos to Cosmos* (New York, Pocket Books, 1989).
32. Brian Swimme and Thomas Berry, *The Universe Story* (San Francisco, HarperCollins, 1992), p. 242.
33. Ibid., p. 242.
34. Ibid., pp. 249–61.
35. John Haught, *The Promise of Nature* (Mahwah, Paulist Press, 1993), pp. 104–5.

Chapter 4: Eco-theology from the South

1. Those wishing to refer to a wider spread of literature need to consult the excellent bibliography compiled by Ernst Conradie. E. Conradie, *Christianity and Ecological Theology: Resources for Further Research* (Stellenbosch: Sun Press, 2006). This bibliography lists sources from across the globe, but is particularly useful in pointing to texts that are published from the perspective of the South.
2. For further discussion see C. Deane-Drummond, *Theology and Biotechnology: Implications for a New Science* (London, Geoffrey Chapman, 1997), pp. 105–32.
3. A. G. Frank, *Capitalism and Underdevelopment in Latin America: Historical Studies of Chile and Brazil* (New York, Monthly Review Press, 1969).
4. G. Gutiérrez, *A Theology of Liberation* (revised edn, London, SCM Press, 1988); *The Power of the Poor in History* (London, SCM Press, 1983).
5. This case study is drawn from Sarah White and Romy Tiongco, *Doing Theology and Development: Meeting the Challenge of Poverty* (Edinburgh, St Andrew's Press, 1997), pp. 154–8.
6. Ibid., p. 158.
7. Leonardo Boff, *Ecology and Liberation: A New Paradigm* (Maryknoll, Orbis Books, 1995).
8. Ibid., p. 89.
9. Ibid., p. 125.
10. Ibid., pp. 128–30.
11. Leonardo Boff, *Cry of the Earth: Cry of the Poor* (Maryknoll, Orbis Books, 1997).
12. Ibid., p. 71.
13. Ibid., p. 104.
14. Ibid., p. 111.
15. Ibid., p. 112.
16. Ibid., p. 113.
17. Ibid.
18. His writing is prolific in this area. Some core examples of his work include, for example, S. McDonagh, *To Care for the Earth: A Call to a New Theology* (London, Geoffrey Chapman, 1986); *The Greening of the Church* (London, Geoffrey Chapman, 1990); *Passion of the Earth: The Christian Vision to Promote Justice, Peace and the Integrity of Creation* (London, Geoffrey Chapman, 1994).
19. For a critical discussion see C. Deane-Drummond, *The Ethics of Nature* (Oxford, Blackwell, 2004), pp. 162–85.
20. Boff has taken this into account in his admission of the 'permanent message of original peoples', but his emphasis on the earth understood as a global organism

remains intact. Boff, *Cry of the Earth*, op. cit., pp. 122–7.

21. R. Cooper, 'Through the Soles of My Feet: A Personal View of Creation', in D. Hallman (ed.), *Ecotheology: Voices from South and North* (Geneva, WCC, 1994), pp. 211–12.

22. G. Tinker, 'The Full Circle of Liberation', in Hallman (ed.), *Ecotheology*, op. cit., pp. 218–24.

23. Ibid., p. 220.

24. S. McKay, 'An Aboriginal Perspective on the Integrity of Creation', in Hallman (ed.), *Ecotheology*, op. cit., pp. 213–17.

25. P. Tolliday, 'Ecotheology as a Plea for Place', in D. Edwards (ed.), *Earth Revealing, Earth Healing* (Collegeville, The Liturgical Press, 2001), p. 188; full article, pp. 177–93.

26. S. K. Gitu, *The Environmental Crisis: A Challenge for African Christians* (Nairobi, Action Publishers). I am grateful to Ernst Conraide for pointing me to this source.

27. E. Conradie, 'Christianity and the Environment in South Africa: Four Dominant Approaches', contribution to edited collection in Public Theology, Beyers Naude Centre for Public Theology, *in preparation*.

28. S. Schama, *Landscape and Memory* (London, Fontana Press, 1996).

29. For discussion see the helpful chapter by Stephen Downs, 'The Landscape Tradition: A Broader Vision for Ecotheology' in Edwards (ed.), *Earth Revealing*, op. cit., pp. 1–18.

30. Marthinus L. Daneel, 'Earthkeeping Churches at the African Grass Roots', in Dieter T. Hessel and Rosemary Radford Ruether (eds.), *Christianity and Ecology: Seeking the Well Being of Earth and Humans* (Cambridge, Harvard University Press, 2000), pp. 531–52.

31. Cited in Daneel, 'Earthkeeping Churches', op. cit., p. 545.

Chapter 5: Eco-theology from the East

1. John Zizioulas, also known as Metropolitan John of Pergamon, delivered three lectures to King's College, London in January 1989 on 'Preserving God's Creation'. They were subsequently published in a number of places – for example, *King's Theological Review* (1989, 1990); *Sourozh* (1990); and *Theology in Green* (1993). He has also been actively involved in Inter-Orthodox and ecumenical conferences that highlight environmental concerns. See Metropolitan John of Pergamon, 'Orthodoxy and the Problem of the Protection of the Natural Environment', in *So that God's Creation Might Live: The Orthodox Church Responds to the Ecological Crisis* (The Ecumenical Patriarchate of Constantinople, 1992), pp. 19–28; 'Ethics versus *Ethos*: An Orthodox Approach to the Relation between Ecology and Ethics', in *The Environment and Ethics: Summer Seminar on Halki* (Ecumenical Patriarchate of Constantinople, 1995), pp. 25–7; 'The Book of Revelation and the Natural Environment', in S. Hobson and J. Lubchenco (eds.), *Revelation and the Environment* AD *95–1995* (Singapore/River Edge, USA/London, World Scientific, 1997), pp. 17–21. For a more recent statement see J. Zizioulas, 'Symbolism and Realism in Orthodox Worship', *Sourozh*, 79 (February 2000), pp. 3–17.

2. P. Gregorios, *The Human Presence: An Orthodox View of Nature* (Geneva, WCC,

1978), p. 25. Other meanings of 'nature' include the non-human, the natural as opposed to the contrived, and nature as opposed to 'history' or 'culture'. Theologians similarly have set up a contrast between 'nature' and 'grace' in Roman Catholic traditions, or between 'natural' and 'revealed' theology in Protestant traditions.

3. This is, of course, hardly true for those more innovative contemporary liturgies that make a conscious effort to be aware in an ecological sense – such as, for example, those from the Iona community in Scotland, or others that draw on, for example, a Celtic theme.

4. Nativity, Vespers, from *The Festal Menaion*, trans. Mother Mary and Kallistos Ware (London, Faber and Faber, 1969), p. 254. Also cited in E. Theokritoff, 'Creation and Salvation in Orthodox Worship', *Ecotheology*, 10 (2001), pp. 97–108. Note that the particular use of the Bible by the early Church fathers was conducted without the strictures of modern scriptural exegesis.

5. Vespers for 2 January, Apostikha cited in Theokritoff, 'Creation and Salvation', op. cit., p. 99.

6. Theokritoff, 'Creation and Salvation', op. cit., p. 103.

7. Ibid., p. 104.

8. Ibid., p. 107.

9. John Zizioulas, 'Preserving God's Creation: Lecture 3', *King's Theological Review*, Vol. XIII (1990), p. 5. For a similar argument published more recently see J. Zizioulas, 'Man the Priest of Creation', in A. Walker and C. Carras (eds.), *Living Orthodoxy in the Modern World* (London, SPCK, 1996), pp. 178–88.

10. Zizioulas, 'Preserving God's Creation: Lecture 3', op. cit., p. 5.

11. Ibid., p. 5.

12. Ibid.

13. E. Theokritoff, 'Creation and Priesthood in Modern Orthodox Thinking', *Ecotheology*, 10.3 (2005), pp. 344–63.

14. This is the view expressed by Alexander Schememann. See A. Schememann, *For the Life of the World* (Crestwood, St Vladimir's Seminary Press, 1973), p. 73.

15. Theokritoff, 'Creation and Priesthood', op. cit., p. 360.

16. For a useful, more detailed discussion of this aspect see A. Nesteruk, *Light from the East* (New York, Fortress Press/Augsburg, 2003), pp. 101–9.

17. Ibid., p. 105.

18. K. Ware, 'God Immanent yet Transcendent: The Divine Energies According to Saint Gregory Palamas', in P. Clayton and A. Peacocke (eds.), *In Whom We Live and Move and Have Our Being: Panentheistic Reflections on God's Presence in a Scientific World* (Grand Rapids (USA)/Cambridge (UK), Eerdmans, 2004), pp. 157–68. See also contributions to this volume by A. Louth, pp. 184–96 and A. Nesteruk, pp. 169–83.

19. Ware, 'God Immanent yet Transcendent', op. cit., p. 159.

20. Ibid., p. 160.

21. Ibid., p. 167, italics mine.

22. For further comparison with Solovyov and Florensky, see my discussion in C. Deane-Drummond, *Creation through Wisdom* (Edinburgh, T. & T. Clark, 2000), pp. 78–91.

23. See, for example, his earlier work, *The Unfading Light*; excerpts in English in R.

Williams, *Sergii Bulgakov: Towards a Russian Political Theology* (Edinburgh, T. & T. Clark, 1999), pp. 149–52; S. Bulgakov, *Sophia: The Wisdom of God: An Outline of Sophiology* (Hudson, NY, Lindisfarne Press, 1993).

24. See, for example, S. Bulgakov, *The Comforter*, trans. B. Jakim (Grand Rapids, Eerdmans, 2004), pp. 191–2.

25. Ibid., p. 194.

26. Ibid., p. 195.

27. Ibid., p. 199.

28. Ibid., p. 200.

29. Ibid., p. 201.

30. See, for example, S. Bulgakov, *The Bride of the Lamb*, trans. B. Jakim (Grand Rapids, Eerdmans, 2002), p. 196.

31. In this respect Bulgakov may have misunderstood evolutionary theory. He contrasts sharply randomness with design. See, for example, *The Comforter*, op. cit., pp. 207–8 and *The Bride of the Lamb*, op. cit., p. 197. Although the origin of life is only dimly understood according to evolutionary principles, so his charge that 'out of nothing comes everything' stands in this respect, many theists would now accept an element of randomness as integral to development. His alternative theory, based on a divine life-force and divine 'seeds', comes over as somewhat naïve in the light of evolutionary hypotheses, unless they are understood in a metaphorical sense.

32. Bulgakov, *The Bride of the Lamb*, op. cit., p. 198. His equation of 'amoral nature' with evil spirits is unconvincing in that it sets up a dualism in the created world, though given the difficulties associated with evolutionary theodicy, it is understandable that he uses angels and spirits as a way out of the problem. For further discussion of this aspect, see Chapter 9.

33. For discussion see Anestis G. Keselopoulos, *Man and the Environment: A Study of St Symeon* (Crestwood, St Vladimir's Seminary Press, 2001), pp. 94–5.

34. Ibid., p. 107.

35. The concept of co-creation is rarely used, but found in St Symeon in the context of a discussion about talents and charisms received as gifts. Ibid., p. 113.

36. Ibid., pp. 128–9.

37. Ibid., citing St Silouan the Athonite, p. 137.

38. Fr Makarios, 'The Monk and Nature in the Orthodox Tradition', in Metropolitan John of Pergamon, *So that God's Creation Might Live*, op. cit., pp. 41–8.

39. See Williams, *Sergii Bulgakov: Towards a Russian Political Theology*, op. cit. Bulgakov was critical of political ideologies, including socialism, for their inhuman treatment of persons as anomic individuals, but his critique lacks any concrete alternatives. See Williams' discussion of the topic, pp. 229–36.

Chapter 6: Eco-theology from the West

1. A good example of this sort is to be found in Philip Sherrard's work, such as P. Sherrard, *Human Image: World Image* (Ipswich, Golgonoosa Press, 1992).

2. M. Northcott, *The Environment and Christian Ethics* (Cambridge, Cambridge University Press, 1996), p. 41.

3. Modern science does not have to show these qualities and naming Francis Bacon as a scapegoat in this respect ignores other strands in his work that are more

benign in tone. See, for example, Alistair McGrath's discussion in *The Re-Enchantment of Nature* (London, Hodder and Stoughton, 2002), pp. 59–61.

4. Northcott, *The Environment and Christian Ethics*, op. cit., pp. 164ff.

5. M. Northcott, *A Moral Climate* (London, DLT, 2007).

6. The use of Bookchin is strictly illustrative here; other examples of social/political theorists could be discussed – for example, socialist ecology that draws on Marxist frameworks.

7. Deep Ecology argues for a new ontology – that is, a new structured relationship between humans and nature. It would be mistaken, however, to suggest that there are no ontological elements in Bookchin – for example, his belief that humans are by nature social.

8. See, for example, Andrew Light, 'Reconsidering Bookchin and Marcuse as Environmental Materialists', in A. Light (ed.), *Social Ecology after Bookchin* (London, The Guildford Press, 1998), p. 348.

9. See M. Bookchin, *The Philosophy of Social Ecology: Essays on Dialectical Naturalism* (2nd edn, London, Black Rose Books, 1996), pp. 147–83.

10. See, in particular, Peter Scott, *A Political Theology of Nature* (Cambridge, Cambridge University Press, 2003), pp. 109–35.

11. J. Clark, 'Municipal Dreams: A Social Ecological Critique of Bookchin's Politics', in Light (ed.), *Social Ecology after Bookchin*, op. cit., pp. 137–91.

12. Scott, *A Political Theology of Nature*, op. cit., pp. 130–5.

13. Ibid., p. 234.

14. This section draws on C. Deane-Drummond, 'Biotechnology: A New Challenge to Theology and Ethics', in C. B. Southgate (ed.), *God, Humanity and the Cosmos: A Companion to the Science and Religion Debate* (2nd edn, London, Continuum, 2005), pp. 361–90.

15. For an anthology addressing these issues see C. Deane-Drummond and B. Szerszynski (eds.), *Re-Ordering Nature: Theology, Society and Genetics* (London, Continuum, 2003).

16. John Cobb is an influential writer in this vein; see J. B. Cobb, *Is it Too Late?* (Beverley Hills, Bruce, 1972).

17. Philip Hefner, *Technology and Human Becoming* (Minneapolis, Fortress Press, 2003).

18. For discussion see UNEP, *Global Environmental Outlook 3 Report* (London, Earthscan, 2002), pp. 18, 126. The Cartagena Protocol was 'developed to ensure that recipient countries have both the opportunity and the capacity to assess risks relating to GMOs, and to ensure their safe transfer, handling and use', p. 126.

19. Ibid., p. 332.

20. Note, this legitimacy is not to be understood in a legal sense, but in the sense of the Government's failure to take account of public opinion, even while commissioning work that would allow such opinions to be aired and discussed.

21. The difference in reaction to medical genetic technologies compared with genetic modifications of crops is likely to be related to the idealised perception that medical GMOs are far better understood and regulated compared with GM crop plants.

22. Peter Scott, 'Anarchy in the UK: GM Crops, Political Authority and the Rioting of God', *Ecotheology*, 11.1 (2006), pp. 32–56.

23. Ibid., p. 54.
24. See Nina Witoszek, 'Globalisation and Sustainability: A Humanist Agenda', *Ecotheology*, 11.3 (2006), pp. 269–82.
25. Sigurd Bergmann, 'Atmospheres of Synergy: Towards and Eco-Theological Aesth/Ethics of Space', *Ecotheology*, 11.3 (2006), pp. 327–57.
26. Consider, for example, changes to the journal *Ecotheology* from one that was initially entirely focused on Christian thought, to wider agendas, eventually evolving into the *Journal for the Study of Religion, Nature and Culture* in 2007.

Chapter 7: Biblical Eco-theology

1. Of course, there are some more conservative Christian groups that have relatively recently opposed reading the Bible as a mandate for ecological practice, more often than not because of suspicions about 'New Age' or pagan influences. Other targets for such suspicion were authors such as Matthew Fox, who encourages a form of spirituality that is detached from traditional views of sin and redemption. I suggest that this suspicion, although present some quarter of a century ago, has largely faded. It is now far more common, even among conservative Christians, to endorse ecological practice.
2. Lynn White, 'The Historical Roots of Our Ecologic Crisis', *Science*, 155 (10 March 1967), pp. 1203–7.
3. In this regard Ernst Conradie argues from the Reformed tradition that such confession needs to be set in the context of the way it was used fruitfully by the South African Church in the situation of apartheid, where admission of guilt was often difficult, as, in a way analogous to climate change, actions which supported such a structure were more often than not disguised from view. E. Conradie, 'Confessing guilt in a context of climate change', lecture delivered to the Centre for Religion and the Biosciences, 28 February 2008.
4. Arnold Toynbee, 'The Religious Background of the Present Environmental Crisis', in David and Eileen Spring (eds.), *Ecology in Religion and History* (New York, Harper and Row, 1974). It is also worth noting that other historians, such as Peter Harrison, point to the historical aspects of the interpretation of the text of Genesis. White, he believed, was correct to identify dominion as a theme that was read off from Genesis, but wrong to suppose that this interpretation was characteristic of the medieval period. See Peter Harrison, 'Having Dominion: Genesis and the Mastery of Nature', in R. J. Berry (ed.), *Environmental Stewardship: Critical Perspectives: Past and Present* (London, Continuum, 2006), pp. 17–31.
5. Commentaries on White's thesis continue to be aired even in more recent literature. For some examples see H. Paul Santmire, *Nature Reborn: The Ecological and Cosmic Promise of Christian Theology* (Minneapolis, Fortress Press, 2000), pp. 10–15; Steven Bouma-Prediger, *For the Beauty of the Earth: A Christian Vision for Creation Care* (Grand Rapids, Baker Academic, 2001), pp. 72–86; Alister McGrath, *The Re-Enchantment of Nature: Science, Religion and the Human Sense of Wonder* (London, Hodder and Stoughton, 2002), pp. xv–xvii, 28–31; Ellen Bernstein, *The Splendour of Creation: A Biblical Ecology* (Cleveland, The Pilgrim Press, 2005), pp. 110–15; as well as discussion in R. J. Berry (ed.), *Environmental Stewardship*, op. cit.
6. Paul Santmire, *The Travail of Nature: The Ambiguous Ecological Promise of*

Christian Theology (Philadelphia, Fortress Press, 1985).

7. For discussion of this see Francis Watson, 'Strategies of Recovery and Resistance: Hermeneutical Reflections on Genesis 1—3 and its Pauline Reception', *Journal of the Study of the New Testament* (1992), pp. 79–103.

8. These are helpfully summarised in Calvin B. de Witt, 'Creation's Environmental Challenge to Evangelical Christianity', in R. J. Berry (ed.), *The Care of Creation: Fostering Concern and Action* (Leicester, Inter-Varsity Press, 2000), pp. 65–7. His earlier paper articulated four main principles: the *earthkeeping* principle; the *Sabbath* principle; the *fruitfulness* principle; and the *limits* principle. See Calvin de Witt, 'Ecology and Ethics: Relation of Religious Belief to Ecological Practice in the Biblical Tradition', *Biodiversity and Conservation*, 4 (1995), pp. 838–48.

9. See, for example, R. J. Berry. (ed.), *When Enough is Enough: A Christian Framework for Environmental Sustainability* (Nottingham, Apollos/IVP, 2006).

10. Conradie discusses in some detail the different aspects of sin and its ecological ramifications. Ernst Conradie, *An Ecological Anthropology: At Home on Earth?* (Aldershot, Ashgate, 2005), pp. 184–202.

11. Ibid., p. 202. This quotation neatly summarises the rationale for dealing with Christology, theodicy and eschatology in the chapters following.

12. Such traditions also need to be brought alongside the New Testament accounts.

13. Richard Bauckham, 'Stewardship and Relationship', in R. J. Berry (ed.), *The Care of Creation*, op. cit., pp. 99–106.

14. For example, the text on the Evangelical declaration on the care of creation; see Berry (ed.), *The Care of Creation*, op. cit., pp. 17–22, but also in statements by Pope John Paul II in an address to a general audience on 17 January 2001, where he claimed that humanity was no longer the Creator's steward, but a despot. This text was cited in The Catholic Bishops' Conference of England and Wales' document, *The Call of Creation: God's Invitation and Human Response: The Natural Environment and Catholic Social Teaching* (London, Catholic Communications Service, 2002), p. 5. It is also noteworthy that stewardship is emphasised less in the latter document than other aspects, such as the status of creation (see below), especially in relationship to other ethical demands, such as concern for the poor.

15. Mary Grey, *Sacred Longings: Ecofeminist Theology and Liberation* (London, SCM Press, 2003). I will return to a discussion of this work in more detail in Chapter 11.

16. For report see http://www.environment.co.za/topic.asp?TOPIC_ID=1641, accessed 3 March 2008. This website also gives references to other Churches that have responded to the challenge of climate change, including a statement to the UN Climate Change conference in Bali in December 2007 from the the World Council of Churches, who claim that 'Societies must shift to a new paradigm where the operative principles are ethics, justice, equity, solidarity, human development and environmental conservation'; this call was associated with a more explicit rallying cry, 'This far and no further: act fast and act now!'.

17. Claus Westermann, *Blessing in the Bible and the Life of the Church*, trans. Keith Crim (Philadelphia, Fortress, 1978).

18. Paul Santmire, *Nature Reborn: The Ecological and Cosmic Promise of Christian Theology* (Minneapolis, Fortress Press, 2000).

19. Richard Bauckham, 'Joining Creation's Praise of God', *Ecotheology*, 7.1 (2002),

pp. 45–59.

20. For commentary, see D. E. Gowan, *From Eden to Babel: A Commentary on the Book of Genesis 1—11* (Grand Rapids, Eerdmans, 1988), p. 26.

21. Scholars who wish to emphasise this aspect include, for example, C. Westermann, *Genesis 1—11, A Commentary*, trans. John J. Scullion (London, SPCK, 1984); G. von Rad, *Genesis* (London, SCM Press, 1972), pp. 55, 57. Although more appealing theologically, the creation story in Genesis does not answer the question as to whether the initial creative activity of God was 'out of nothing' in the beginning or not; see Westermann, p. 174.

22. Robert Murray, *The Cosmic Covenant* (London, Sheed and Ward, 1992), p. 34.

23. Santmire, *Nature Reborn*, op. cit., pp. 33–4.

24. Murray, *The Cosmic Covenant*, op. cit., p. 169.

25. For a helpful commentary on the principles see Norman Habel, 'Introducing the Earth Bible', in Norman C. Habel (ed.), *Readings from the Perspective of Earth, The Earth Bible 1* (Sheffield, Sheffield Academic Press, 2000), pp. 25–37; The Earth Bible Team, 'Guiding Ecojustice Principles', in Habel (ed.), *Readings from the Perspective of Earth*, op. cit., pp. 38–53; The Earth Bible Team, 'Conversations with Gene Tucker and Other Writers', in Norman Habel and Shirley Wurst (eds.), *The Earth Story in Genesis, The Earth Bible 2* (Sheffield, Sheffield Academic Press, 2000), pp. 21–33.

26. Paul Trebilco, 'The Goodness and Holiness of the Earth and the Whole Creation (1 Timothy 4:1–5)', in Habel (ed.), *Readings from the Perspective of Earth*, op. cit., pp. 204–20.

27. Gunther Wittenburg, 'Alienation and Emancipation from the Earth: The Earth Story in Genesis 4', in Habel and Wurst (eds.), *The Earth Story in Genesis*, op. cit., pp. 105–16.

28. Terence E. Fretheim, 'The Earth Story in Jeremiah 12', in Habel (ed.), *Readings from the Perspective of Earth*, op. cit., pp. 96–110.

29. As discussed in Brendan Bryne, 'Creation Groaning: An Earth Bible Reading of Romans 8:18–22', in Habel (ed.), *Readings from the Perspective of Earth*, op. cit., pp. 193–203.

30. Keith Carley, 'Psalm 8: An Apology for Domination', in Habel (ed.), *Readings from the Perspective of Earth*, op. cit., pp. 111–24.

31. Norman Habel, 'Geophany: The Earth Story in Genesis 1', in Habel and Wurst (eds.), *The Earth Story in Genesis*, op. cit. pp. 38–9.

32. I will discuss the wisdom traditions in the New Testament in a later chapter on Christ and ecology. There is also further elaboration of woman wisdom in the chapter on eco-feminism.

33. Norman Habel, 'Where is the Voice of Earth in the Wisdom Literature?' in Norman Habel and Shirley Wurst (eds.), *The Earth Story in Wisdom Traditions, The Earth Bible 3* (Sheffield, Sheffield Academic Press, 2001), pp. 23–34, esp. p. 24.

34. For a fascinating account, see N. Habel, 'The Implications of God Discovering Wisdom in Earth', in Ellen van Wolde (ed.), *Job 28: Cognition in Context* (Leiden, Brill, 2003), pp. 281–97.

35. Norman Habel, 'Earth First: Inverse Cosmology in Job', in Habel and Wurst (eds.), *The Earth Story in Wisdom Traditions*, op. cit., pp. 65–77.

36. Habel, 'The Implications of God Discovering Wisdom', op. cit., p. 292.
37. The Patristic interpretation of the Wisdom of God existing as God's *energeia*, as discussed in Chapter 5, would rely on the concept of wisdom pre-existing in God. Leo Purdue follows this interpretation in relation to the Job passages. See L. Perdue, *Wisdom and Creation: The Theology of Wisdom Literature* (Nashville, Abingdon, 1994), p. 186.
38. Habel challenges us to go further than this and suggests that God *acquires* Wisdom from creaturely wisdom, using the more common interpretation of Proverbs 8:22 to mean 'acquire' rather than 'create'.
39. See Denis Edwards, *Jesus the Wisdom of God* (Maryknoll, Orbis Books, 1995), p. 28.
40. Space does not permit a discussion of prudence in an environmental context, but some examples may be found in C. Deane-Drummond, *The Ethics of Nature* (Oxford, Blackwell, 2004).
41. C. Deane-Drummond, 'Living from the Sabbath: Developing an Ecological Theology in the Context of Diversity', in Denis Edwards and Mark Worthing (eds.), *Biodiversity and Ecology as Interdisciplinary Challenge, Interface 7/1* (Adelaide, ATF Press, 2004), pp. 1–13.
42. For discussion of this aspect of exegesis see Norman Habel, 'Geophany: The Earth Story in Genesis 1', in Habel and Wurst (eds.), *The Earth Story in Genesis*, op. cit., pp. 38–9.

Chapter 8: Ecology and Christology

1. John Hall's most important books are *Imaging God: Dominion as Stewardship* (Grand Rapids, Eerdmans, 1986); *The Steward: A Biblical Symbol Come of Age* (2nd edn, Grand Rapids, Eerdmans, 1990).
2. Of course, biblical exegesis might be suspicious of linking references to Christ with Genesis 1:28, but the idea of Christ as a second Adam is defensible, as will be discussed further below.
3. For a discussion of this aspect, see Duncan Reid, 'Enfleshing the Human: An Earth-Revealing, Earth Healing Christology', in D. Edwards (ed.), *Earth Revealing, Earth Healing* (Collegeville, The Liturgical Press, 2001), pp. 69–84.
4. Ernst Conradie has pointed to the exclusive focus on the human, that is, the anthropocentrism pervading much Western, especially Protestant theology, where consideration of wider cosmological aspects in theology fades with the rise of modern science, for science is now given the high ground in descriptions of nature. This move also leads to a turn to the human subject and corresponding reduction in the idea of God as Creator to internal, existential notions of God in relation to the human subject. E. Conradie, *An Ecological Christian Anthropology: At Home on Earth?* (Aldershot, Ashgate, 2005), pp. 129–34. The lack of confidence in cosmological descriptions is also related to postmodern perspectives and the resistance to any form of 'grand narrative' that has heavily influenced theological discourse in recent years.
5. There is a difficulty that may become apparent to some readers, in that broadening of the scope of the incarnation's significance might imply that all of nature becomes divine. Sallie McFague's significant contribution to eco-theology tended to go rather too far in blurring the distinction between God and creation to such

an extent that Jesus and the earth become one in their divinisation. She draws back from a thoroughgoing pantheism by suggesting that the reality of God is not identical with or exhausted by the planet. What happens to the significance of Christ in such a view? He seems to disappear altogether as a theological paradigm. S. McFague, *The Body of God: An Ecological Theology* (Minneapolis, Fortress Press, 1993), p. 149. I will return to McFague's contribution in Chapter 11.

6. Paul Santmire's book is instructive here: *The Travail of Nature: The Ambiguous Promise of Christian Theology* (Philadelphia, Fortress Press, 1985).

7. The translation is taken from Michael Trainor, 'Celebrating Biodiversity: The Hymn to Christ in a Letter from Ancient Colossae' (Col. 1:15–20), in Denis Edwards and Mark Worthing (eds.), *Biodiversity and Ecology* (Adelaide, ATF Press, 2004), pp. 65–71.

8. Scholars divide on whether this letter was written by Paul or an author with Pauline sympathies after Paul's death, but the authorship is not pertinent to the discussion here.

9. Homer Kent, Curtis Vaughan and Arthur Rupprecht, *The Expositor's Bible Commentary with the New International Version: Colossians* (Grand Rapids, Zondervan Publishing, 1996), p. 89.

10. G. B. Caird, *Paul's Letters from Prison* (Oxford, Oxford University Press, 1984), p. 175.

11. Ibid., p. 178.

12. Markus Barth and Helmut Blanke, *Colossians: A New Translation with Introduction and Commentary*, The Anchor Bible, trans. Ashid B. Beck (New York, Doubleday, 1994), p. 246.

13. Trainor, 'The Hymn to Christ', op. cit., pp. 68–9.

14. Ibid., p. 70.

15. For further discussion of biblical interpretation, see Chapter 8.

16. Conradie, *An Ecological Christian Anthropology*, op. cit., p. 66.

17. Sittler took his inspiration from Colossians 1:15–20, discussed below. J. Sittler, 'Called to Unity', in S. Bouma-Prediger and P. Bakken (eds.), *Evocations of Grace: Writings on Ecology, Theology and Ethics* (Grand Rapids, Eerdmans, 2000), pp. 38–50.

18. See, for example, further discussion of this topic in C. Deane-Drummond, 'Shadow Sophia in Christological Perspective: The Evolution of Sin and the Redemption of Nature', in *Theology and Science*, 6.1, 2008, pp. 13–32.

19. J. Moltmann, *The Way of Jesus Christ* (London, SCM Press, 1990).

20. Matthew Fox, *The Coming of the Cosmic Christ: The Healing of Mother Earth and the Birth of Global Resistance* (San Francisco, Harper and Row, 1988).

21. For more discussion of Matthew Fox's view, see C. Deane-Drummond, *Creation through Wisdom: Theology and the New Biology* (Edinburgh, T. & T. Clark, 2000), pp. 40–2.

22. Although Moltmann pointed to this failure to discuss cosmic Christology in *The Way of Jesus Christ*, op. cit., p. 374, n. 3, he offered little explanation as to why this was the case. The failure also does not apply to Eastern Orthodox reflection on Christology, as noted by Sittler, 'Called to Unity', op. cit., p. 43.

23. He follows Galloway in naming and shaming the Middle Ages as a period when nature became disparaged, though this is a simplistic view of Aquinas' under-

standing of nature, for while he believed supernatural grace could be 'added' to nature, nature itself was good in as far as it emerged from God's gracious acts in the creation of the world through secondary causes and according to natural law. If anything, Aquinas put greater emphasis on the worth of the natural and the secular, following Aristotle, compared with Augustine, who was more deeply troubled by the idea of original sin.

24. Sittler, 'Called to Unity', op. cit., p. 45.
25. He suggests that the doctrine of the Trinity naturally followed from further reflection on the text. See J. Sittler, 'Chapter 2: Essays on Nature and Grace', in *Evocations of Grace*, op. cit., p. 116.
26. Ibid., p. 124.
27. V. Rossi, 'Christian Ecology is Cosmic Christology', *Epiphany*, 8 (1987), pp. 52–62.
28. Ibid., p. 54.
29. In his desire to counter what he believes are heretical tendencies in those theologians who have absorbed evolution into their faith, it is unfortunate that Rossi has castigated those attracted to biocentrism as equivalent to making a contract with the devil, for he believes a pernicious stream of thought follows from deifying the universe. He is also careful to reject scientism, rather than science as such, though this takes careful reading of his text. 'Ecology as science is of universal validity, applicable to all areas of life. Ecology as religion is a disaster, a Pandora's box releasing all manner of evils into the world.' Ibid., p. 62.
30. See, for example, Teilhard de Chardin, *The Human Phenomenon*, trans. Sarah Appleton Weber (Brighton, Sussex Academic Press, 1999). For a more specific reference to his cosmic Christology, see *L'activation de l'énergie* (Paris, Seuil, 1965).
31. Teilhard, *The Human Phenomenon*, op. cit., p. 152.
32. Teilhard de Chardin, *How I Believe*, trans. R. Hague in *Christianity and Evolution* (New York, Harcourt Brace Jovanovich, 1971), pp. 96–132.
33. This is the view, for example, of Paul Santmire; see, for example, *Nature Reborn* (Minneapolis, Fortress Press, 2000), pp. 53–5. However, he may not have fully appreciated the influence of Eastern traditions on Teilhard, which would have countered such a view by seeing unification as flowing from God to all things through the Logos. Further discussion of Teilhard's thought in relation to ecology is in C. Deane-Drummond (ed.), *Teilhard de Chardin on People and Planet* (London, Equinox, 2006).
34. Teilhard de Chardin, 'My Fundamental Vision', trans. R. Hague in *Towards the Future* (New York, Harcourt Brace Jovanovich, 1975), pp. 164–208, esp. p. 198.
35. The figure here also takes its cue from that of wisdom, but it culminates in announcing that love as being that of the Virgin Mary. For the original text see Teilhard de Chardin, 'The Eternal Feminine', trans. R. Hague in *Writings in Time of War* (New York, Harper and Row, 1968), pp. 191–202. For further discussion see C. Deane-Drummond, 'Sophia, Mary and the Eternal Feminine in Pierre Teilhard de Chardin and Sergei Bulgakov', *Ecotheology*, 10.2 (2005), pp. 215–31.
36. For a helpful discussion see Robert Faricy, 'The Exploitation of Nature and Teilhard's Ecotheology of Love', *Ecotheology*, 10.2 (2005), pp. 181–95.
37. This vision seems to have stemmed from his experiences in the trenches in World

War I, where he acted as a stretcher bearer. An account is in 'Christ in the World of Matter', in *Hymn of the Universe, Hymne de l'univers* (Paris: Seuil, 1961), pp. 39–51 and discussed in Faricy, 'The Exploitation of Nature', op. cit., p. 189. It should also be noted that unlike Santmire, critics of Teilhard at the time of his writing such essays accused him of being pantheistic.

38. His lack of attention to suffering makes it understandable that he has been accused of over-optimism, though this is not strictly true, as he is more aware than most of the reality of suffering. His difficulty, perhaps, like many others who adhere to a process vision of reality, is that suffering is considered inevitable in the movement towards unification. For further discussion of the theme of suffering in creation, see Chapter 9.

39. His earlier work, *The Crucified God* (London, SCM Press, 1974), widened to consider more explicit cosmic dimensions in *The Way of Jesus Christ* (London, SCM Press, 1990).

40. *The Way of Jesus Christ*, op. cit., p. 278.

41. Ibid., p. 280.

42. Ibid., p. 282.

43. Ibid., p. 291.

44. There are popular accounts of Christology that do make steps in this direction, as in, for example, J. Jones, *Jesus and the Earth* (London, SPCK, 2003); and E. Echlin, *Earth Spirituality: Jesus at the Centre* (London, John Hunt, 1999).

45. David Wenham, 'Kingdom and Creation from Jesus to Paul: Does the New Testament Give us an Ecological Mandate?', *Theology in Green*, 3 (July 1992), pp. 27–38.

46. Ibid., p. 33.

47. Keith Carley believes that the psalm is in effect an apology for domination. See K. Carley, 'Psalm 8: An Apology for Domination', in N. Habel (ed.), *Readings from the Perspective of Earth* (Sheffield, Sheffield Academic Press, 2000), pp. 111–24.

48. Michael Trainor, 'And on Earth Peace … (Luke 2:14). Lucan Perspectives on the Earth', in Habel, *Readings from the Perspective of Earth*, op. cit., pp. 174–92.

49. Trainor believes that the cosmological duality of heaven and earth has negative ecological consequences, as it speaks of a restoration of a hierarchy of heaven and earth, God and humanity.

50. Trainor, 'And on Earth Peace', op. cit., p. 190.

51. For discussion see Vicky Balabanski, 'An Earth Bible Reading of the Lord's Prayer; Matthew 6:9–13', in Habel, *Readings from the Perspective of Earth*, op. cit., pp. 151–61.

52. C. E. Carlson, 'Wisdom and eschatology in Q', in J. de Lobel (ed.), *Logia – The Paroles de Jesus (The Sayings of Jesus)* (Leuven, Leuven University Press, 1982).

53. James Dunn, *Christology in the Making* (London, SCM Press, 1989).

54. Dunn believes that the earliest expression of Wisdom Christology is in 1 Corinthians, and this then spread to Colossians 1, Hebrews 1:2, Matthew and John; ibid., pp. 211–12.

55. Denis Edwards seems to take this stand in *Jesus, the Wisdom of God: An Ecological Theology* (Homebush, St Pauls, 1995), see pp. 145–9.

56. See Deane-Drummond, 'Sophia in Christological Perspective'.

57. Edwards believes that in this respect Wisdom Christology has an advantage over Son of God Christologies, which he believes are docetic – that is, they do not do justice to Christ's human nature. Ibid., pp. 57–9. Such Son of God Christologies may be a reaction to the opposite tendency that seems to me to be rather more common – that is, too great an emphasis on the human nature of Christ.
58. Ibid., pp. 62–3.

Chapter 9: Ecology and Theodicy

1. Some authors, such as Southgate and Robinson, have resisted using the term 'evil', and prefer to use the term 'harm' as 'evil' when applied to the natural sphere on the basis that it might imply maleficent moral action. I am less convinced that 'evil' carries such connotations when used in the context of natural evils, since it is used habitually in the philosophical literature, and the use of the word 'harm' might entail a different danger, namely that it might give connotations of a certain lack of severity or seriousness. See C. Southgate and A. Robinson, 'Varieties of Theodicy: An Exploration of Responses to the Problem of Evil based on a Typology of Good/Harm Analysis', in Nancey Murphy, Robert J. Russell and William Stoeger (eds.), *Physics and Cosmology: Scientific Perspectives on the Problem of Natural Evil* (Berkeley and Vatican City, CTNS and Vatican Observatory, 2008), n. 4. I am particularly grateful to the authors for letting me read this chapter before publication.
2. Christopher Southgate, personal communication. I find the term 'biophysical evil' confusing, as biophysics in bioscience means biophysical processes that are physical in nature – that is, the use of physics to describe what is happening in the biological world. To name suffering in this way is, it seems to me, odd.
3. Space does not permit a full treatment of this issue here. See Marc Bekoff, *Animal Passions and Beastly Natures: Reflections on Redecorating Nature* (Philadelphia, Temple University Press, 2006); Frans de Waal and Peter Tyack, *Animal Social Complexity: Intelligence, Culture and Individualised Societies* (Cambridge, Harvard University Press, 2003).
4. Brian Davies, *The Reality of God and the Problem of Evil* (London, Continuum, 2006), p. 5, n. 1.
5. Although scholars were reluctant at the start to 'read into' animal behaviour parallels with human emotional states, such reluctance has some analogy with the reluctance to believe that animals that scream following physical torture are really suffering pain. I have also gradually become more convinced myself that animals are far more sophisticated in their emotional behaviour than we have given them credit for in the past.
6. Christopher Southgate comments on the work of Keith Ward in this respect in C. Southgate, 'God and Evolutionary Evil: Theodicy in the Light of Darwinism', *Zygon*, 37.4 (2002), pp. 803–21. Ward's most recent book does discuss this issue, though he believes that much of the suffering of the non-human world is a result of 'anthropomorphising' – that is, a reading into the pain of the world what it might be like from our point of view. See K. Ward, *Pascal's Fire* (Oxford, One World, 2006), p. 72.
7. See Ward, *Pascal's Fire*, op. cit., p. 72.
8. David L. Hull, 'The God of the Galapagos', *Nature*, 352, pp. 485–6.

9. Ibid., p. 486.
10. Southgate, 'God and Evolutionary Evil', op. cit. See also C. Southgate, 'Creation as Very Good and Groaning in Travail: An Exploration in Evolutionary Theodicy', in Ted Peters, Gaymon Bennett, Martinez Hewlett and Robert John Russell (eds.), *The Evolution of Evil* (Dordrecht: Vandenhoek and Rupprecht, 2008. I am grateful to the author for permitting me to read this article before publication.
11. Holmes Rolston III, *Science and Religion: A Critical Survey* (2nd edn, Philadelphia, Templeton Foundation Press, 2006), p. 133.
12. Although there may be adaptations to local ecological niches that do not entail combat or 'struggle' as such, Rolston believes that it is significant that the language of struggle is no longer used.
13. Denis Edwards has considered this problem in his essay, 'Celebrating Eucharist in a Time of Global Climate Change', *Pacifica*, 19 (February 2006), pp. 1–15.
14. Ernst Conradie, 'Confessing Guilt in the Context of Climate Change', lecture delivered to the Centre for Religion and the Bioscience, University of Chester, 28 February 2008. Of course, loss of habitat and species destruction are also a contributory factor in climate change, so the two issues are interlaced, but the rhetoric of climate change all too often tends to come back to negative impacts and injustices in relation to human communities, and the destruction of species that are not directly contributing to climate stability represents an evil that goes beyond the remit of climate change as such.
15. Rolston, *Science and Religion*, op. cit., p. 133.
16. A. Plantinga, *God, Freedom and Evil* (London, George Unwin, 1975).
17. This is the view of, for example, Kenneth Surin, *Theology and the Problem of Evil* (Oxford, Blackwell, 1986).
18. See Southgate and Robinson, 'Varieties of Theodicy', op. cit. I am not suggesting that Southgate and Robinson are limited to this kind of argument; I am merely pointing out that their term for this category is 'developmental good harm analysis', whereas I prefer the simpler 'process arguments', though this should not be confused or aligned with 'process theology'.
19. Keith Ward, in his most recent book *Pascal's Fire*, op. cit., remains anthropocentric in his focus in that he says that God is an 'ultimate mind of the universe', that suffering is 'a necessity of the natural order' and that the potentiality for self-aware human beings inevitably 'contains negative destructive elements as well as positive constructive ones' (pp. 71–8). In this he seems to be combining process and possibility, but interpreted particularly in the light of human suffering. It is ironic, perhaps, that he reads those who are worried about suffering in the non-human world or those who are concerned with why God does this as interpreting from too human a perspective. His vision of God is one who seems to act as an intelligent designer, but who has to accept pain: 'there is nothing that even God can do about it' (p. 75).
20. For a good example, see Arthur Peacocke, 'The Cost of New Life', in J. Polkinghorne (ed.), *The Work of Love: Creation as Kenosis* (London, SPCK, 2001), pp. 21–42.
21. Southgate, 'Creation as Very Good', op. cit.
22. The idea of 'selving' in Southgate implies a teleological process, though I am not intending to imply that his thinking is *confined* to this category. He offers a com-

bination strategy which is helpful, but by his own admission (personal communication, December 2006), this includes 'the recognition that selving requires suffering, and a conviction that the triune God suffers with the suffering', which I find problematic, and even though the edge is taken off this somewhat by his idea that 'there is a redeemed existence for creatures which have known no creaturely flourishing', it is the idea of a requirement for or *necessary* suffering which I find difficult.

23. A subsequent chapter will deal with the specific aspect of how eschatology might be envisaged from an ecological point of view. I am certainly not arguing *against* eschatology and its place in a construction of theodicy; rather, it is necessary as one strand of the argument, rather than the first step.

24. Authors drawn to eschatology include, for example, Southgate, Haught, Russell, Edwards, McDaniel and Ward, while Robin Attfield and Holmes Rolston find this less necessary. See, for example, Robin Attfield, *Creation, Evolution and Meaning* (Basingstoke, Ashgate, 2006).

25. In spite of this proviso, his understanding of atonement still seems to draw primarily on those models which make most sense in the human sphere.

26. For a discussion of their interrelationship see Bruce Barber and David Neville, *Theodicy and Eschatology* (Adelaide, Australian Theological Forum, 2005).

27. Southgate and Robinson name this within a broad category of property-consequence good harm analysis (GHA). Although this is an accurate definition, it strikes me that it is unnecessarily complicated terminology, especially for pedagogical purposes. Aetiological GHA has also been used for this category.

28. John Polkinghorne brought this term to general attention in his *Science and Providence: God's Interaction with the World* (Phildelphia, Templeton Foundation Press, 2005).

29. This also seems to be the view preferred by John Polkinghorne, but he does not develop the idea. See, for example, *Science and the Trinity: The Christian Encounter with Reality* (London, SPCK, 2004).

30. Ruth Page, *God and the Web of Creation* (London, SCM Press, 1996), p. 101.

31. Ibid., p. 105.

32. Other terms that have been used for this view are 'axiological' or 'constitutive' good harm analysis.

33. These examples are cited in Southgate and Robinson, 'Varieties of Theodicy', op. cit.

34. Marilyn McCord Adams, *Horrendous Evils and the Goodness of God* (Ithaca, Cornell University Press, 1999).

35. This view was advanced by theologians such as C. E. Rolt at the turn of the last century. For discussion of his *The World's Redemption*, see Adams, *Horrendous Evils*, op. cit., pp. 70–4. Difficulties with this view include its passivity in the face of suffering.

36. See D. Allen, 'Natural Evil and the Love of God', *Religious Studies*, 16 (1980), pp. 439–56.

37. Adams, *Horrendous Evils*, op. cit., pp. 161–2.

38. Davies, *The Reality of God*, op. cit.

39. Southgate, 'God and Evolutionary Evil', op. cit.

40. Applying kenosis to language about God and God's creativity is, nonetheless,

problematic, for it implies a questionable spatial metaphor of God. In this I agree with Southgate, 'Creation as very Good', op. cit.

41. Davies, *The Reality of God*, op. cit., p. 168.
42. Denis Edwards, 'Why is God Doing This? Suffering, the Universe, and Christian Eschatology', in Nancey Murphy, Robert J. Russell and William Stoeger (eds.), *Physics and Cosmology: Scientific Perspectives on the Problem of Evil in Nature* (Berkeley and Vatican City, CTNS and Vatican Observatory, 2007). I am grateful to the author for letting me read this article before publication.
43. Edwards, 'Why is God Doing This?', op. cit.
44. I will return to a discussion of Edwards' views on eschatology in a later chapter. Here he speaks of 'inscription' of creaturely being into the memory of God, which presumably does mean that even suffering is somehow caught up into God's being.
45. See Southgate, 'God and Evolutionary Evil', op. cit., and developed further in Southgate, 'Creation as Very Good', op. cit.
46. Discussion of this aspect is in Southgate, 'Creation as Very Good', op. cit.
47. See Edwards, 'Why is God Doing This?', op. cit.
48. Bulgakov intereprets the Fall as being in the spiritual angelic realm first, but evil is 'created by creatures' as a 'parasite of being' due to the existence of creaturely self-determination and creativity expressed as creaturely freedom. While the language of angels might seem archaic today, his insistence on the ontological grounding of evil could be extended to creaturely being as such, not just humanity. He also believes that, in the light of evolutionary knowledge, we should not read the accounts of the Fall of humanity in the same way as other events, such as the downfall of Israel. See, *The Bride of the Lamb* (Grand Rapids, Eerdmans, 2002), pp. 153, 168–9.
49. In this particular context I have chosen to capitalise 'Divine Sophia' and leave 'creaturely sophia' and 'shadow sophia' in lower case in order to highlight this contrast.
50. Southgate seems to rely on this interpretation of the Fall in order to discount it as a viable subject for discussion in evolutionary terms. See Southgate, 'Creation as Very Good', op. cit.
51. For discussion see C. Deane-Drummond, *Creation through Wisdom* (Edinburgh, T. & T. Clark, 2000).
52. I will come back to a discussion of the kenosis of the Spirit as wisdom in the work of Bulgakov in the following chapter.

Chapter 10: Ecology and Spirit

1. J. Moltmann, *God in Creation* (London, SCM Press, 1985), p. 99.
2. He develops an even greater focus on the experience of the Spirit in the Christian community in a later work, *The Spirit of Life* (London, SCM Press, 1992). This book makes only passing reference to the work of the Spirit in non-human creation.
3. Moltmann, *God in Creation*, op. cit., p. 100.
4. Ibid., p. 101.
5. Moltmann, *The Spirit of Life*, op. cit., p. 51.
6. Further discussion of eschatology – that is, the future life of the cosmos – will follow in a later chapter.

7. Ruth Page, *God and the Web of Creation* (London, SCM Press, 1996), p. 44.
8. J. Moltmann, *The Way of Jesus Christ* (London, SCM Press, 1990).
9. Ibid., p. 296.
10. Ibid., pp. 296–7.
11. For a discussion of the use of ecology in Moltmann, see C. Deane-Drummond, *Ecology in Jürgen Moltmann's Theology* (Lampeter, Edwin Mellen Press, 1997).
12. See, for example, G. Altner, *Natutvergessenheit: Grundlagen einer umfassenden Bioethic* (Darmstadt, Wissenschafliche Buchgesellschaft, 1991), pp. 14–18, 55–70; *Fortschritt wohin? Der Streit um die Alternative* (Neukirchen-Vluyn, Neu-kirchener-Verlag, 1984); G. Altner (ed)., *Ökologische Theologies: Perspektiven zur Orientierung* (Stuttgart, Radius Verlag, 1989).
13. Other German scholars would disagree with Altner in as much as they retain Trinitarian concepts, such as Christian Link, who incorporates the evolutionary history of nature into the Trinity, understood historically. This bears some resemblance to Moltmann's later eschatological works. C. Link, *Schöpfung*, op. cit., p. 527.
14. Mark Wallace, *Fragments of the Spirit: Nature, Violence and the Renewal of Creation* (Harrisburg, Trinity Press International, 2002).
15. Ibid., p. 136.
16. Ibid.
17. Moltmann, Primavesi and Wallace seem to accept Gaia as an appropriate interpretation of life processes on earth, but give it different significance in their theologies.
18. Wallace, *Fragments of the Spirit*, op. cit., p. 143.
19. This view is also developed further in his more recent work, *Finding God in the Singing River* (Minneapolis, Fortress Press, 2005).
20. Wallace, *Fragments of the Spirit*, op. cit., p. 144.
21. Ibid., p. 148.
22. Ibid., p. 154.
23. Wallace, *Finding God in the Singing River*, op. cit., pp. 122–36.
24. Ibid., p. 126.
25. The idea of cruciform nature is taken up in the chapter on theodicy, and is problematic where it is linked specifically to positive goals for creation, as it seems to justify, rather than protest against the injustice. Wallace has consistently, and correctly, in my view, argued against those forms of theodicy that seek to justify what he calls 'recalcitrant evil', in which he includes environmental mass death. See *Fragments of the Spirit*, op. cit., p. 182.
26. Denis Edwards, *Breath of Life: A Theology of the Creator Spirit* (Maryknoll, Orbis Books, 2004).
27. Ibid., p. 30.
28. Ibid., p. 34.
29. Ibid.
30. Ibid. Chaotic systems are predictable and even 'determinative', which makes identifying contingency and/or the work of God with such systems somewhat problematic. Bob Russell, personal communication, March 2007.
31. Edwards, *Breath of Life*, op. cit., p. 34.
32. In a previous work I suggested that Edwards focuses on the work of the Spirit in

emergence of the new at the expense of naming the work of the Spirit in creature-ly being. Deane-Drummond, *Wonder and Wisdom* (London, DLT, 2006), p. 104. I wish to retract this criticism in as much as I failed to appreciate the extent to which Edwards acknowledges the active presence of the Spirit from the beginning of creation.

33. The work of the Word in creation is related to the idea of the cosmic Christ, which is dealt with in another chapter.
34. Edwards, *Breath of Life*, op. cit., p. 49.
35. I will take up the idea of the Spirit groaning with all creatures in evolutionary processes in a later chapter.
36. Edwards, *Breath of Life*, op. cit., p. 119.
37. Ibid., p. 46.
38. Ibid, p. 109.
39. His chapter 'Come Holy Spirit, Renew the Whole of Creation' in *History and the Triune God* is significant, as it was published after his earlier work, *God in Creation*. See J. Moltmann, *History and the Triune God* (London, SCM Press, 1991), pp. 70–89.
40. Originally published in German in 1998, this work is now available in English. Sigurd Bergmann, *Creation Set Free: The Spirit as Liberator of Nature* (Grand Rapids, Eerdmans, 2005).
41. Ibid., pp. 48–9.
42. Ibid., p. 71.
43. Ibid., p. 81.
44. Gregory resists alternatives, such as Sabellianism, which collapsed differences within the Godhead, or Arianism, which weakened the role of the Son.
45. Bergmann, *Creation Set Free*, op. cit., p. 85.
46. Ibid., p. 87.
47. Ibid., p. 120.
48. Ibid.
49. Ibid., pp. 121–2.
50. Ibid., p. 167.
51. Ibid., p. 292.
52. Ibid., p. 319.
53. See my earlier work, *Creation through Wisdom* (Edinburgh, T. & T. Clark, 2000), ch. 4, 'The Spirit of Holy Wisdom'.
54. Irenaeus, *Demonstration of the Apostolic Teaching*, trans. from the Armenian by J. A. Robinson (London, Black, 1920), ch. 5.
55. See Augustine, *On the Trinity*, XV.27.28.
56. S. Bulgakov, *The Comforter*, trans. from Russian by Boris Jokim (Grand Rapids, Eerdmans, 2004), p. 187. The fact that he called his book on the Holy Spirit, *The Comforter*, out of many possible titles for the Holy Spirit, does at least show that he has high regard for the feminine status of this title.
57. *Perichoresis* is understood to mean the mutual indwelling of each of the persons in the Trinity.
58. Elisabeth Johnson, *She Who Is* (New York, Crossroad, 1992), p. 124.
59. Hildegard, *Scivias*, cited in Johnson, *She Who Is*, op. cit., pp. 127–8.
60. Johnson, *She Who Is*, op. cit., p. 134.

61. Ibid., p. 135.
62. Moltmann uses the Jewish idea of *zimzum*, or inner withdrawal in God, to describe his understanding of kenosis. Edwards (*Breath of Life*, op. cit., p. 109) also speaks of the inner withdrawal of love to let a creature be itself, and describes this as 'making space', but this seems to be an existential idea related to common human understanding of loving relationships. It is not clear, in other words, how far he understands this as a spatial withdrawal.
63. Bulgakov, *The Comforter*, op. cit., pp. 219–20.
64. Ibid., p. 220.

Chapter 11: Eco-feminist Theology

1. Heather Eaton, *Introducing Ecofeminist Theologies* (London, Continuum, 2005), p. 3. This variety has been characteristic of eco-feminist thinking for some time; see, for example, Mary H. MacKinnon and Moni McIntyre, *Readings in Ecology and Feminist Theology* (Kansas City, Sheed and Ward, 1995). It is also noteworthy that many writers in this collection identify with postmodernity, but it is understood to mean that which challenges the patriarchal concerns of modernity, rather than a radical critique of all realist notions on which environmentalism depends.
2. For a helpful overview of these positions, see Eaton, *Introducing Feminist Theologies*, op. cit., pp. 64–6.
3. Susan Griffin, *Woman and Nature: The Roaring Inside Her* (London, The Women's Press, 1984).
4. C. Christ, 'Rethinking Theology and Nature', in J. Plaskow and C. Christ (eds.), *Weaving the Visions: New Patterns in Feminist Spirituality* (San Francisco, Harper and Row, 1989), p. 321; full article, pp. 314–25.
5. Eaton, *Introducing Ecofeminist Theologies*, op. cit., pp. 72–6.
6. R. Radford Ruether, *Gaia and God: An Ecofeminist Theology of Earth Healing* (London, SCM Press, 1993).
7. R. Radford Ruether, *Introducing Redemption in Christian Feminism* (Sheffield, Sheffield Academic Press, 1998), p. 119.
8. M. Grey, *The Outrageous Pursuit of Hope: Prophetic Dreams for the Twentyifirst Century* (London, Darton, Longman and Todd, 2000).
9. Ibid., p. 49.
10. Ibid., p. 57.
11. Mary Grey, *Sacred Longings: Ecofeminist Theology and Globalization* (London, SCM Press, 2003).
12. S. Alaimo, *Undomesticated Ground: Recasting Nature as Feminist Space* (New York, Cornell University Press, 2000), p. 182 (italics mine).
13. See, for example, R. Radford Ruether, *Women Healing Earth: Third World Women on Ecology, Feminism and Religion* (London, SCM Press, 1996).
14. M. J. Ress, *Ecofeminism in Latin America: Women from the Margins* (Maryknoll, Orbis Books, 2006), p. 202.
15. For an overview of these issues see H. Eaton and L. Lorenzen, *Ecofeminism and Globalisation; Exploring Culture, Context and Religion* (Lanham, Rowman and Littlefield, 2003), pp. 41–71.
16. H. Eaton (ed.), *Special Issue: Gender, Religion and Ecology, Ecotheology: The Journal of Religion, Nature and Environment*, 11.4 (2006). See, in particular, for

example, Anne Marie Dalton, 'Gender and Ecofeminism: Religious Reflections on a Case Study in Soc Son, Vietnam', *Ecotheology*, 11.4 (2006), pp. 398–414.

17. I raised a similar point in Chapter 6.
18. S. McFarland Taylor, 'Eating Spirit: Food, Faith and Spiritual Nourishment in the Lives of Green Sisters', *Ecotheology*, 11.4 (2006), pp. 445–64.
19. For a historical survey see Eaton, *Introducing Ecofeminist Theologies*, op. cit., pp. 38–58.
20. Gillian McCulloch, *The Deconstruction of Dualism in Theology: With Special Reference to Ecofeminist Theology and New Age Spirituality* (Carlisle, Paternoster Press, 2003).
21. See, for example, Susan Parsons, *The Ethics of Gender* (Oxford, Blackwell, 2002).
22. G. Jantzen, *God's World: God's Body* (London, DLT, 1984); Sallie McFague, *The Body of God: An Ecological Theology* (London, SCM Press, 1993).
23. G. Jantzen, *Becoming Divine: Towards a Feminist Philosophy of Religion* (Manchester, Manchester University Press, 1998).
24. Ibid., p. 269.
25. McFague, *Body of God*, op. cit., pp. 133–4.
26. S. McFague, *Life Abundant: Rethinking Theology and Economy for a Planet in Peril* (Minneapolis, Fortress Press, 2001).
27. Ibid., pp. 138–41.
28. Ibid., p. 141.
29. Ibid., p. 168. For comment on this approach to Christology see Chapter 8.
30. Ibid., p. 170.
31. Ibid., p. 201.
32. A. Primavesi, *Sacred Gaia: Holistic Theology and Earth System Science* (London, Routledge, 2000).
33. For a thorough treatment of this view see Maria Mies and Vandana Shiva, *Ecofeminism* (London, Zed Books, 1993). Shiva has also been particularly critical of biotechnology and its impact on poor communities, as discussed in Chapters 2 and 6.
34. Such a view is also characteristic of ecology in general; see C. Deane-Drummond, *Biology and Theology Today* (London, SCM Press, 2001), pp. 45, 74.
35. Primavesi, *Sacred Gaia*, op. cit., p. xii. She has also published *Making God Laugh: Human Arrogance and Ecological Humility* (Santa Rosa, Polebridge Press, 2004). Much of this book is reworked material from her earlier books and articles, and not specifically a discussion of Gaia. It seems to be directed particularly at those Christians who claim to know what God wants for either people or the earth. She believes that such arrogance leads to only one response from God – namely, peals of laughter.
36. Primavesi, *Sacred Gaia*, ibid., p. xvii.
37. Ibid., p. xvii.
38. Ibid., pp. 37–8.
39. Ibid., p. 37.
40. Ibid., p. 7.
41. Ibid., p. 8.
42. Ibid., p. 9.

43. Ibid.
44. Deane-Drummond, *Biology and Theology Today*, op. cit., p. 174.
45. Primavesi, *Sacred Gaia*, op. cit., p. 10.
46. Ibid., pp. 15–23.
47. For further discussion about the problems associated with holistic environmentalism, see D. E. Marietta, *For People and the Planet: Holism and Humanism in Environmental Ethics* (Philadelphia, Temple University Press, 1995), pp. 49–68.
48. Primavesi, *Sacred Gaia*, op. cit., p. 29.
49. Ibid., p. 160.
50. Ibid., p. 166.
51. Ibid., pp. 170–1.
52. Ibid., p. 179.
53. L. Osborn, 'Archtypes, Angels and Gaia', *Ecotheology*, 10 (2001), p. 15.
54. Notably Charlene Spretnak, but also Carol Christ; see C. Deane-Drummond, 'Creation', in S. Parsons (ed.), *Cambridge Companion to Feminist Theology* (Cambridge, Cambridge University Press, 2002), pp. 190–205.
55. Primavesi, *Sacred Gaia*, op. cit., pp. 121–36.
56. L. Osborn, 'Archtypes, Angels and Gaia', op. cit., p. 12.
57. C. Spretnak, *States of Grace: The Recovery of Meaning in a Post Modern Age* (1st edn 1991; New York, HarperCollins, 1993), pp. 135–6. For further discussion see Deane-Drummond, *Biology and Theology Today*, op. cit., pp. 169–70.
58. Primavesi, *Sacred Gaia*, op. cit., p. 175. This notion is also developed in her subsequent book, *Gaia's Gift: Earth, Ourselves and God after Copernicus* (London, Routledge, 2003).
59. Deane-Drummond, *Biology and Theology Today*, op. cit., p. 180. It has also been observed by others; see Osborn, 'Archetypes, Angels and Gaia', op. cit., p. 18.
60. Deane-Drummond, *Biology and Theology Today*, op. cit., p. 179.
61. Susan Hawthorne, *Wild Politics: Feminism, Globalization, Diversity* (Melbourne, Spinifex Press, 2002).
62. Ibid., pp. 31–42.
63. Ibid., p. 159.
64. C. Deane-Drummond, *Creation through Wisdom* (Edinburgh, T. & T. Clark, 2000).
65. It is significant, perhaps, that her original article on 'The Wisdom of Gaia' is republished in her most recent book, *Making God Laugh*, op. cit., pp. 145–61.
66. For further discussion, see Deane-Drummond, *Creation through Wisdom*, op. cit.
67. Aquinas cites Psalm 103:4.
68. Aquinas, *Summa Theologiae*, Vol. 8, 'Creation, Variety and Evil', trans. T. Gilby (Oxford, Blackfriars, 1967), 1a Qu. 47.1.
69. Grey, *Outrageous Pursuit*, op. cit., p. 87. I find the connection between wisdom and Griffin's work less convincing in that while wisdom theology is creation theology, wisdom also maintains a distinction between the divine and the earth in a way that is not apparent in Griffin's approach.
70. Grey, *Outrageous Pursuit*, op. cit., pp. 93–8; see also C. Deane-Drummond, 'Come to the Banquet: Seeking Wisdom in a Genetically Engineered Earth', *Ecotheology*, 9 (July 2000), pp. 27–37.
71. C. Deane-Drummond, 'Sophia: The Feminine Face of God as a Metaphor for an Ecotheology', *Feminist Theology*, 16 (1997), pp. 11–31. Anne Clifford has also

written on the promise of Sophia for eco-theology in Anne M. Clifford, 'Feminist Perspectives on Science: Implications for an Ecological Theology', *Journal of Feminist Studies in Religion*, 8 (1992), pp. 65–90.

72. Although James Lovelock originally wanted his theory to be considered seriously by scientists purely as science, the fact that religious writers such as Primavesi have taken up his theory and used it to construct an alternative theology is a position that he now seems to welcome.

73. See, for example, Caitlin Matthews, *Sophia: Goddess of Wisdom: The Divine Feminine from Black Goddess to World Soul* (London, HarperCollins, 1991). Sophia has some parallels with Gaia in that both have been incorporated into goddess theologies.

74. E. A. Johnson, *She Who Is: The Mystery of God in Feminine Theological Discourse* (New York, Crossroad, 1992).

75. For further discussion of this idea see C. Deane-Drummond, *Wonder and Wisdom: Conversations in Science, Spirituality and Theology* (London, DLT, 2006). For discussion of the importance of wisdom in economic and political critiques, see the discussion in earlier chapters.

Chapter 12: Eco-eschatology

1. This is repeated in various volumes. The most notorious, perhaps, is Jürgen Moltmann, *Theology of Hope: On the Grounds and Implications of a Christian Eschatology* (London, SCM Press, 1967).

2. J. Lovelock, *The Revenge of Gaia* (London, Penguin Books, 2006). It is significant, perhaps, that he evokes the importance of the emotion of wonder as a way of appreciating life on our planet.

3. Ibid., p. 189.

4. Christopher Rowland, *The Open Heaven* (London, SPCK, 1982), p. 38.

5. I will deal with more specific ethical discussions in the postscript.

6. Margaret Barker, *The Lost Prophet: The Book of Enoch and its Influence on Christianity* (London, SPCK, 1988), p. 38.

7. Maragaret Barker, *The Older Testament: The Survival of Themes from the Ancient Royal Cult in Sectarian Judaism and Early Christianity* (London, SPCK, 1987), p. 29.

8. Stephen Smalley comments on this aspect in *The Revelation to John: Commentary on the Greek Text of the Apocalypse* (London, SPCK, 2005), pp. 524–5.

9. Margaret Barker, *The Revelation of Jesus Christ* (Edinburgh, T. & T. Clark, 2000), pp. 364–7.

10. I will come back to a discussion of the resurrection again below.

11. Philip Edgcumbe Hughes, *The Book of Revelation: A Commentary* (Grand Rapids, Eerdmans, 1990), pp. 221–2. For commentary on Colossians 1:20 see the chapter on Christology.

12. See Nicholas Lash, *Holiness, Speech and Silence* (Aldershot, Ashgate, 2004).

13. Hans Urs von Balthasar, *Mysterium Paschale*, trans. with an Introduction by Aidan Nichols (T. & T. Clark, Edinburgh, 1990), pp. 51–2.

14. Ibid., p. 53.

15. Rosemary Radford Ruether, *Sexism and God-Talk* (London, SCM Press, 1983), pp. 257–8.

16. Von Balthasar, *Mysterium Paschale*, op. cit., pp. 137–8
17. Jürgen Moltmann, *The Way of Jesus Christ* (London: SCM Press, 1990), p. 294.
18. C. E. B. Cranfield, *The Epistle to the Romans*, Vol. 1, 1-VIII (Edinburgh, T. & T. Clark, 1975), p. 412.
19. James Dunn, *Word Biblical Commentary, Romans 1—8* (Dallas, Word Books, 1988), p. 467.
20. Ibid., p. 471.
21. Jürgen Moltmann, *The Coming of God* (London, SCM Press, 1996), p. 231.
22. Jürgen Moltmann, *The Experiment Hope* (London, SCM Press, 1975), p. 52; see also *The Future of Creation* (London, SCM Press, 1979), pp. 29–31.
23. Moltmann, *The Coming of God*, op. cit., p. 260.
24. Ibid., p. 263. Yet Moltmann is possibly inaccurate to equate Aquinas with a circular view of history, for his sense that all things begin in God and end in God could be interpreted in terms of the new, not simply a circular return. In fact he does this himself by declaring that the new creation will find its consummation in God, and God will be all in all.
25. Ibid., p. 266.
26. Ibid., p. 273.
27. Ibid., p. 279.
28. Ibid., p. 294.
29. Ibid., p. 295.
30. Jürgen Moltmann, *God in Creation* (London, SCM Press, 1985), p. 87.
31. Moltmann, *The Coming of God*, op. cit., pp. 318–19.
32. Ibid., p. 318.
33. Ibid., pp. 326–30.
34. Ibid., pp. 338–9.
35. Moltmann, *The Way of Jesus Christ*, op. cit., p. 256.
36. Ibid., pp. 258, 303.
37. Ibid., p. 258.
38. Ibid., p. 262.
39. G. Liedke, *Im Bauch des Fisches: Ökologische Theologie* (4th edn, Stuttgart, Kreuz-Verlag, 1984), pp. 165–200. See also Ulrich Duchrow and Gerhard Liedke, *Shalom: Biblical Perspectives on Creation, Justice and Peace* (Geneva, WCC, 1989), pp. 59–78.
40. Ernst Conradie, *Hope for the Earth* (Bellville, University of the Western Cape, 2000), p. 338. For a more detailed account see E. Conradie, 'Resurrection, Finitude and Ecology', in T. Peters, R. J. Russell and M. Welker (eds.), *Resurrection: Theological and Scientific Assessments* (Grand Rapids, Eerdmans, 2002), pp. 277–96.
41. For Whitehead see A. N. Whitehead, *Process and Reality: An Essay in Immortality* (1st edn 1929; 2nd edn New York, Harper and Row, 1957).
42. Conradie, *Hope for the Earth*, op. cit., pp. 342–3.
43. John Haught, *God after Darwin* (Boulder, Westview Press, 2000), p. 43.
44. Ian Barbour, 'God's Power: A Process View', in J. Polkinghorne (ed.), *The Work of Love: Creation as Kenosis* (Grand Rapids, Eerdmans, 2001), pp. 1–20.
45. Conradie, *Hope for the Earth*, op. cit., p. 373.
46. Ibid., p. 373.

47. Ibid., p. 374.
48. Jürgen Moltmann, *In the End: The Beginning* (London, SCM Press, 2004), p. 150.
49. Denis Edwards, 'Every Sparrow that Falls to the Ground: The Cost of Evolution and the Christ Event', *Ecotheology*, 11.1 (2006), pp. 103–23.
50. Ibid., pp. 117–20.

Postscript

1. I refer the reader to international efforts among religious groups to foster changes in practices and attitudes. One of the first major meetings on religion and environment took place in 1986 for the 25th anniversary of the World Wide Fund for Nature in Assisi, Italy. In 1992 religious representation was present at the United Nations conference on environment and development in Rio de Janeiro, Brazil. In 1993 200 religious leaders signed 'Towards a Global Ethic' at the Parliament of World Religions in Chicago, United States. 1995 saw the launch of the Alliance of Religions and Conservation that works with major world faiths in encouraging conservation projects. Between 1996 and 1998 Harvard University hosted a series of conferences on religions of the world and ecology, including a Forum on Religion and Ecology. Such public meetings are a visible sign of a much stronger groundswell of religious practices that seek to engage with conservation practice and strategies for earth care through, for example, deliberate attempts to be accountable in ecological terms. Specific organisations include Christian Ecology Link (CEL), as well as, increasingly, groups that emerge from developmental agencies, such as CAFOD, that have become more consciously 'green' in their thinking and practice, normally under the label of sustainability.

2. A term coined by Pope John Paul II. See, in particular, Catholic Bishops' Conference of England and Wales, *The Call of Creation* (London, Catholic Communications Service, 2002), p. 5.

3. The Five Marks of Mission are (1) To proclaim the Good News of the Kingdom; (2) To teach, baptise and nurture new believers; (3) To respond to human need by loving service; (4) To seek to transform unjust structures of society; (5) To strive to safeguard the integrity of creation and sustain and renew the earth. Arguably, eco-theological praxis would not just be focused on (5), but would also incorporate ecological insights into *all five marks of mission*, including proclamation of the good news as ecological as well as encompassing humanity, and especially more practical aspects such as baptism, where water is symbolic of the close interconnection between all life forms. For this reason, the fifth mark of mission should be the first priority, rather than the last, in its present position implying incorrectly that ecological practices are an afterthought, having dealt first with the human community.

4. These are wholly unnecessary sufferings, the deaths of individual creatures and the exploitation and eventual extinction of species due to human interventions and activities.

5. I am referring here to the work of pioneering international organisations like *A Rocha*, but there are others that would also fall into this category.

6. Dave Bookless, 'Mission and the Environment in London and India: A Personal Reflection' (personal communication).

7. See, for example, D. T. Hessel, *After Nature's Revolt: Eco-justice and Theology*

(Philadelphia, Fortress Press, 1992), L. Ramussen, *Earth Community: Earth Ethics* (Maryknoll, Orbis Books, 1996). More recent sources by these authors include L. Ramussen, 'Environmental Racism and Environmental Justice: Moral Theory in the Making?', *Journal of the Society of Christian Ethics* 24.1, pp. 3–28; D. T. Hessel, 'The church ecologically reformed', in D. T. Hessel and L. Ramussen (eds.), *Earth Habitat: Eco-Injustices and the Churches's Response* (Minneapolis, Fortress Press, 2001), pp. 185–26. A further significant text in this vein is Willis Jenkins, *Ecologies of Grace: Environmetal Ethics and Christian Theology* (Oxford and New York, Oxford University Press, 2008). *Ecologies of Grace* illustrates the integration between theological reflection and practices that informs the particular approach to theology taken in this book. However, Jenkins' starting point is one that is more self-consciously ethical, and he then moves to consideration of how particular practices such as justice, virtues, stewardship and reconciliation are supported by particular theological traditions. For example, he finds the environmental virtues in Thomas, including ecojustice, while he finds themes of reconciliation and stewardship in Barth, and more cosmic dimensions in Maximus and Bulgakov. I welcome this discourse at the boundary of theology and ethics, and especially the ecumenical approach to eco-theology that I believe is vitally important to sustain. Although I have concentrated in this text on theology, this should not give the impression that ethical issues are less important, rather, with Willis, much eco-theology emerges in the context of ethical ferment. Given that this book was published just as mine was going to press, I was unable to do it full justice here.

8. Declaration on the Environment signed by Patriarch Bartholomew I of Constantinople and Pope John Paul II, 10 June 2002 (italics mine).

9. Pope John Paul II, 19th January 2001, to a general audience in St Peter's square, taken from 'Ecological Conversion', http://conservation.catholic.org/john_paul_ii.htm , accessed June 13th, 2007. The significance of the term *human ecology* in the work of Pope John Paul II should be noted, in that he takes up a secular term and uses it in order to develop his own distinctive position on the integration of human and creaturely life. This subject is being actively pursued at present by my doctoral student at Chester University, Fr Peter Conley.

10. Denis Edwards, *Ecology at the Heart of Faith: The Change of Heart that Leads to a New Way of Living on Earth* (Maryknoll, Orbis Books, 2006).

11. I have discussed this matter in more detail elsewhere: see C. Deane-Drummond, 'Living from the Sabbath: Developing an Ecological Theology in the Context of Biodiversity', in Denis Edwards and Mark Worthing (eds.), *Biodiversity and Ecology: An Interdisciplinary Challenge* (Adelaide, ATF Press, 2004), pp. 1–14.

12. C. Westermann, *Genesis 1—11, A Commenatary*, trans. John J. Scullion (London, SPCK, 1984), pp. 171–5.

13. Ibid., p. 172.

14. See R. J. Berry (ed.), *When Enough is Enough: A Christian Framework for Environmental Sustainability* (Nottingham, Apollos/Inter-Varsity Press, 2007).

15. The redemptive theme in the texts on the seventh day was often missed in early biblical scholarship.

16. Space does not permit discussion of how these themes might be developed in this context.

17. Robert Murray, *The Cosmic Covenant* (London, Sheed and Ward, 1992).
18. For a fuller discussion, see C. Deane-Drummond, *The Ethics of Nature* (Oxford, Blackwell, 2004).
19. See, for example, S. Boumer-Prediger, *For the Beauty of the Earth: A Christian Vision for Creation Care* (Grand Rapids, Baker Academic, 2001).
20. It would be inappropriate to list all the different practical projects on offer at present. However, one notable example is the green audit being undertaken at present by all Anglican churches in the United Kingdom. Ministers are asked to assess how much energy their churches use, with a view to recording an improvement in efficiency in future years as the monitoring continues.
21. See C. Deane-Drummond, *Wonder and Wisdom: Conversations in Science, Spirituality and Theology* (London, DLT, 2006).

Index